.39

.023

.16

Living As Light:

The Awakening of Mystical Consciousness©

*Offering Words of Hope and
Consolation in Times of Trauma*

BY
BRENT M. BAUM, STB, SSL, ICADC, LISAC, CCH

Published by Healing Dimensions, ACC
Printed by West Press
Tucson, Arizona

Living As Light
The Awakening of Mystical Consciousness

Published by:
Healing Dimensions, A.C.C.
5675 North Camino Esplendora #6137
Tucson, Arizona 85718
Phone: (520) 615-9247
Web Site Address: www.healingdimensions.com
Also Visit: www.michaelsgift.org

Edited by Antoinette Kleinpeter and Linda Ladner
Cover Illustration and Design by Christy McMearty
Portrait Photograph by Philip Ramackers
Layout and Manufacture by West Press
Cover Production by West Press
Printed in the United States of America

Library of Congress Cataloguing-in-Publication

Baum, Brent M.
Living as light: the awakening of mystical consciousness
By Brent M. Baum, 1st ed.
p. cm.
Includes bibliographical references.
ISBN 978-0-9661990-2-4
Library of Congress Control Number (LCCN): 2006935495
1. Mysticism   2. Spirituality   3 Mind and Body
4. Energy Psychology   5. Consciousness

I. Title   II. Author

CONTENTS

Preface

By Sharon Wegscheider-Cruse

Humility in the artist is his frank acceptance of all experiences,
Just as Love in the artist is simply that sense of Beauty
That reveals to the world its body and soul.

Oscar Wilde

The words "courageous, intuitive, holy, spirited, healing and wise" kept coming to me as I read Brent's most recent book. It seemed as though I was on the journey of his life and his inspired learnings as he presented his truth through his journey inward. This journey he describes so well as "the only true safe place." The excitement of this presentation is in the merging of the principles of science and spirituality. I felt drawn to the expanded ideas surrounding what it is to experience mystical intimacy, healing and the power of truly "letting go".

Brent takes us on his lifetime quest through his exploration in archeology and the connections we have with each other on a very cellular level. He helps us build bridges to those who have gone before us. We learn about how we store our memory through the trance experience and how trauma becomes part of who we are. Then he helps the reader to understand how and why we need to take the necessary steps to heal that trauma.

Early in my career, I learned from another powerful healer. Her name was Olga Worrall. Olga and her husband Ambrose were introduced to me by one of my early mentors, Virginia Satir. She took me to Baltimore to meet the Worralls and both she and I experienced a healing with Olga. She was a renowned mystic who practiced her healing mission in a very simple manner - the laying on of her hands.

When I met Brent, I found that he, too, is a healer and a mystic with an incredible ability to verbalize and explain the lessons he is so able to teach. I have personally experienced his healing power. His life story is told in rich and fine detail in this book; he shares his simple and profound truth. His book informs us of the value of visual imagery, the dangers of auditory over-stimulation, explains the dangers of terrorism, and the culture's fascination with reality television shows. Then he is able to take us to the healing we can find by the empowerment of ourselves and others. He helps us to find balance by understanding karma and how to resolve our own healing. He inspires us by helping us find our own ability to become a visionary. His book is a wake-up call to our own development.

This past year, I had an experience of sharing with a dear friend who had lost a loved one in a senseless traffic accident. I remember telling her that you do not get over a death – you survive and get through a death. I related to Brent when he says – we do not get over trauma, we get through trauma. Brent says, "Trauma is often a wake-up call. It helps us move from complacency and apathy to opportunity and change."

Scientists who investigated Olga Worrall's powers were left awed by them. Brent as well goes beyond the level of scientific explanation. He challenges our belief systems, our old perceptions and earlier standards of healing. All those who work with others can profit by his teachings.

In working with others, we must each "clear our energy field". We must finish our unfinished business. Then we will find our own light, our own power and our own ability to become a healer. Brent takes the mystery of that possibility and shows us how to tap into our own abilities to heal.

An important part of his message is that each of us can become priestly, can find our true light and can be with someone else in their search for their own power and spirituality. Abundance is available to each of us. This book is eye opening and directs each of us to a shift of consciousness. Some of the most courageous and revealing questions and answers that the book raises are around the subjects of sexuality, religious addiction, gay marriage, celibacy, co-dependency, trauma, healing and hope. The information provided is groundbreaking and clear.

It is inspiring to learn about the powers of our fantasy, our daydreaming, and our times in meditation and prayer. This book is very important to those in medical systems, educational systems, religious systems and the addiction treatment system. It is an awakening.

There is a new vision that can promote and encourage integrative medicine, holistic healing, greater inner wisdom, more complete health, a time of abundance and success in the way we live. Brent's book can bring us that vision.

Sharon Wegscheider-Cruse, MA
Author, Trainer, Healer and Family Therapist

Acknowledgments

Though it may seem strange, my first word of thanks goes to trauma! Without its lessons and challenges I would not be anywhere near as passionate as I am about my "mission." Along with this, I must thank you, my teachers, particularly those of you who appeared as clients and who found the courage to face your own traumas and make the journey within to find solutions. The truth of this was revealed when I realized that nearly all of the truly life-changing career opportunities I have had occurred through the intervention of you who practice Twelve Step programs and, who, from your own wisdom and experience, glimpsed the potential of this work when I was only marginally aware. If not for the pioneering work of Sharon Wegscheider-Cruse, I doubt that I would have been as inspired to move into the field of counseling and psychotherapy. Under the promptings of Nancy Meyer and Don Lavender, I began my own paradigm shift. A special word of gratitude I offer to Wyatt Webb who intervened to bring me to Miraval – a tremendous spiritual springboard for connecting with so many resources for healing.

Among those on my indomitable support team, I want to thank Antoinette Kleinpeter, Kenny Kleinpeter, Linda Ladner, Steve Potocki, Jeanette Arnold, Audrey Kirk, Gennie Landry, Diana Cronan, Jason Henderson, Roberta Guillory, Vicki Bentley, Rosemary Vaughn, Yvonne Hedeker, Madelon Mitchum, Fran and Ray Lemkul, Jayne Weingart, Ellen Katz, Tim Frank, Beverly Sincavage, Lila Cherri, Sharron Raymond, Dawn Whiting, Karen Restivo, Maya and Tom Sharp, Deborah Titus, Kristen Trahan, Suzanne Honda, Marcia Howton, Chris Oehrle, Soram Khalsa, Mariko Tanaka, Ronnie and Betty Falgout, the "Lightbearers" Healing Group, "Angel" Gail Konz, Gladys Strohme, Reed Brown, and many others. Among the institutions, organizations, and communities that have supported me are the administration and staff of Cottonwood Treatment Centers, the Miraval staff, Unity Christ Church of Gaithersburg, Maryland, Nancy Marder and the Infinity Foundation in Chicago, Arden Shore Children and Family Services, the Cenacle Retreat Centers, Sr. Joan and St. Mary of the Pines Retreat Center, and all of the other spiritual communities that have hosted me and supported the dissemination of this message of healing. To the archaeology community that inspired my passion to unearth the past, I offer my heartfelt gratitude: Uncle Mel, Joe Seger, Paul Jacobs and the Lahav Research Project. I wish to express a special word of thanks to my parents and brother who continue to guide me in spirit, and my sisters Peggy, Margie, and Carole who have been unceasing in their encouragement and support over the years. To the medical team in spirit who are ever present and effective in ways that I will probably never fully understand, I offer my heartfelt gratitude. May this momentum of love and support touch every heart seeking comfort and guidance on the *via negativa* and the path to mystical awakening.

Introduction

I offer you this work as an introduction to a new way of being in the world. In the clearing and healing of the bodymind, a new way of knowing and perceiving self emerges. This changes our manner of perception from a static, trauma-based frame of reference, to one that is dynamic and flowing – a non-threatening mode of embracing all experience as an invitation to master our perception. This new way of perceiving self is "light-based." In coming to know ourselves as dynamic fields of light at play in a universe of images, our focus is able to change. The ability to focus is directly related to our ability to create, and for this very reason, the reclamation of our power to focus is of revolutionary importance – just how revolutionary you will see in the pages that follow. The truth of the matter is that we have been "in trance" for at least 1.5 million years on this planet – before we were even verbal! These static states of consciousness induced by trauma added a density to our self-definition that left us trapped in physicality and materiality. This protective encoding began with the occurrence of our earliest stages of evolution and the traumas that accompanied them. Over time, the weight and burden that we accumulated was incorporated into the bodymind and our belief systems. Eventually we were no longer able to distinguish between our true nature and the perceptions imposed by trauma. Our self-understanding was profoundly shaped by this accumulating static and eventually supplanted our luminosity with its own binding and restrictive physics. In the advent of our new findings about our universe, quantum physics, and the power that we possess to alter our states of consciousness, we are emerging from our 1.5 million year old trance and coming into our power. The ability to reclaim our power and to master our states of consciousness becomes paramount for our coping with change and trauma in our lives. Meditation, prayer, healing, intimacy, safety, and mystical oneness – all flow spontaneously when we discover our innate ability to move fluidly as light within a world of illusion.

The implications of what you are about to experience here are immeasurable. If you "get it," you will see the vulnerability of the forces that have so readily hypnotized us and sustained our powerlessness over these last millennia. In the recognition of your power, you will move from any residual sadness, anger, fear, and shame from the past into a place of compassion and gratitude, for it is here that all of our traumas and encumbrances resolve. In embracing this message, you will find true freedom – an expansion of mind that integrates all within a simplicity that we believed lost. There is both teacher and mystic within the very fabric of your being; the mystery school that you seek was so deeply embedded in the matrix of your consciousness that it is inseparable from who you are. The spirituality and luminosity that accompanies the authentic self emerges spontaneously with the resolution of our "trances." The intimacy, joy, abundance, and serenity that so readily follow suggest that we were destined for an Edenic existence, not removed from such possibility by some primordial failure. The reclamation of our capacity to manifest, a power closely tied to the mastery of our quantum projectors – our minds, holds the key to the transformation and healing of our world. The evidence of this I have laid down in the pages that follow.

These reflections come at a time when all of the many faces of our global experience are presented to us in incredible sensory detail and within a millisecond of cyber communication. The moment we awaken and begin expanding our awareness we are flooded with more information and sensory communication than we have ever witnessed in our previous evolution. The mind as our quantum projector of reality becomes quickly overtaxed using the traditional parameters that were established by family, religious, societal, political, and educational systems. Though we may attempt to reset those boundaries that would enable us to handle the onslaught of such expanding consciousness, we find ourselves seduced nonetheless. In the barrage of sensory overload, we are tempted to withdraw from this bombardment, but to do so is to risk finding ourselves caught off guard, pulled along in the landslide of opinion and thought that surrounds us and is so desperately trying to regain some semblance of order and control. We end up as participants in the drama regardless of how strongly we try to distance ourselves from the violence and its presentation. This, we are coming to realize, is the responsibility and the gift that comes with being a creator on the level of quantum perception. In coming out of the inhibiting altered states of consciousness induced through trauma, we move into a new era where we are the conscious creators of our lives, our bodies, marriages, occupations, and communities, rather than its victims.

Years ago, when I began to glimpse the untapped reserve of power that we possess to heal ourselves, I was overwhelmed with a sense of urgency. As I began to integrate these resources and envision a method of delivery, a hope was born that effective personal healing might reduce the occurrence and impact of trauma in our world. In working with the American medical personnel and officers of the Oklahoma City bombing, I was profoundly moved by the heroic efforts of the rescue personnel who traumatized themselves in their efforts to save the injured. A few years later, working with those involved with TWA Flight 800 in New York, I first heard the sadness and terror that resulted from the personal loss and confusion regarding this mysterious airplane disaster. This event began to prepare us for what was yet to come. At each stage when I witnessed and felt the actual traumatic imprinting of these events, I experienced a stronger impetus to provide more effective intervention for those overwhelmed by such experiences. Just as I thought we had seen the worst, however, a greater trauma arose. With September 11, 2001, the whole picture changed. What was a sense of urgency became a mandate for healing. Millions were affected at the same millisecond in time! Never was there a trauma that overwhelmed so many simultaneously. The first plane caught many off guard, while the impact of the second plane was viewed "live" as we watched the events unfold. We entered a new millennium with "trauma" as the principal theme. I found hope in the Red Cross asking individuals and media to cease their constant replay of the imagery of September 11th. However, not long after, the media discovered "reality TV" and the capacity to hypnotize a viewer to the screen by stimulating adrenaline flow and triggering previous (hypnotic) states of overwhelm. Following the events of September 11, 2001, the terrorists noted our media obsession and our vulnerability. Before long, we were involved in a war whose strategists were consciously employing media tactics that involved videotaped beheadings and the deliberate use of trauma induction as a legitimate psychological weapon. With instantaneous global communication, it was almost impossible to block the broadcast of the videotapes. And at a time nearing the end of 2004, when the news carried the latest reports of the war on terrorism, nature itself gave us cause to reexamine our definition of global trauma. A tsunami of unimaginable power slammed into Indonesia and many other countries leaving entire cities and populations annihilated in its wake. And even as we continued to rush resources to the aid of those ravaged by the tsunami, Hurricane Katrina devastated major cities in the Southern United States, killing thousands and leaving hundreds of thousands homeless, including some of my own family members. The impact of this event was also global, affecting the world economy, the internal balance of power, and the false assumptions we held about our preparedness to deal with trauma on such a scale. We are now beyond "urgency" when it comes to addressing the individual and collective impact of trauma. And this impact is truly personal. Each image we have witnessed in these years triggers our personal adrenaline response and also causes a corresponding repression of our immune system. We no longer have the luxury to repress and ignore our individual and global moments of overwhelm – not, at least, if we are to live healthily.

In my own small way, I have sought in these last two decades to discover effective methods to break the cycle of traumatic encoding. This search has known profound moments of success; however, the lessons learned must now expand to a much larger traumatized population – a global one! It is in the transfer of these lessons of empowerment to each of us that our greatest hope for healing arises. As we resolve the estrangement from self and others that millennia of trauma have imposed on us, we become available to participate in this healing and awakening of humanity. As we move past the trauma-imposed constraints of the "ego," infinite possibilities unfold before us for healing and transformation. In inviting you on this journey, I offer for your reflection an excerpt of the vision statement that my friend Yvonne Hedeker and I wrote as we founded a charity to address the global impact of trauma. The starting point of all healing is the self!

> We believe that all persons possess an innate ability to heal, given the proper tools and resources. We hold that personal transformation creates the foundation for global change. We are committed to reducing the impact and recurrence of trauma in our world.
>
> Michael's Gift Vision Statement

CHAPTER 1

℘℧

THE INVITATION

The invitation was inscribed and embedded deep within us before we were very conscious as a species. It was present from our earliest inception but became buried beneath millions of years of memory – genetic and traumatic imprinting. It has remained intact and still stands. It is an offer of intimacy – not intimacy as it was typically modeled for us, but, rather, the capacity to merge with another as light, generating the ability to heal, love, and let go. This involves our capacity to release all that we are not and to discover the magnificence that we truly are.

In every age and time there are words of comfort and reassurance that help us to see our way through the darkness. Every exile or loss, individual or collective, will summon from deep within us a prophetic voice, an Isaiah or Jeremiah who reminds us that we possess all the resources necessary to restore focus and return home after exile. In an age where terrorism finds ever-new forms of self-expression, a light arises from within to meet the challenge. This radiance allows us to navigate the unfamiliar paths and keeps us safe. Safety is the preoccupation of our day and time. But such a challenge is, ultimately, an inner one. It tenders an invitation to navigate ourselves differently. The almost palpable fear emerging from the events highlighted around us summon a reserve of power held for just such a challenge. The turbulence of the past decade encourages a flight within – not so much to hide from the new storms arising, but to find and address the actual source of our emotional discontent. This inward journey brings us to a creative point where our histories, our choices, and our traumas all converge. It is here at this nexus in the search for understanding and solutions that something new is born.

Science and spirituality are converging to teach us about consciousness and perception. From a "quantum" perspective, what we perceive we create. Global traumas of recent years have riveted our perception and unwittingly drawn us into their manifestation. As a side effect of this siphoning of our creative energy, we are becoming more attentive to the objects of our focus. September 11th does not just happen "out there," we discover, but is an image constructed and felt in the depths and movements of our visionary mind. Responsibility comes with the power of perception. Through this creative force we discover that the boundaries of our inner world and our outer world are not as clear-cut as we thought. We are immersed in depths of perception for which we were never prepared. We are more profoundly connected to our world, its inhabitants, and even this body that mediates our perception. There are gifts and challenges that come with such heightened relationship.

This book is about mystical intimacy – not intimacy as it was typically modeled for us by parents, teachers, religion or society, but true oneness: the capacity to merge with another as light, generating the ability to heal, love, and let go. This involves our capacity to release all that we are not and to fill the emptiness with the magnificence that we truly are. I am going to talk about our mastery of consciousness and the invitation to embrace the fullness of our destiny and nature. As part of this evolutionary unveiling, we will examine the opportunities we now face to use our spiritual resources to transform our relationships, our bodies, our minds, and the world around us. As a "side effect" of this shift in consciousness, I suspect that we will find an intimacy greater than we imagined possible, a new model for interpersonal relationship and social interaction, and the power to heal many of our diseases. The source of this power may surprise you.

At heart, I am a radical pragmatist. As a child, I wanted to be an archaeologist and to actually uncover and touch the richness of our history. I later did this, digging in Israel as part of an excavation for over thirteen years. When, as a child, I decided I wanted to make more of a difference in our world, I followed the local, culturally endorsed model for healing and became a priest. Upon discovering that the traditional systems actually remembered little of the healing sciences that came naturally to my mother and me, I promptly diverged onto my own path. In the frustration that those I attempted to assist in healing were trapped in parts of their minds that I was not trained to address or access, I used my own intuitive thinking and research skills to create a more effective path. The most important lesson of all was that of self-trust and empowerment. The riches and blessings of my journey form the backdrop for the lessons which I am obliged to share. Many of us have digested reams of material that have nurtured our intellects and minds through many stages of personal and spiritual growth. The multitude of self-help books have inspired and challenged our growth, predisposing us for change and honing our willpower. In speaking to the intellect, however, they did not always reach those places where our pain holds us captive. It is the place of memory and is largely non-linear: it involves the flow of consciousness and our power to master it. Therefore, this mystical journey that I propose to you is pragmatic beyond description. It hints at a physics of mysticism about which I shall discourse from my limited human experience. But this discussion is not abstract or designed to inspire your intellect so much as it is intended to summon your power and to create a bridge. This bridge, once erected, offers the opportunity to realize our deepest hopes and dreams. It is very real and very much about the infinite resources we hold within. It is also timely. The heart of our discussion centers on our capacity to create relational bridges. We may call this search "relationality," "spirituality," or "intimacy" – it is the same connection that we all seek. All of our emotions are relational bridges. I have learned this through both love and trauma. Let us take a look at our capacity to link heart to heart.

Some time ago, while visiting Evanston, Illinois, I had the privilege to view the film: *What the #$*! Do We Know!?*[1] A tremendous portion of that film resonates with what you will encounter in this text. The chapters of this text were nearing completion when this movie surfaced. Much of this work is about the power of perception and the empowerment occurring through application of the principles of quantum physics. While feeling validated by the findings and shared experiences of the interdisciplinary pioneers in the film, I became profoundly aware of the gap that was reflected when it came to explaining how we might become empowered enough to become "unstuck" from our unconscious perceptions, beliefs, addictions, and behaviors. This entire text is devoted to the liberation of the bodymind from its 1.5 million years of unconscious evolution and encoding. While the interdisciplinary perspective that I offer is somewhat unique, many of us have found ourselves reaching the same conclusions, irrespective of our paths.

The past decade has revealed much about the creative power of perception: what we focus upon we become; what we carry within we attract. The act of observation is not passive, but creative. So says quantum physics. In a world where victim-hood is, for many, a preferable escape or safer illusion of being, discussions of power raise skepticism, confusion, and even anger. To make things even more challenging, we discover that our emotions unite us in an instant with a person, circumstance or event, bridging the limits of space and time. My mother taught me this simple principle as a child. It sparked within me a passion to understand her capacity to feel in her body the events that happened to her children. I knew that I was committed to this quest when I suddenly sat upright in bed in Rome, Italy, at the moment of her death in Louisiana. I had been awakened by a sudden shift from within and not by anything outside in the cool silence of the city of Rome that night. I always knew that I would feel the moment of her passing; there was that much love present, and its power transcended space and time. She died beneath her favorite painting acquired from our old church: "Simon of Cyrene takes up the cross." How appropriate for a woman who spent so much of her life with the ability to feel and ease the pain of others.

Power reveals itself to us at some of the most unexpected moments and in some of the most unpredictable ways. Originally, I thought that the power to heal, for instance, was the proprietary right of the ministers and priesthood of our world. While in formal ministry as a Catholic priest, I never felt any energy exchanges from my hands, but within three months of leaving "formal" ministry, with plans to begin full-time teaching, my hands seemed to become active and led me to a spontaneous healing of my own body. I never made it to a traditional teaching position at a university or to the Jesuits who had invited me to join them. In my current healing work, I do not formally affiliate with any one system or belief, for the nature and scope of my work is truly universal ("katholikos" in the original Greek means "universal"). The demands of the energy coming from my hands dictated their own path. I did not discover until a few years ago that I had a great uncle on my mother's side of the family who could also send some form of light or healing energy from his hands, beginning his service to others as I had – healing viruses like herpes simplex (warts) and other skin disorders. Ironically, it was actually my second cousin, a nun, who provided me with the details about this! My first realization that I could send some form of healing energy to others through my hands was, in fact, an accidental occurrence of which I was oblivious until my friend told me what had happened: healing the skin ailment in his feet that had already defied medical intervention. Power introduces itself to us in truly unanticipated and surprising situations. Thomas Kuhn, in his book, *The Structure of Scientific Revolutions,* states that this is the way of authentic paradigm shifts in consciousness.[2] These revolutionary changes often come in the most unexpected and spontaneous ways.

We are at the beginning of a great awakening of consciousness, a great paradigm shift in intimacy. The illusions of separation that allowed me to remain estranged from you and vice versa are dissolving. Some of this is by necessity. Hidden behind the dense energies of my traumas I did not have to feel your pain, but I was also more alone. Trauma imposes a weight and a density on the bodymind. In the process it provides an insulation to keep me from internalizing further pain. With the weight of my own trauma history to mask my fear and pain, I do not have to attend so closely to your own. Such numbness is not selective, however, for as we block our pain, we reduce our capacity for happiness – for this too comes through the same emotional channels. As I commit to my own spiritual healing and "lighten up," I discover that I can increasingly feel the moments of your pain and, by joining with you, facilitate our mutual healing. Freed from the illusions and burdens of these states, I can feel the authenticity of your hurt and sadness, for we are truly parts of each other. This mandates that I continue my own clearing so that the energies being released do not backup into my own system. The deeper we commit to loving another, the more the physics of spirituality demands of us. The more I commit to my personal healing, the more deeply we are energetically joined. With this promise of heightened intimacy, I desire to be present to you without burdening our exchange with the pain and powerlessness imposed by my past.

The trances imposed by our life traumas keep us separated from each other. "Trauma" is the label that we give to those trances that are induced through physical or emotional overwhelm. We have all known such moments of encoding, given the sensitivity of the nervous system. Our degree of encoding varies, however, and is relative to the quality and vulnerability of the boundaries that provide our security. The earlier in our lives that we experience a boundary violation, the more potent will be the emotional charge of the trance that follows. While it is true that we move in and out of altered states of consciousness many times an hour, including those states of fantasy and daydreaming that carry us through difficult times, it is the painful trance induced by overwhelming stress and trauma that poses a problem. Our minds are instantly seized by these moments of pain and pulled out of present time, removing us from authentic presence and communication. At such moments I act from fear and the script, no longer hearing you as you are, but receiving your words through the filters of my own history and pain. This aloneness is not acceptable to me. To walk the path of beauty I will have to make myself authentic first. This is within my grasp. From this place, then, I may recognize you, remember you, and truly know you. Intimacy flows freely in such a place.

In our current world, the trances come rapidly: several every hour. Pain induces this automatic protective reaction we call "trance." It is mostly a subconscious and automatic protection deeply rooted in our physiology and nature. Due to the excess of visual imagery, auditory over-stimulation, etc., we are apparently producing too much adrenaline. Under repeated sensory bombardment with stress and trauma-inducing images, our immune systems are slowing their production of T-cells to allow for increased steroid hormone production in order to assist us in dealing with crisis. Our endocrine systems are over-taxed. If we do not curb or address this over-stimulation of our senses, we will become ill. This is our wake-up call. Have you been wondering about the remarkable rise in autoimmune disorders over these last years? One source is obvious: how long have we been living in crisis or its replayed images?

Media has discovered that ratings rise when the population is hypnotized to the screen by the triggering of adrenaline-producing altered states. This has given rise to "reality TV" and the proliferation of trauma-based imagery and advertising. We are captured by images that in any way resemble our own encoded states of consciousness. The triggering of our traumatic memories gives rise to increased steroid hormone production (adrenaline), endorphins, and encephalins that are generated within the bodymind to produce the necessary "fight, flight, or freeze" response to crisis. They offer the momentary promise of strength, calm, and clarity to address the crisis. This is the lure of the trigger. This system, however, was not designed to be running continuously.

Global trances like that induced on September 11th of 2001 mandate our self-care. Any "terrorism" left unresolved in our personal or collective history surfaces, I assure you, under the continuous replay of archetypal images of boundary violations and trauma. Terrorists choose archetypal symbols or values to induce the greatest fear in the largest percentage of the population. They attack our common symbols of industrial achievement, economic prosperity, defense, and democratic rule. At such moments of invasion, we spontaneously "trance" to protect ourselves. It would appear that we have been trancing – repressing our pain subconsciously and automatically for at least 1.5 million years. We no longer even recognize these altered states of mind from authentic presence. I have seen this in my work with over eleven thousand trauma survivors in these last years. In the worst of cases, we begin to identify ourselves with the pain of the trance imposed by trauma or abuse. We identify ourselves with the shame over time and begin to live from its frequency and level of morality. But such negativity is not our nature and will create a profound sense of loss as we move away from our power and the clarity that emanates from the Source within us. We call ourselves home when we diverge too far from center.

We have come to this planet, earth, for purposes of empowerment – for both self and others. Many souls in feminine form have come to reclaim their power from oppressive persons and systems: embracing their strength and autonomy in this lifetime. Many, in masculine form, have come to surrender their illusions of power to find the strength that comes from tenderness and vulnerability. All come to find balance.

As we begin this journey, I share one prayer that I find helpful. I am uncertain of its origin, but I have made some modifications as a result of my own meditations. It is patterned after the traditional language of the "Our Father."

> *Prime Creator, Intelligent Infinity, the One Source of All,*
> *Which dwells in perfect balance,*
> *Sacred is the vibration of the Logos,*
> *May the plan of our higher selves be realized*
> *As we surrender to the Divine within.*
> *May we manifest our place in the plan.*
> *May we experience all we need to overcome.*
> *Teach us to release and empty that we may be filled!*
> *Guide us through the shadows of our fears,*
> *That we may be freed of the illusions of separation,*
> *For ours is the wisdom, the power and the glory,*
> *Beyond time and space.*
> *So be it.*

(Modified Version, Original author, Unknown)

CHAPTER 2

ಶಲಞ

"VISIONS AND DREAMS"

Then afterward I will pour out my spirit upon all mankind.
Your sons and daughters shall prophesy,
Your old men shall dream dreams,
Your young men shall see visions.

(Book of Joel 3:1-2)

The paths we tread as beings of light cannot be navigated by the rational mind alone. If I had tried to use pure rationality to direct my life decisions, I doubt that I would be doing the healing work I do today. I was first taught by the "visionary" abilities of others about our capacity to transcend the limitations of the rational mind. My mother was the first to teach me about our mystical natures: There is a way of "seeing" that transcends the traditional laws of physics but is sometimes more real than the current "scientific" world we know. She demonstrated the importance of this knowledge when I was once in a car accident. When I eventually called her three hours after the accident, I discovered that she had been meditating or praying, waiting for my call. She even pinpointed the time of the accident as 3:23 p.m. and stated that she felt in her body the moment that the accident occurred – growing "ice cold" and feeling a wave of fear pass over her. This "feeling" had led her to pray for my safety; I had no doubt that it helped. In another demonstration of her ability to connect with her children, she called the Veteran's Hospital where my brother Jerry was domiciled. She asked what had happened to him, whereupon the hospital employee informed her that the ambulance was arriving at that moment to take him for x-rays. He had apparently fallen and broken his ankle, but the employee was disgruntled because no one was supposed to inform her of the accident until a formal diagnosis had been obtained and emergency care fully provided. The employee thought that a co-worker had called her prematurely and "broken protocol." Her empathy and vision at moments of crisis led me to respect the authenticity and importance of her type of perception. She experienced an episode of this nature with each of the children in our family. Over time I came to realize that such "sight" is not relegated to the few, but is inherent to our nature as spiritual beings. Like many of us, I was skeptical about any abilities of my own and required the assistance of some "messengers" to change this belief. These guides appeared quite spontaneously and gently directed me down the path that I now walk. My hope is that the personal insights I gained from these "angels" can, likewise, facilitate your own spiritual progress in a manner that honors your own timing and spiritual evolution. Perhaps these accounts may ease your own transition.

I recall that one of my friends in the college seminary, Isaac, around 1977, stated that he had experienced a series of dreams which indicated that in the future I would be doing some type of healing work with my hands. I responded skeptically at the time, commenting that I had never felt any such abilities in my hands or anywhere else. Isaac stated that this was not too surprising, but added that some people were able to tap into the consciousness or energy surrounding the body and could read or "see" events, truths, and facts about life that resided in this emanation of consciousness. Isaac stated that his grandmother could do this as well. He added that some people are more naturally oriented to be "receivers," sometimes getting spontaneous images while in the presence of others. Others, he indicated, are predisposed as "senders" who possess a presence or energy field that enables others to see images like those he had been receiving. Over time I came to realize that we are all capable of both: receiving and sending energy as part of our nature as beings of light. At that early stage in my own development, I remember just shrugging and wondering what all this weirdness meant. Though we were in a Catholic seminary at the time, I wasn't sure how strictly orthodox this would be considered. I was erroneously imprinted with the message during my religious instruction that mysticism was restricted to the few and the gifted – those who were strictly chosen by God! Such spiritual gifts could not be earned or acquired in any way. I wondered where my mother and Isaac fit into the bigger picture of things, since both of them seemed fairly normal to me, but definitely gifted. I also was not sure how I felt about being one who helped others to see images or memories. Looking back, I think that Isaac was a blessing who provided one of the first steps to prepare me for what was to come. Over twenty-five years later, I know a great deal more about the science of consciousness and our mystical nature. Even the religious systems have come around a bit more since then. One of my spiritual directors, Janusz Ihnatowicz, from my college years entitled his doctoral dissertation: "The Ordinary Mysticism of the Laity." His premise was that there existed a vast number of unknown or "anonymous" mystics who were simply ordinary, everyday people who meditated and prayed on a daily basis, and who were profoundly contributing to the whole of spiritual consciousness. I believe this to be true. He helped to normalize mysticism for me by his teachings and example.

Another stepping-stone presented itself in my college years through my friend Alfred who shared a vivid dream in which he swore I had been a priest-healer in "another lifetime." I humored him and brushed it off, but the truth remained that his description annoyed and disturbed me – and for a variety of reasons. For one, Alfred's dreams had often proved prophetic and usually held at least a grain of truth. The second reason was more theological in nature. Given the Catholic fervor about making sure that we make the most of this lifetime in case it is the only one we have, the whole reincarnation issue was something not to be discussed openly. When I later asked one of our more conservative bishops about this, he quietly commented that the truth was that we just do not know if past lives exist or not. Since we cannot prove it either way, he elaborated, the church has traditionally taught that we should all just focus on the present lifetime and make the most of it. I recalled that my mother had experienced six miscarriages and stillbirths; the notion of reincarnation offered some consolation when I thought of the lost opportunities of those lives ended so prematurely. In the interim, I remained open to the discussion and found it surprising to discover that Hassidic Judaism had always taught a doctrine of reincarnation or "transmigration." Rabbi Yonassan Gershom's work: *Beyond the Ashes: Cases of Reincarnation from the Holocaust*[3] was a real eye-opener and affirmation for me. I was surprised to learn from the Catholic scholars that even St. Jerome, renowned for his linguistic and literary talents – having translated the Bible into Latin from the Greek and Aramaic, believed that he did so easily because he had been a scribe in a former life. It impressed me that a Catholic "Saint" believed in other lifetimes. The book by Dr. Brian Weiss, *Many Lives, Many Masters*,[4] wherein he chronicled the spontaneous appearance of regression into past lives and the resolution of all of his clients' pain symptoms during therapy, also had a profound impact on me, but this occurred after I had already entered the therapy field. Even prior to this, however, when I had first left formal ministry and was considering a career shift into the therapy field, I remembered Alfred's dream, but only after experiencing some very vivid dreams of my own.

When I left formal ministry and was considering full-time teaching, perhaps even responding to an offer to join the Jesuits, I had a series of very powerful dreams that affected me profoundly and redirected me to the healing sciences. In the most vivid of these, I was one of three students (scribes) in training in a red granite chamber inside a pyramidal structure. Our instructor, a splendidly attired priestess opened an ornate golden shrine and removed a scroll from it. She unrolled the scroll, whereupon I discovered that I could read the writing easily. I awakened from the dream, feeling disappointed that the world I currently lived in did not seem anywhere near as spiritually nurturing as the culture of my dream. The dream and its mindset, in some ways, seemed more real than that of the waking world. When I finally checked the history books to determine the validity of the unusual names from the scroll, the names and locations were real and could be dated precisely to four thousand years ago.

The strongest support for the existence of "past life" perception was of a profound nature and occurred unexpectedly during a training workshop with Gail Konz, a world-renowned intuitive and healer. During the final exercise of her workshop, I was flooded with an inexplicable energy and startled by a body of emotion that emanated from the area of my solar plexus and, much to my surprise, was even physically felt by those seated nearest me. From its nature and intensity, I knew instantly that this force was most certainly not the product of any accumulated experience in this lifetime. Being predominantly "clairsentient" or "kinesthetic" – one who feels memories and issues rather than a "clairvoyant" who sees such images, I was overwhelmed by the profound recollections of having spent eons with her in friendship and service in the past. I no longer merely "believed" in past lives, I remembered from a profound level in my being that such depths of relationship do exist and remain intact over vast expanses of time. This generated quite a shift from my traditional religious upbringing, but was undeniable in its reality and impact upon my spirit and my work.

In the final analysis, however, we need not become overly concerned with the question of "past lives." The fact remains that any unresolved issues that we hold from "the past" are fully linked to this lifetime and the body that we now manifest. This is the "karma" referred to in many religious systems. "Karma" is precisely this: the unfinished lessons of the past carried into this lifetime/this body in order to facilitate resolution and healing; it is simply the "unfinished" or incomplete memory or scene, imprinted in our consciousness with "less than love" present. It is a deficiency of love, light captured in the matrix of consciousness on an energetic level. This "blueprint" we bear with us as lessons on an energetic and spiritual level as we evolve upward. Recently, while working with a gifted client who identified herself as a medical intuitive, she described the interrelationship she saw between the energetic "blueprint" of previous lifetimes and the merging of this pattern with the physiological structure and DNA of her body from the moment of conception onward. She was able to see a specific pattern of trauma that was intergenerational through her mother and used her perception to address this trauma that re-presented itself during the earliest stages of this lifetime. As she reframed this experience, we both felt, at the same moment, a strong energy release from her nervous system. I have never felt such releases when the claims are imaginary or spurious in nature.

Over the past fifteen years, I have witnessed over a thousand such instances of "past life" memories that presented as actual trances encoded as pain in the current body of the client. In the development of my work, however, I often wondered why so few of my clients accessed "past life" memories if they were as powerful and real as some claimed. Over time I came to realize that this physical body and its memories serve as the perfect vehicle for our spiritual evolution. All memory is accessible from the current body that we manifest. This body mirrors our blueprint accurately. By focusing on its pain and triggers, the blueprint and unfinished lessons of the soul are revealed. Before developing the sensitivity in my hands, I was not convinced about the authenticity of past lives, and while I am not sure that such a label is the most accurate to describe this phenomenon, my hands have never lied to me when it comes to the pain of an actual traumatic event. In the end, quantum physics teaches us that time is merely a matter of perception, and all lifetimes actually co-exist simultaneously, in a manner of speaking. Hence, the notion of "past" lives may be somewhat inaccurate. Given our need to communicate using the predominant "linear" language of our day, it suffices.

From my work, there are suggestions that the trauma metaphor itself actually transcends any single lifetime and serves as the perfect vehicle for resolving "karma" and any long-standing trauma from other places and times. Resolution of such metaphors, therefore, can have a tremendous impact by clearing all of the pattern's temporal occurrences. However, I have also seen individuals dismiss the body's present cues and focus on "past life" memories as a way of avoiding current responsibilities and the pain of the wounded voices of this lifetime. An excessive focus on the issue of past lives can sometimes be a matter of avoidance or ego. In general, it would appear that the body memories that we now hold only demand a return to absolute origin when the "emotional charge" of the precipitating act is greatly stronger in the "past life scene" than its manifestation in this lifetime. The invitation of all memory is integration and the maturing of love. It is a delight to be able to share the resources now available for such multi-dimensional healing.

The dreams, visions, and memories we each hold are all articulations occurring within the sacred arena that we now call "holographic space." It is this multi-dimensional realm of the mind that hosts our every thought and movement in time. Michael Talbot, in his book, *The Holographic Universe,*[5] laid out for us the physics which explains our visions, our mystical phenomena, and even our capacity to transcend the limits of space and time. We shall examine various aspects of this ability in the chapters that follow, for such vision is our nature, not the exception. As we open to the vast realms accessible through the unconscious mind, we embrace our mystical natures and come to know ourselves as the visionaries we all are.

CHAPTER 3

∾⃝

"THE WAKE-UP CALL"

There are no accidents.
Every moment of existence is a summons to awaken!

Buried beneath the surface of our existence is both mystery and perfect wisdom. It beckons us in infinite and often unnoticed ways. We usually remain true to this voice without consciously realizing it. This wisdom comprehends what we call accident. It invites our pain, our mistakes, and our traumas as invitations to awaken. It utilizes our seemingly fruitless efforts to produce fruit recognizable only decades later. Such wisdom contextualizes everything we have ever known and experienced within a meaningful matrix. It embraces our rage, futility, and grief as anticipated outbursts while loving us all the while. It perceives death, defeat, and victimhood as the retractive forces that catapult us the greatest distances toward enlightenment.

Though we, as human beings, are prone to doubt ourselves and our connection to the wisdom that resides within, life speaks to us through circumstances and events that seem "accidental" at first, but which, over time, reveal a purpose and a plan: they reveal a perfection. There is a unity and flow that underlies every thought and action – a force of attraction that frequently discloses itself through our passionate attachment to persons, places, and events. These voices of attraction insert themselves in such a manner that they force us to reexamine our relationship to self and other. Though largely an unconscious process until now, we are gaining momentum as we ride upon these waves of consciousness, driven inevitably into the necessary realization that, ultimately, there is no private pain. We are all so interconnected. These lessons of intimacy do not come easily to us due to this investment of "ego" and our age-old mechanisms of defense. We surround ourselves with beliefs that maintain the illusions of separateness that keep us from personalizing and owning the pain we feel. The effort to which the universe will go in order to help us transcend these barriers to conscious awakening is almost unfathomable. It is at once humbling and startling to realize that our histories are filled with moments when the universe repeatedly extended its hand, inviting us to step out of our illusory world-view, to meet all the disparate parts of ourselves – an invitation to healing and enlightenment.

I share with you a touching experience of my own, not so much a lesson about myself as it is a study in the importance of reclaiming ourselves individually and collectively from the past. Looking back, I must laugh at my own degree of resistance and the subsequent measures that were required to shift my thinking and "nudge" me onto the right path. In reflection, I think that I must have been a "slow learner" to have positioned myself where I would be forced to manually extricate myself from my own spiritual entrapment in history. Archaeology, my first love as a child, was to be the passionate vehicle for this awakening.

It was the most remarkable experience that has ever happened to me – unearthing another human being, my height, my age, from a period in human evolution with which I had been obsessed until the day I removed his skull from the ground. He died when the cave collapsed on top of him, probably while he was sleeping. The hearth still held ash from the fire at his feet. I discovered that we could even determine the contents of his last meal from the remains left in the area of the stomach around the skeleton. The five thousand seven hundred year old unfired "green ware" was still green when I excavated it from the collapse. He apparently startled when the earthquake collapsed the cave sheltering him, because his arm was raised and his mouth opened in a cry. Undoubtedly, it was the most poignant moment of trauma that I had ever been privileged to witness or to discover and excavate. My only claustrophobic reaction had occurred while climbing through a Bar Kochba cave in Israel. I could certainly relate to his predicament. Curious coincidence! Or so I thought at the time.

Ten years prior I had been ordained as a priest and, within a month, left to continue my studies with the Pontifical Biblical Institute in Jerusalem, an extension of our post-graduate studies in Rome. I had arranged the program, having a deep passion for archaeology, which, in fact, pre-dated my interest in ministry. During my nine-month stay in the program in Jerusalem, we studied archaeology with the Hebrew University, and I had the opportunity to live in the Jesuit house located across from the King David Hotel. A big advantage of this and a factor that would later shape my archaeological experience was the fact that the Jesuit residence housed the premier Chalcolithic archaeology collection for the whole Middle East. These were the excavation finds from Teleilat Ghassul[6], excavated by Robert North, S.J., who had been my professor in Rome. The Chalcolithic period had been a great fascination for me, evidencing painted frescos of a spiritual nature hundreds of years before most cultures and even

16

before biblical times. The Chalcolithic inhabitants of this region seemed a largely pacifistic, creative culture with a mysterious, revolutionary talent for artistic expression and innovative ideas. They introduced the "lost-wax" method of casting copper as evidenced in the remarkable finds of Nahal Hever, *The Cave of the Treasure*[7]. This period pre-dated Abraham and other historical biblical figures by over 1400 years. The Chalcolithic period has been estimated to have lasted from approximately 4500-3700 BC.

I had found myself fairly obsessed with the study of flint tools, particularly those manufactured during the Chalcolithic period. During the excavation of 1992, in niches all around the body, we found flint tools virtually identical to those that I had touched and photographed in the Jesuit Museum ten years prior. I was the only person that had ever gone to the trouble of photographing the entire Chalcolithic collection up to that point in time. I couldn't help myself! Touching these ancient objects electrified me. There was an inexplicable magnetism associated with anything related to this particular period of human history. A few days prior to the finding of the skeleton, at a point slightly higher in elevation than that of the body, I had found a pinkish quartz wadi (river) pebble resting on the founding stone of a collapsed column. I knew that this stone was the "hammer stone" used for the manufacture of his flint tools, though the elevation differences would never allow us to prove such. The flint typologist from the Cobb Institute of Archaeology at Mississippi State University informed us that a quartz wadi pebble was known to be the perfect manufacturing tool of the period. Several days prior, I had sensed the finding of such a stone though I cannot explain this in words. It was as though I knew where it was to be found. Three days later, upon removing a bit of soil and seeing two front teeth looking at me from the soil, I knew that there was more to the emerging scene: there was a body reclining on the floor of the cave. The fact that we actually uncovered what I had suspected unnerved me. What did this all mean? What was my connection to this site and this ancient traumatic event? Was it luck? Somehow we had managed to blindly create and position four areas of excavation precisely over the center of a collapsed cave – a cave that happened to collapse with its occupant(s) inside. It was not in any way visible from the surface of the site. When the director first told me to begin excavation on the surface in a given direction, I remember correcting him and him acceding to my suggestion without protest. Why had I insisted on the direction change? I have come to appreciate my intuition as reliable over these years, but still marvel at my unconscious use of my skills at that time in my life. I still recall Gary Zukav's message in *The Seat of the Soul,* that humankind's path of evolution until now has been predominantly unconscious from unconscious intentionality.[8] I did many things unconsciously in those days.

The day before the scheduled removal of the skeleton and all surrounding artifacts from the site, I had the strongest impulse to return alone to the site before sunset. We had completed photographing the site, an event that had included a visit from the director of the American Schools of Oriental Research, Dr. Bill Dever, and some of the journalists and staff from National Geographic. I returned to Site 101, finally alone with the remarkable finds and all the visible evidence of the cave's collapse. I removed the tarp covering the skeleton, and in a private gesture born from the deepest admiration for the beauty, antiquity and vulnerability of the moment, moved my hand slowly over the body from the skull downward and prayed that all residual energies of this being and this lifetime be released to their appropriate place in the spiritual order of the universe … that the spirit of the man who had remained to reveal so much to us, so much later in history, find rest. I did this quite naturally, and felt a calm and peace afterwards.

The strangest effect of this whole experience, however, occurred the afternoon after we had finally removed the skeleton from the excavation and prepared it for transport to Mississippi State University for further examination. Up until that time I had been unable to shake the feeling that it was absolutely necessary for me to do archaeology and to continue excavating. I had to pursue my work with the research project. Termination was unthinkable; I had to return to dig the following summer. That afternoon, one of my colleagues asked me for the umpteenth time whether I would be returning next summer to resume excavation as I had over the past twelve years, and I remember turning to him and responding: "I don't think so. I feel like I've finished what I need to do for now." At that point, I remember pausing in shock and realizing that I truly felt very differently inside than I had since my childhood. Something inexplicable had been completed that day. I knew that it occurred when I removed that resistant, implacable skull from the ground. Somehow, that act, completed something in me that had been insatiable to that day. Something about the completion of that site of excavation changed the dynamics inside me. Suddenly my energies had a new direction and I was free to move forward in a new way. I no longer felt torn by opposing directions in my life. One very powerful voice had been silenced. My own trauma resolution had begun. Little did I know that my real excavation of human trauma had just commenced!

The power of this kinesthetic experience of uncovering a 5,700-year-old instant of trauma with all of its detail intact changed something for me. It touched my heart in a profound way. Trapped though he was by a moment in time, his trauma would offer to us remarkable knowledge and wisdom several thousand years later. His death would become a treasure to us -- so far removed from his original culture and time. In our excavation in the Middle East, we had never recovered the body of a Chalcolithic man intact in its original context. In fact, we rarely found any cemeteries or bodies from this period at all, a rather strange and unexplained phenomenon.

Intuition offers us knowledge and direction by tapping into those resources that transcend the rational mind and the ego. We frequently make some of our best decisions from this place though they may not appear logical at the time or fully explicable from the standpoint of the rational mind. In my own case, I can certainly state that my intuition was always faithful to me. It allowed me to learn more quickly and to consolidate the information into a process that could more readily be taught to others once the dynamics were understood. I now know that we are all capable of developing such a connection between our minds, our hands, and our bodies. The sensitivity in my hands that I developed over those thirteen years of excavation was very helpful and led me in ways that even now I cannot fully understand. I could feel densities in soil texture that allowed me to trace the outline of a deteriorating mud brick wall so precisely that the director of the French excavation, visiting our site, asked where I had received such training. I still recall the time my hands reached out and overturned a pottery handle covered in dirt ... one amid hundreds unearthed by the rains of winter in Israel. We were visiting the site called Lachish, mentioned in numerous biblical passages (cited in the biblical books of Joshua, II Kings, II Chronicles, Nehemiah, Isaiah, Jeremiah, and Micah)[9]. Why I picked up this particular handle amid the hundreds exposed above ground I will never fully grasp. It actually felt as though the object had called out to me! It was only days later, when I washed the dirt from it that I realized that it was a lamelek pottery handle, bearing the seal of the King of Israel. In Hebrew, la means "to/for," and melek means "king." Such stamped handles date to the period of the divided monarchy between 900-700 BC. The archaeologists of the Hebrew University archaeology staff confirmed this after examining it, whereupon I became a footnote in a research article, a specified spot on a map, and the proud possessor of an authentic pottery seal of the King of Israel (they released it back to me saying that I could "keep it since we have nicer ones in our collection at the Department of

Antiquities.") It has proven a wonderful teaching tool for both children and adults alike who have few authentic tactile contacts with the history about which most have only read.

The capacity we possess to focus thought, energy and light into our hands mirrors the enhanced ability we hold to affect the human body and the material world as we know it. This connection that we possess between our minds and our bodies – particularly our hands, served as the bridge between my scientific training and the intuitive faculties which were evidenced by my mother, my great uncle, and eventually, by myself. Looking back, I really think that the years of practice in feeling vibrational differences in soil types set the stage for the later development in distinguishing vibrations with my hands. It also trained me in scientific method. Such manual training provided an experiential knowledge that has allowed me to train others at a pace far more accelerated than my own labored pace. Little did I know the depth of excavation to which these "trusty" hands would eventually commit me, and what a difference they would eventually make in the lives of so many trauma survivors.

Sigmund Freud recognized the value of touch in the recovery of memory. He utilized massage on occasion to stimulate the body to help his clients recover from amnesia. Freud also utilized archaeology as a metaphor to illustrate the importance of understanding our past. He recognized that, unless we embrace our past, we will never understand fully who we are – particularly if these events exert a certain traumatic power and control over us in present time.

From my own experience I now understand that we cannot dismiss the seeming "ruins" or painful events of our past. They are best integrated within our experience as wisdom and lesson. On a more spiritual plane, I have found that such life experiences magnificently set the stage for the emergence of our life mission or purpose. Wisdom is revealed in the remarkable details of our lives, though we may not understand the intricacy and precision of the path when we are still in the "trenches." In retrospect, we will find ourselves amazed at the value and perfection of events that, at the moment of their occurrence, seemed to us chaotic and confusing.

In extricating our spirits from the layers of the past, we come to realize that traumatic events are not always what they appear to be. Such overwhelming events form the backdrop for the orchestrations of the "higher mind." This mind is multi-dimensional in nature and sees beyond the blind constraints of ego. This larger vision offers us the capacity to find meaning and depth in experiences that seem hollow and pointless at first glance. I sometimes remind my clients who have experienced miscarriages that my own mother experienced six miscarriages or stillbirths prior to the births of my sister and me. In the midst of profound trauma was created an opening and a timely opportunity for my sister and me to enter. Looking back, I can see that the timing of these events was perfect! I find it interesting that I eventually became a trauma therapist and that she leads one of the nation's leading programs that assists one of the most traumatized populations on our planet: the deaf-blind! Were there influences at work in our family history that served to stimulate our search for such purpose and meaning in our lives? My sister and I believe this to be the case. Our souls/higher selves can use what the "ego" even calls tragedy to serve its own growth and enlightenment. Life changes and traumas occasion shifts in perception that are pivotal in our spiritual growth and maturation. Great passion frequently emerges directly from our encounter with these transformative moments. Our life mission is readily defined through the sculpting of our identity by those "dark" experiences that help us to determine what is consonant with and what is alien to our nature. All too often the traumas and "inexplicable" events of our lives serve as the very "wake-up" call that we require to move us out of complacency and to open us up to previously unfathomable opportunities.

CHAPTER 4

℘Ⴉ℘

"FROM SOLID TO LIGHT"

It is inevitable that, as we relinquish our over-identification with the slowed-down, crystallized, dense energy we know as matter, we come to experience ourselves as light. Secure as Light, everything changes.

If you were to join an archaeological excavation, as a new archaeology student, you would be taught to feel the difference between a rock and soil, a mud brick and rain-deposited sediment, a piece of pottery and a flint blade. Each material sends its own resonance through the handle of the digging tool – the "patish," and this vibration allows you to know something of its nature before you can even observe it with your eyes. Dr. Paul Jacobs, one of my earliest instructors, taught me well and would set me onto tracing elusive midden (domestic living) surfaces that undulated and were even interrupted by rain and debris. I enjoyed these challenges. I never imagined, however, that one could actually drop the patish and that the hand itself could be used to feel vibrational differences in any form of matter. This "leap" emerged over time.

When I completed my training in Rome in 1984, I spent some time in training with the Remote Sensing Laboratory at the John C. Stennis Space Center in Bay St. Louis, Mississippi. My goal was to explore possible applications of satellite scanner technology to improve archaeological methodology by replacing the random surface survey approach with scanner data that was far more precise. They had already located prehistoric occupational sites along the Nile while accidentally engaging the Shuttle Imaging Radar-B. Though my personal project never quite came to fruition, I gained some critical information. From eight hundred nautical miles above the earth, we possessed, already in 1982, the capacity to distinguish one type of vegetation or plant from another; we could locate large marijuana fields or cocoa plants from such scanners. Man-made structures appeared distinctive under the scrutiny of the scanners. Further investigation revealed to me that each form of matter possessed its own "spectral signature." I immediately realized that something as complex as the energy system of the human body would also evidence a unique signature at each moment of consciousness.

In your body, with your unique DNA, personal perceptions, memories, history, and feelings, each moment of consciousness is a "spectral" work of art. Kirlian photography had suggested this, though with a greatly averaged and diminished capacity for articulation of the field. Consciousness itself, I knew, was fluid, constantly changing, and varied from moment to moment. If it was, indeed, true that we experienced from fifteen to fifty trance states an hour with the respective body changes, the human energy field would prove infinitely complex and changing -- reflecting the many shifts in consciousness. Each state, in fact, each moment of consciousness, I realized, possessed the unique signature of our personal energy system. This information would later prove most valuable in recognizing the uniqueness of the power we hold to heal our own memories. Initially, I was led to believe that such energy signatures were only recognizable by specially calibrated scanners such as those developed by my colleagues at the Remote Sensing Lab. A number of those brilliant scientists I befriended and enjoyed while sharing hours of enlightening discussions regarding our various fields of specialization. I was particularly amused when I found out that they initially thought I was at the lab to help develop a "Vatican spy satellite system," since "00120 Vatican City State" had been my address for five years in Rome, though our college was officially outside the walls of the Vatican.

Some time passed before I made the connection with that remarkable summer at the Remote Sensing Laboratory in Mississippi, realizing that our human bodies, particularly the hands, appear to possess the capacity for scanning distortions, not unlike the calibrated scanners with which I was acquainted from the lab. One of the first surprises in the evolution of my own sensitivity was the realization that, as I cleared my own memories and "dense, heavy" electromagnetic encoding, I was able to sense more from my clients. In meditation I would notice that I was able to sense the movement of energy in my body where previously I had only felt heaviness and solidity. After a time, I started to become aware that the light feeling of flowing energy was the norm, whereas the heaviness of the body was the illusion that we have been reduced to by the feeling of physical density induced from our trauma memories. Over time I noticed that the increased energy flow in my body became so intense that I could only feel the energy – I was no longer aware of my "physical body" at all! With this expanded definition of "self" – learning to perceive myself as light or energy, the rules of human interaction began to change.

Early on there were suggestions that our true nature is one of light, and that much of the apparent heaviness of the body is the by-product

24

of encoded trauma. Perhaps our heaviness is largely due to our "domestication," as Don Miguel Ruiz so aptly phrased it in *The Four Agreements*.[10] In the "breaking" or fragmentation of our spirits, much is lost. And having been domesticated during our evolution, we have lost our capacity for fluid movement as light and energy. I finally asked the question: Well, if humankind has been encoding trauma for 1.5 million years, what exactly is our "intended" perception of self – what are we capable of becoming as spiritual beings? Perhaps we are light-beings and were not intended to live by the perceptions of the density and burden that so many centuries of trauma have subconsciously imposed? Was this heavy energetic congestion merely the by-product of trauma? How was such a burdensome energy impacting our capacity to heal and recover from illness and depression? What would we become without such density?

The answer to this last question, I realized, was suggested by my own mother: she had always demonstrated abilities that defied the "solid" world-view of the old Newtonian physics. She could "feel" my car accident in Lake Charles, my sister's miscarriage, and my brother's broken ankle. Similarly, I felt the moment of her death all the way from Rome, Italy. Clearly there was something that suggested a capacity for connectedness that moved us beyond the current level of scientific explanation. In *The Holographic Universe*,[11] Michael Talbot had discussed the "holographic" nature of reality as a quantum perception of light images projected from some unknown and inexplicable source. This idea I found comforting and consonant with my family's physics. My mother picked up images and sensations without regard for distances or time. I learned from her example. I later applied it in a moment of desperation when my friend Doug had urgently asked me to meditate and send him light to alleviate a very painful glandular inflammation. That night, I sat down to meditate and visualized him seated in front of me. Closing my eyes, I scanned his body with my hands, locating pain sites and sending to those sites the colors that came to me. I did so at each site where I felt pain in my hands. I felt warmth and the disappearance of the pain over each site. A few weeks later I spoke with him again and heard him say: "You did the meditation that I asked you to do that night, didn't you?" "Of course!" I responded. He said: "I knew it! All my pain went away that night and only recently has started to return." I assured him that I would continue to send him "light," all the while, amazed that the holographic visualization had worked so well. Perhaps prayer was simply a matter of moving beyond our illusions of separateness and connecting as light with light.[12] It certainly worked with Doug! I encourage you to try this exercise with friends and loved ones in need of healing.

I am now certain that trauma and all forms of "incomplete" memory contribute to our illusions of separateness by adding a heavy, dense electromagnetic quality to our holographic bodies. This is not to say that the body is not "real." But it IS saying that reality is holographic: meaning that all reality is a matter of perceiving the refraction of light multi-dimensionally. It is all about perception.

In training individuals to utilize their skills to facilitate the healing of others, I require that they make efforts to "clear" their own energy fields – taking advantage of opportunities to resolve the dense energies of their own trauma histories. It is in the clearing of these denser energies that the spiritual mobility of the light being truly occurs.

CHAPTER 5

ಐಐಐ

"OUR SOURCE OF SAFETY"

Our greatest and most challenging lesson is that true safety resides within us. We thought that hiding in the dark would bring safety, but Darkness is at home there. We are most safe in our radiance where we cannot even be seen except by those who live at that same frequency. That which dwells in darkness is blinded as it approaches the light. In our truth resides our safety.

Hidden beneath the dense illusion of our trauma-based perceptions is pure light. This light offers safety and completeness. It is the only safety we truly possess. This is one of our hardest and most important lessons. Trauma imprints on most of us at such a young age that we get stuck in our early development, still waiting for the safe rescuer-nurturer to arrive. We continue looking outward for safety: expecting our parents, our educators, our religious and societal systems to "complete" us; we turn to food, drugs, alcohol, work, relationships, power, money, sex, adrenaline, exercise, swamis, gurus, diets, religion and a host of other promising authoritative systems, looking for an external source of comfort and safety. But this is a challenge that these "resources" cannot resolve for us. The reason is this: they are not the source of our blockage; we are! Let us take a look at the physics of safety.

As we shine outward into the universe, we summon to ourselves others of like kind. If we carry the imprint of a traumatic event or individual within our field unresolved, we radiate outward white light everywhere except in our field where we continue to hold the darkly-framed image of the specific abuse or deprivation. Outward into the universe we shine except where we are using our creative power to contain the pain and darkness of our trauma. This precise trauma profile, though subconsciously and automatically encoded, creates a "dark spot" imprinted over our light core. As a result, a specific void, or vacuum, is created by this absence of light, summoning every individual or event that fits this dark hole or profile in our field of consciousness.

This is the physics of consciousness. We summon those very beings whose imprints we hold. If I carry unresolved abuse from an alcoholic or emotionally unavailable father, for instance, I will rapidly summon other individuals or systems that fit this profile on a subconscious level. The inherent magnetism created by this void feels perilously close to the intense draw of love. Quite frequently, we cannot tell the difference. When our ninety-three percent subconscious mind holds traumatic imprints, we can create an intense vacuum that will seek to fill itself. In creating from the void, we usually retraumatize ourselves. Until we correct or complete our subconsciously imprinted, trauma-based definitions of love, we will continue to manifest from the void. Such relationships will offer an opportunity to mirror our unfinished "business," affording an opportunity for personal and, perhaps, mutual healing, otherwise resulting in divergent paths when one individual heals the void when the other does not. When I left ministry, my oldest sister and I started dating members of the same family at the same time in a city of three hundred thousand persons without consciously knowing it. The physics is clear.

At the time of this writing, I have had the opportunity to immerse my hands in the immediate energy fields of many thousands of people. These experiences were both humbling and transformative. There are untold numbers of lessons to be shared from such intimacy with the delicate energies of this sacred space. As one client began to speak of the traumas that she had "already addressed," mentioning the name of her ex-husband, my hands began to ache and suddenly burn, revealing sadness and an unresolved anger that kept her attached to him emotionally, in spite of her conscious efforts to move on with her life. In my hands there was evidenced a sure knowledge that she remained with him in one or more scenes of grief and anger in her subconscious. Another individual stated that all of her memories of sexual trauma had been addressed in past therapy, while, at that moment, my hands began to ache with the naming of her perpetrators: the subconscious revealing through her body and its fields that there were some unresolved issues that she could not yet consciously admit.

Paramount in importance is the fact that what I am describing are *stages of sensitivity that we all will experience* as part of clearing and healing our memories. I was told years ago by one of my spiritual teachers that I should document the changes that I would experience as I became more effective at perceiving the various movements of energy during the healing process. The reason for his recommendation became obvious: *They are routine stages through which we will all pass as we rise in consciousness and open to our true spiritual capacity for intimacy.* This has proven true in my training of over fifteen hundred individuals in these last years. But how eager are we as a society to embrace such a heightened capacity for intimacy? Such spiritual awareness greatly modifies our concept of safety. The issue changes from "How far away can I get from this violence so distant from my own nature?" to "What can I do to facilitate the healing of this aspect of consciousness of which I am a part?" When we discover the interconnectedness of all living beings, separating or "dissociating" ourselves tends to reinforce the trauma pattern rather than resolve it. When we stop pushing away the most wounded elements of our society and embrace them as parts of ourselves, we will move beyond justice to mercy, compassion, and authentic healing. Our prison system is a prime example of this. When we dissociate others from ourselves and induce further shame in them, we intensify their addictive and compulsive tendencies; this is simply the natural by-product of shame induction. When an individual is shamed s/he is more likely to act out those negative subconscious imprints; the trauma patterns have been strengthened by additional abuse. By applying dissociative controls, society, as a whole, will not be safer in the long-term picture of things.

On the one hand, it sure seems easier when our lives are not so interconnected – when we can neither validate nor negate the claims made by others about the nature of reality, as they perceive it. If we are truly separate, we do not have to know the degree of pain that others experienced at a moment of abuse or trauma. In fact, if we are so different and separate from each other, I cannot even feel your pain; such a thing should be impossible. This is convenient. In our detachment and disconnectedness, we can live our own lives without any awareness of the overlapping nature of consciousness, energy fields, and emotions. Violence can occur "out there," but it ultimately remains fairly distant and separate from our personal world. Hunger and deprivation can remain far from my world. There is, in a sense, an incentive to remain hidden behind the dense energies of our own shame and personal trauma histories. There are tremendous implications if we accept our natural capacity to recognize and feel what is authentic, what is true. To reach this place of awareness, however, we cannot continue to deceive ourselves, pretending that certain painful experiences have had no impact on us. We cannot simply push our emotional pain out of mind. (The farthest away we will ever push an unresolved traumatic experience is a millisecond anyway.) There is only one mind and it embraces all! Denying or ignoring the existence of the wounded parts of us is not safety. Remember? We attract what we truly bear within our field of consciousness. External reality will act as a quantum mirror: creating exactly according to our degree of resolution/irresolution. The

29

more we deny or treat as entertainment the violence of our history, the more likely we are to project or manifest a large scale or global trauma from the collective subconscious. The subconscious accepts as reality whatever images we present to it whether they are viewed as entertainment or actual "news" – though even here the boundaries are becoming blurred.

The question of safety, therefore, becomes a personal one. To heal oneself is to heal the world. Of course, this is true only if all is interconnected – only if there is, in fact, only one mind that connects all. If we are all expressions of the one flow of consciousness, it would surely explain why I can feel your pain. It would explain how I can feel your release of anger just as you feel it – how I can know in an instant that buried beneath your anger is a sadness which burdens your heart – or that buried beneath your sadness is a shame which stings my hands as you repeatedly stab yourself with thoughts of judgment and self-recrimination. We walk through this world with faces that seek to mask our pain. We hide behind the illusions and densities of the five senses. What happens when we learn to transcend the physical world of the five senses and embrace our greater capacity for intimacy? What happens to our world when we gain the capacity to feel through the masks? Are we ready for the invitation and changes that this promises us?

The only true safety is the clarity and luminosity of self. Jesus sought to deliver this message over two thousand years ago. "Light from light" is the phrase used to describe Jesus in the liturgical creed of the Catholic tradition. The light source is within. Spirituality originates from within. The shadows of the outer world are projections of that which we hold within our creative consciousness. "Do you not see that nothing that enters a man from outside can make him impure; that which comes out of him, and only that, constitutes impurity" – Jesus states in the Gospel of Mark (7:15). If you wish to know the clarity of your heart, examine the events and relationships that you manifest in the outer world. They are absolute mirrors of the light or shadows kept in the filter of the emotional body, the "pain body," as Eckhart Tolle calls it.[13] Our unresolved emotional pain, trapped statically in the cells and fields of our bodies, will alter the emanations of light to create the patterns of our outer world. We are not the victims of this world. We are its creators – sculpting it by our love and our hate, our joy and our rage.

Rather than continuing to manifest our outward reality from these subconscious influences, we are approaching a time in our evolution when we will have conscious choice. The clearing of the emotional body restores our intentionality, enabling us to make new choices, conscious choices, rather than leaving us resigned to the world that appears before us as it is projected to us through the filter of our pain histories. Our safety, therefore, resides in our healing and the clearing of our intentionality – in the release of those outdated intentions that are imposed from moments of fear, trauma, and self-doubt. As adults, safety and the lack of safety have much to do with our subconscious influences and attractions.

More recently I have begun doing workshops at Miraval (located North of Tucson, Arizona) with Wyatt Webb, author of the book: *It's Not About the Horse – It's About Overcoming Fear and Self-Doubt.*[14] During these workshops, I marvel at the lessons about our power to create and maintain safety. In the "Equine Experience," the attendees are asked to perform certain tasks with the horse. When there is no response from the horse, or when the individual puts him/herself in harm's way, Wyatt inevitably pulls him/her aside and asks when, where, and how this pattern originated. "How long have you been placing yourself in dangerous situations while you're trying so hard to get your needs met?" As soon as the trance, the memory source of the boundary damage and danger, is resolved within the psyche, the horse responds immediately. We can then perform our task from an innate ability to do so – from a place of centeredness, safety, and self-respect. It is in the wounding of our boundaries and self-respect that we attract to ourselves the shadow experiences that endanger us. The implications here are immense.

If we are, for instance, predisposed to alcoholism through family history and genetics, the denial of the presence of this disease will not foster our safety; blindness to our alcoholism will enable the disease to progress unabated. It will also attract to us others of like kind. To embrace our "truths" is the only sure path to safety. I saw Wyatt work with one of my clients who was struggling with issues regarding his sexuality. His denial of his feelings also "closed off" an authentic part of himself and compromised his interactions with others – including the horse, during one of Wyatt's therapeutic exercises. He learned that he could not deny essential aspects of his nature and expect authentic intimacy from the restrictive world he subsequently created. In addition, the denial of his feelings and orientation placed him in a position of living with no healthy emotional or sexual outlets supportive of his nature. The danger in living from such a place is that the ensuing repression leads to compulsion, addiction, and depersonalized "acting out" behaviors that wound the psyche. When we deny such powerful aspects of our personhood, we act from an imbalanced and even dangerous place. When we move into denial about essential aspects of our being, we make decisions from a myopic and skewed perspective. True safety comes, I reminded him, from embracing our truth and attracting those situations and individuals that support authentic growth. In denying our truth, we detach from the source and become vulnerable to many extraneous influences. The voice of trauma will draw to itself others of like kind. In embracing our truth, in whatever form it takes, we live and act from our alignment with the truth and the Higher Mind. Our responsibility, therefore, is to live fully from the integrity offered by our "truth" and our connection to the Source. When we are bombarded by the voices and messages of trauma, we are unable to attend to the voice of our Higher Self directing us to safety, intimacy, abundance, and fulfillment. As we resolve the false messages induced through trauma, we are free to listen to the voice of our intuition gently guiding us through the perils of our trauma-laden world. This capacity to be attentive to the movements of consciousness and to act from our truth is the only path to true safety.

Take a moment to do this exercise. Imagine yourself free, if only for a moment, of all trauma and pain. Picture yourself connected to the river of white light that is our Source. Visualize yourself as a sphere of silver or golden-white light. As you move through your life and resolve your trauma memories, you complete the dark imprints (which create vulnerable openings) that were left in your field through trauma; you seal those openings and fully become that sphere of metallic-white light. If someone then approaches you with the same positive frequency or intention, they can easily see and connect with you. This light-boundary is fully permeable and familiar as would be one silver light being to another. On the other hand, if others of dark intention or "negative" emotional states approach you, they have difficulty seeing you in your truth without blinding themselves and experiencing their own pain. Those that live in caves cannot simply walk out into the light without being blinded by the contrast. The closer they approach you in an effort to render harm, the more difficult you are to behold. Your true safety, therefore, is to be found by standing in your truth, your integrity. You are safe by simply being the silver or golden-white light that you are. In this highest frequency of light, you simply mirror back anything that does not pertain to you or your journey. You are easily able to not take things personally and can readily discern what is yours from what is not. When you find your boundary integrity violated or absent in your daily life, look for the source of the intrusion. Though it may appear to originate from the outside, there is usually an earlier memory or trauma already at work in your system that left an opening for this to occur. As we heal these "incomplete" states of consciousness, we become invulnerable to the old patterns and triggers. They no longer affect us. As we radiate outward from the source within, we need only abide in our truth to know safety, love, and authentic intimacy.

CHAPTER 6

℘℃℞

"BECOMING TRANSLUCENT"

*All of our relationships change when we are no longer
separated by illusions of separation and the trauma that
maintains density and darkness in the bodymind. We are truly
parts of each other; we are aspects of the One Mind.*

It is simple and natural for anyone to learn to feel consciousness
as a flow of energy in the bodymind and its meridians. Acupuncture
has become an accepted practice in Western medicine. The reason for
our natural ability to sense energy flow through the nerve plexes of the
body is that sites of encoded trauma – domestic violence, anger, fear,
shame, abandonment, grief, and pain all exist as distinctive frequencies
within the fields of consciousness. They are forms of energy. Despite
the variety of hands-on energy applications now developed, there
remains no faster way to learn the frequencies of traumatic encoding
than to have your hands near the principal nerve center(s) at the
moment of release. I share the stages of my own energetic awakening
to help accelerate your own and to assist you in assimilating these
lessons. My first experience in physically feeling the encoded trauma
of another was something of a shock!

The first instance in which I felt trauma release from the body
of another person was actually something of an "accident." A family
friend asked me to use the energy of my hands to "get rid of" her
migraine, having heard about some of my successful attempts at
healing conditions among my family members. This woman turned
out to be a friend of my oldest sister and heard about my efforts despite
my determination to keep this information from going public. She
stated that she would have to leave the treatment center if I did not
help her resolve her migraine first, since "the migraine makes me light
and sound sensitive … and talking will only make it worse." When
I attempted to use the energy of my hands to release her migraine
pain, however, the pain actually increased in intensity as she suddenly
accessed the scene of abuse which was the source of the intense pain
in her head. It was as though her bodymind would not allow me access
to the system – I was not communicating in her own language. When
she indicated that her pain was due to a flashback that she was having
about her father, I immediately turned to the reframing technique I

had developed for releasing the emotional charge of stored memory: By creatively visualizing the "corrected" image and sending this feeling through the cells and fields of her body, she taught her subconscious that she now possessed the capacity to create safety in her life, whereupon the subconscious released its protective hold on the pain of the original memory. When she visualized her solution: her father getting treatment for his alcoholism much sooner than he did, thereby allowing her to sleep peacefully at night without abuse, she saw the colors of pink and silver appear in her mind's eye. Upon moving these colors through her body, the pain of the original encoding began to release from the cells and fields of her body. What was most startling, however, came from the fact that I had forgotten to remove my hands from the sides of her head. As a result, when she began the reframing technique, I was surprised to feel increasing discomfort in my hands as she entered more deeply into the memory. As soon as she was able to visualize an image of safety and move the colors of this scene through her body, I felt waves of pain leaving her head and passing through my hands. As she moved the emotional solution through her body, I felt the pain that had been constant suddenly become intermittent with waves of decreasing intensity leaving her head. After three minutes, the pain waves ceased. I waited another minute and asked her about the migraine: "Oh, that left about a minute ago," she responded. I realized that I had felt the moment when the pain began to release as well as the final waves. For the first time, I actually felt the pain of another's abuse leave the cells and fields of the body. I could feel the peace and calm that remained as well.

Initially, I thought this experience to be an exception, but, as I placed my hands besides the head of other clients during such reframing, the perceptions were the same. The variations introduced themselves as different types of emotional release, but all were easily felt. Routinely, anger was an intense burning, domestic violence a very real physical pain, abandonment a coolness over heart and solar plexus, death a stabbing pain, shame and guilt a stinging sensation, nerve damage an ice cold feeling … to name only a few. Some of my colleagues attempted to make this perceptive ability my gift alone, until I demonstrated the process and watched them experience many of the same sensations at their very first attempt.

Excited about the results I witnessed, I was eager to use the process to begin releasing some of my own "density." What became a vital message to share with all was the realization that, as I utilized the reframing process on myself, I began to experience an increase in sensitivity due to the release of the dense energies of my traumas. When I cleared my head traumas, for example, I could suddenly feel the migraine pain of another in my head as well as my hands; this made a certain sense, however, now that the flow of energy in my own nerve centers was less "congested." I began to see certain beneficial effects to the healing of ones own memories and nerve centers. At least, I hoped it would prove beneficial. I did start to notice that, as I cleared more and more of my own memories, my enhanced sensitivity gave rise to certain social consequences. I could be sitting next to someone on a plane, for instance, and my head might start throbbing with a pain that was entirely new to me. On most occasions, I tactfully engaged the adjacent passenger in conversation whenever possible and enquired about any injury related to the symptoms I was experiencing. I was, in every case that I can currently recall, fairly accurate and identified a precipitating trauma. In one situation when I had to share a bed with a visiting colleague, I started to fall asleep only to find myself awakened with the most excruciating head pain on the side of my body nearest my companion. I managed to resolve the pain through meditation and did not want to wake him, but recalled enough of the pain the next morning to enquire about any injury he had ever had to the left side of his head and torso. He looked surprised but admitted that at three months old his alcoholic father had fractured his skull, "beating me to a pulp," whereupon he was "unrecognizable" to his family in the hospital. I offered to reframe these memories with him but also secretly questioned whether I wanted to pursue developing such enhanced sensitivity in a world where such events were possible. I had never felt the violence done to another as though it was actually my own pain until that experience. It was an eye-opener! I also felt more compassion for this individual when the reality of his pain physically passed through me. "Compassion" means to "suffer with" (from the Latin words, passio, meaning "suffer" and, cum, meaning "with"). Our personal concept of intimacy changes as we resolve our traumas and become more sensitive.

There are no words to describe adequately the spiritual intimacy of the moment when you feel the pain of a specific trauma leave the body of another person. I still recall most vividly our family friend who allowed me to energetically witness the moment when she reframed and healed her incest memory – and her migraine as well. It is at once humbling, transforming, and grounding to feel the reality of another's trauma as ones own physical pain. There is a privilege and level of intimacy that surpasses anything that I had ever hoped to experience in ministry. We feel more spiritual from such moments – far beyond what many of us were led to expect from traditional religious teachings. I know now that each of us is priestly in nature and capable of what I have felt: of knowing the depth of pain that trauma causes to the human body, mind, and spirit. We are also capable of feeling and facilitating its release. Our whole world changes when we realize that abuse imprints in the bodymind as a detectable physical pain. We leave the imprints of our own shadows in the bodies of others if we traumatize them, but these shadows have substance: they hurt; they have weight and density; they impede energy flow; they diminish the light. I recall one vivid demonstration of this principle.

I was reframing some memories with a young man from South America. As I began the session and scanned his head, I felt an intense physical pain and a burning on the right side of his face. I immediately asked him if he had ever been hit in the face, whereupon his girlfriend burst into tears. I was somewhat confused by her intense response. When I moved through the process to track the pain and asked how old he was when such a violation happened, he stated: "This morning! I told Angela (his girlfriend) that I was leaving her and returning to Colombia, and she slapped me." At that moment his girlfriend began sobbing, horrified that she had again lost control of her anger and that her anger had impacted him on such a profound level. In hitting him, she realized that she reinforced the very communication problems from her unresolved abuse history that had led to the relationship's dissolution. She was also shocked to realize that this abuse was imprinted at such a physical and lasting level – that somehow she had left a part of herself and her violent, abusive energy and history in his face! She was even more appalled that the evidence of this abuse was so readily identifiable to an "outsider." The use of physical force is particularly traumatizing to another when expressed in the facial area. Most of our primary senses are centralized in the face. There are too many nerve endings in the face to not induce trauma from a blow. Such violence can be stored indefinitely as static memory in the cells and fields of the bodymind. This is the power and energetic nature of trauma.

When I began to see the depths of abuse that we as humans are capable of inflicting on the innocent, I began to ask myself if I really wanted to lose my traumas, my protective density that allowed me to define and feel myself as separate from others. Sometimes, I thought, the illusion of clear separation from others felt safer. When I simply stood next to others and found that I could feel their memories, I started to wonder if I truly wanted to continue my spiritual evolution if it meant actually feeling the depths of trauma in the people around me. Wasn't it simpler when I could just stand next to you and take you at your verbal and face value? Did I really want to know that your girlfriend, boyfriend, father, mother, or minister abused you in the past? Did I have to feel the loud declarations of your subconscious mind continuously broadcasting an S.O.S. from your body and its fields? Finally, I asked myself, what if being spiritual meant truly becoming a clear being of light? Wouldn't that leave us just too sensitive to the contrasting darkness of others – perhaps even too sensitive or vulnerable to live calmly in our current world?

Continuing my own healing journey over these last thirteen years, I can definitively state that there are very real consequences to the clearing of ones own field or "emotional body." Ultimately, such clearing proves to be a blessing. Increased sensitivity allows us to listen to the subconscious mind speaking through the body when the conscious mind is confused or disoriented. The conscious mind is only seven percent anyway. The greater wisdom resides in the subconscious and its link to the Superconscious or Divine Mind.

I suspect that we have placed too strong a value on physical sexual intimacy due to the fact that we have been unable to truly merge our "consciousness" with that of another. Being over-defined in our bodies by the density and weight of our traumas, we have missed the capacity for feeling the consciousness of another "pass through" or merge with us. In fact, the "congestion" created by trauma has inhibited such merging. In Oriental mysticism, they referred to this spiritual merger as "tantra." To feel such moments of union is an intimately touching experience. I firmly believe that we have tried to use intense physical sexual experience to substitute for the more subtle levels of intimacy because we have been too "congested" to routinely link with the larger consciousness of our friends and partners. Sexuality becomes reduced to its most intense physical descriptors when we cannot enjoy the greater intimacy that comes from merging our light-body with that of another. When we cannot even perceive ourselves to be such light, due to the imposed density and "solidity" of our traumatic imprints, we no longer expect or understand the larger, more normal context of intimacy. We over-sexualize our concepts of intimacy because we lack the greater spiritual and emotional capacity for true union.

To empathically feel the pain another experienced from a moment of abuse is to create a relational bond that is indescribable. We have not been consistently capable of such intimacy up to this point in our evolution. Compassion increases in proportion to our degree of trauma resolution! There is an additional blessing: the promise of the resolution of our traumas is that we will be able to share the moments of joy and ecstasy on a near physical level as we release the impeding densities of trauma. I think that it is a clear statement about our degree of traumatization that nearly half of all women cannot even reach orgasm – their potential levels of ecstasy, through sexual intercourse. At our most intimate moments, the densities of our imposed individual and cultural traumas remain which impair our ability to know safety and connect profoundly. Our partners cannot know our needs or read our signals when they are buried behind the densities of their own encoded traumas. We cannot recognize our partner's needs when we remain dissociated beneath our own. No, I think it is well worth our while to commit to the clearing of our bodyminds. There we may find true intimacy, relationship, and joy.

I have several friends with whom I have experienced a deeper level of communication as a result of my own personal healing work and the lightness of their energy fields. There is one friend in particular, Matthew, with whom I have experienced a profound connection. On almost every occasion that we have ever visited, there is at least one moment when I comment on a statement or answer aloud a question that he has asked. The problem is that, in each of these instances, he never voiced his thought aloud. The first time that he confronted me with this phenomenon, I realized that I had not really heard him voice his question aloud, but had somehow heard it from within my mind. It sounded as clear as a bell, but simply did not come through my ears. I have seen evidence that as we clear our memories, our capacity for communication and manifestation becomes immediate and direct. Our thoughts, dreams, and intentions can manifest as quickly as we formulate them. Our capacity for bonding with another comes naturally when we are so able to hear the thoughts and sense the emotions of our friends and partners. We will also know when we are not compatible with another individual. This is a logical consequence of removing the blockages to the flow of light – to the flow of consciousness.

Clear communication occurs when we are not pulled out of the flow and exchange of consciousness by trances that seize control of our perception of the other. Because memory is "holonomic"[15] in nature – acting like a hologram, it only takes a fragment of an encoded memory: a word, a phrase, a tone of voice, a smell, a sensation to capture our attention and pull us into other places and times. In the middle of a pleasant conversation we are suddenly irritated and distracted by a turn of phrase, a tone of address that "triggers" a negative experience from the past that threatened our security and safety. Painful memories are stored with their negative charge intact to protect us from the danger of future occurrences. The holonomic nature of encoded trauma memories insures that we will receive a warning when anything similar to an abuse episode nears us. Given the sensitivity of the nervous system, we seem to trigger more frequently when there are significant numbers of unresolved trances in our subconscious minds. It is almost impossible for the current partner to "do right by us" when their very language activates our warning signs of impending retraumatization. If it is true that the average individual trances fifteen to fifty times an hour, I do not know how many conversations we have ever fully attended. The depth of our personal trauma histories compromises the potential for intimate and nurturing communication. We can expect the quality of our relationships to be reduced by the insecurities triggered by our unresolved pain.

On the other hand, the resolution of the dark polarities induced by pain and overwhelm allows for clear and direct communication. As we learn to "complete" the emotional charges (or frames) of our painful memories – those stored with insufficiencies of nurturing or safety, we remove the potential for distraction from the exchange and interplay of white light. I do not "drop out" of the interaction due to a trigger of anger imposed by the intrusion of a memory from an ex-partner. Anger and hatred, for instance, are among the lower frequencies. They pull us out of the fluid exchange of intimacy and nurturing by the density they introduce. From my work with couples, I believe that over ninety-five percent of couples' conflicts do not relate directly to the current relationship. We are so sensitive to our holonomic triggers that our systems react to protect whenever anything even remotely resembling our traumas surfaces. In these cases, we do not even remember the original miniscule issue that sparked the argument due to the intense polarity that is triggered by a word, a phrase, a tone of voice, etc. More aggressive "survival" strategies are introduced to try to win the argument that has taken on a threatening nature due to the memory trigger that has become active. The problem is that we are struggling to survive a transaction that does not really originate or exist in present time. We are trancing.

In my workshops with Wyatt Webb at Miraval, the attendees get a real opportunity to see whether they are able to remain focused in present time in order to communicate with the horse (or with others). It would appear that one must be fully present to make contact with the horse to perform the assigned tasks. When the horse does not respond to you at all, just as the title of Wyatt's first book suggested, it is not about the horse! The non-responsiveness of the horse is not the horse's fault; it, inevitably, is about our inability to communicate due to the presence of a trance. We do not communicate clearly when ninety-three percent of our mind is occupied elsewhere, trapped in an unresolved scene of pain or terror in the past.

Recently I witnessed Wyatt guiding a client who was overwhelmed by a trance state filled with fear. Though Wyatt was communicating clearly how she could connect with the horse, I could see how the fear overwhelmed her and interrupted the communication. She could not "focus" enough to hear his voice or his instructions properly due to the fear. She could not make her body respond in a gentle, clear, but assertive way when her self-control was robbed from her by the trance. Her hands were actually doing the opposite of what she was intending and of what Wyatt was guiding her to do! As Wyatt worked with her, she managed to identify memories at ages three and twelve that left her feeling unsafe around people and, subsequently, the horse as well. Once she made these younger "ego-states" safe, she was able to communicate perfectly with the horse and realize her original intention. The horse responded immediately when she was not preoccupied with the emotions of another place and time that held her nervous system captive.

How often are we looking directly into someone's eyes while we are actually carrying on a dialogue in our heads about an issue entirely different from the present conversation? We trance routinely. I cannot count the number of times that I have spoken with clients who use this trancing ability to think about someone else while they are trying to be sexually intimate with their current partner. This is especially true when the partner has triggered an abuse memory. We use our trancing ability and its fantasy and daydream imagery to modify the circumstances of our current lives – sometimes to just make them more bearable. At other times, we use our trancing to mask or deny deeper feelings and traumas that are trying to get our attention. There are so many survivors who are not able to be sexually intimate or achieve sexual fulfillment unless they are safely dissociated into an altered state at the time. Even in routine conversation, I try to catch myself and return to present time when my trances compromise any exchange.

As we heal our memories, replacing the dark affect with authentic messages of love and white light, our communication is less obscured.

Our fields become more "translucent," so to speak. We begin to "see" each other for who we really are without the baggage of the encoded trances. Without these distortions, we are free to attract persons of like frequency who may be our real soul mates, versus the "unconscious marriage"[16] created by the dark polarities of our unfinished trauma scenes. The aggressive magnetism created by the latter is often mistaken for love, given the intensity of its pull. Our spirits may use such attractions to begin a healing process, but the marriage may turn out to be more about healing the past than authentic communication with each other in the present.

Relationships serve as the perfect mirrors for the presence of our unresolved issues. A partner or friend assists us in healing when s/he calls our attention to the excessive emotional charge of our trance states. I have found that whenever we overreact or find excessive emotional attachment to an issue, we are talking memory! The great difficulty with resolving our own altered states is that, due to their empowerment by the ninety-three percent subconscious mind, they tend to be so effective and overpowering to the psyche when triggered, that we are unable to step back from them to notice their presence before we have "bought into" the trance and begun acting from it. I see this most commonly with what we call "Level Two" trauma – patterns of repeated imprinting that begin affecting the belief system itself and instilling their wounded perceptions as the norm within our psyche. As we progress from the single imprint of "Level One" trauma to repeated imprints, we induce trance states of increasing intensity. They begin to associate and become compounded in the subconscious, forming patterns and archetypes of their own (constituting Level Two). These have increasing power and begin to affect our belief systems and core identity. By the time an individual reaches "Level Three" induction (a relatively uncommon phenomenon), s/he has often succeeded in creating separate personalities to handle the various categories and vast quantities of trauma. The most extreme cases of trauma induction can induce psychosis or a split from reality itself.

Emotional imprinting forms the foundation of the psyche. In observing the patterns of imprinting on over twelve thousand people, I have concluded that there are five principal stages that are involved in our development of both self-worth and shame. We can be imprinted either positively, or negatively. In other words, depending on the nature of the holonomic imprinting, our encoding can be integrative or disintegrative. The five stages are as follows: 1) external introduction, 2) internalization, 3) autonomy, 4) identification, and 5) the spiral.

Initially, the imprinting for self-worth and/or shame originates from outside of us and is temporary. With repeated reinforcement, the imprints are internalized. As this internalization of feelings from the caregiver continues, the imprinting gives rise to a certain independence or self-rule (autonomy) of affect within the psyche. If this continues and is reinforced, the psyche comes to identify itself with this positive or negative affect. Once the system has identified fully with the worth or shame, the smallest external trigger can activate a spiral of emotion now associated with the internalized belief, creating a spiral of confidence and inspiration, or one of shame and powerlessness, depending upon the affect.

One of the side effects of this process, however, is that once shame is induced, it tends to block out other affect or more positive emotions. Depending on the strength of our personal boundaries, once we induce enough negative imprinting, our confidence diminishes and the negative messages begin to dictate our choices. With additional traumatization, we remain in trance so frequently that we begin to identify ourselves with the emotional rule of the trance. We begin to act from and self-reinforce this negative perception, thereby anchoring it within our psyche. With our rational mind and moral intention diminished by the dominance of the immense, subconscious trance state, we begin to act from the distorted perceptions of the subconscious. Once thoroughly induced, this body of consolidated negative perception follows the natural laws of a holonomic trance state: the smallest fragment similar to the encoded body of pain will trigger the whole affect, thereby leading to the "spiral" of negative emotion that quickly overwhelms us. The smallest trigger can send us into an overwhelming spiral of fear, shame, depression, or despair.

When our systems are burdened with the dense electromagnetic baggage of the past, we are not available to receive the infinite wisdom and guidance reaching out to us through the subtle messages of our intuition. We become so preoccupied with survival that we barely find time to pause to reconnect with our inner guidance. The voice of pure consciousness becomes obscured by the intrusive voices of our traumas, our perpetrators, and our negative teachers. By the time we reach these final stages of shame induction, we are routinely repeating to ourselves the negative messages with which we now identify. Until we resolve these static messages from another place and time, we have difficulty attending to the voice of love guiding us to intimacy, abundance, safety, fullness, and joy. This is the true and enduring "dark night of the soul." Our quantum nature dictates that we will create relationships which will mirror to us precisely the state of clarity of our bodymind. We cannot use our subconscious minds as the convenient repositories for our painful, unresolved states of consciousness and, at the same time, keep them from manifesting these distortions. We are simply too powerful as creators. And the subconscious, consisting approximately of ninety-three percent of our mind, will have its say.

Our mandate, therefore, is to bring love and light to complete those unfinished moments of our past. In doing so, we recognize our ability to love and enable the possibility of more authentic connection arising from a place of clear perception. When consciousness is no longer dammed by the need to protect from death and overwhelm, its flow is clear and direct, connecting us to our highest good and most loving relationships. Our intentionality is no longer conflicted by a mere survival ethic, and we proceed to create from a perception of abundance and authenticity. Let us take a look at relationality and creativity as seen from this clarified perspective.

CHAPTER 7

℘℃℞

"MANIFESTING EDEN"

*Eden is more than a mythological place or a material site of
primordial failure. It is a promise and invitation embedded
within the cells of our bodies. It is our spiritual destiny.*

Among the greatest fascinations of modern society are the
mythologies of ancient cultures. Thanks to my Uncle Mel, with whom
I was able to travel and visit many Native American sites, I became
intrigued with archaeology as a child – a love that grew and led to
my involvement in Middle Eastern Archaeology for over thirteen years.
The field of archaeology itself owes a debt of gratitude to another
amateur: Heinrich Schliemann whose passion for the classic mythology
of Homer's work, *The Iliad and the Odyssey* led to his search for and
discovery of the ancient city of Troy. Mythology often captures our most
surpassing articulations of truth. It inspires the search for higher meaning
and frequently lifts us beyond the constraints of any one culture, or belief
system. Mythology moves us beyond the linear mind into the realm
of archetype, transcending any one moment in space and time. These
"higher" lessons frequently form the foundation for our ideals, values,
and morality. By means of its symbolic language, mythology connects
us to the realm of mystical experience through its capacity to bridge
the terrestrial with the celestial – earth-bound with transcendent. Our
current culture and its values were founded on such early mythologies
and their interpretation. Given its inherent symbolic and metaphorical
nature, mythology is profoundly affected by the interpretive stance or
"hermeneutic"[17] of the reader/listener. As we have evolved in these last
decades, our manner of viewing the world has shifted.

As children, our world and its lessons are filtered through a mind
bound to the physical. This is understandable when we realize that our
earliest memory imprints are visual and felt. This physical predisposition
of the "child mind" leads us to interpret our mythologies and stories
literally and concretely. The physical orientation of the "child mind"
becomes restrictive, however, as we evolve into higher awareness.
The child mind interprets the emptiness of emotional abandonment as
hunger, and frequently seeks to compensate physically with food. The
sexually abused teen feels dirty and compulsively washes to remove
a sense of violation that is actually held as memory in the cells and

fields of the body, and cannot actually be found or removed on the surface. Another teen may seek to extract the dirty feeling on the inside by purging the stomach – only to find that the feeling remains despite physical attempts at purification. In a like manner, we have used this physically oriented mind to interpret one of the most potent mythologies in history: Eden.

In our spiritual infancy, we sought security by interpreting Eden physically and literally. With the admission of the possibility of evolution, we moved beyond literal constraints to the power of mythology. For didactic purposes, a physical and literal approach was natural and appropriate in our early spiritual evolution, but we begin to lose the higher meaning and power of the mythology if we stay bound to the hermeneutics of the child mind.

The original authors of the Genesis mythology pointed us toward their intended meaning through a distinctive interplay of words. This language reflected their current understanding of human nature. Having no abstract notion in the Hebrew language for "nature," the authors carefully selected their terms to introduce a higher interpretive key: *Adam* ("man" in Hebrew) comes from the "soil" – *adamah* in Hebrew. We are given a hermeneutic key at the outset to decrypt the higher meanings of the text. Try reading the account while holding in your mind the notion of "soil" as the inherent wisdom and power of human nature. The text continues to reveal itself and its message if we allow ourselves to use its own interpretive key. When we lose touch with our nature, for instance, we now have to "work the soil to make it productive," rather than have it render up its fruit and abundance spontaneously. In this understanding, Eden becomes the metaphor for perfect harmony with our nature: the garden of paradise, of abundance – filled with spiritual intimacy and beauty. We will examine this in more depth in the reflections that follow.

Mythology touches our souls through its symbolism and metaphor. Its language is larger than history, for it is transcendent: it moves us beyond the limits of space and time and is transhistorical. The mind itself encodes experience not only historically, but also transhistorically. Profound experiences and patterns are frequently stored as metaphor and archetypal representations in the bodymind. Researchers have been so preoccupied in observing and proving the unreliability and nonhistorical nature of memory encoding, that they have frequently failed to recognize the precision, beauty, and power of metaphor and archetype in the subconscious. In the case of trauma, for instance, repeated experiences often combine in the subconscious or "blur" together to form a single archetypal representation. This archetypal metaphor frequently carries such power that it transcends any particular moment in its formation or in the individual's history. One client of mine, for instance, noticed that her abused "inner child" always appeared in the same white and pink dress in each of the incest memories, showing the link between all the subsequent abuse episodes and the first horrid violation. The subconscious revealed to her this connection by reminding her in its visual imagery of the innocence lost to the first child in her pretty white and pink Sunday dress. Such archetypal metaphors reveal profound and often hidden connections that magnificently allow for the expedient resolution of trauma without the need to individually reframe each memory. Such archetypal metaphors transcend any single moment of time to capture and articulate a larger truth. Such are the lessons of Genesis and Eden as well. What is the wisdom of human nature revealed in the ancient mythology of these early texts?

Though couched in the language of the "moral failure" model – the predominant paradigm of its day, the text reveals so much more in its language. But let me back up a moment to suggest the higher hermeneutic or interpretive key. If Eden is more than a lesson about a moral failure and is intended to teach us about the power of human nature itself, we must interpret it through the language of total consciousness, and not merely through the rationality and restrictions of the seven percent conscious, moral mind. What is interesting is that the original language of the text transcends the moral failure model of its day. It was about something much greater. Let me set the stage for our interpretation of this lesson: Trauma, as the "via negativa" or negative path to spiritual enlightenment offers us an interpretive key for unlocking the natural power and wisdom of human nature. The loss of Eden is a story about spiritual intimacy and the negative route to empowerment.

When we resolve our negative subconscious imprints, our natural capacity to manifest abundance appears. Trauma inserts a negative intention whose goal is protection and preventing recurrence of the overwhelming experience. It bends our intentionality to its own ends of protection and repression of pain. Unfortunately, in seizing majority control of our mind for its protective purposes, our conscious intentions are pushed aside to maintain survival. From current research, it would appear that we have been in survival mode on this planet for at least 1.5 million years. We have been subconsciously and automatically repressing our overwhelming experiences to survive. It appears that our intentionality was compromised before we were even verbal as a species or very cognitively developed in our evolution. From this perspective, the trauma induction mechanism provides magnificent protection when lightning appears as a mysterious force or is seen as a god intent on destroying us as early man feared. We were clearly dissociating right alongside our earliest stages of moral development, if not prior. Our earliest mythologies, including Genesis, concluded that something profoundly wrong happened in human development – initially concluding that we must have done something wrong. The young child self-references all around him/her, concluding that negative experiences are his/her fault. We have evidently done the same in our spiritual development.

Let us take a more detailed look at the remarkable mythology of the Genesis account. For instance, I was trained to read the text and its manuscript versions in the original Aramaic. Written in the Hebrew language dating to about 1000 BC, the account holds a wealth of ancient knowledge and beliefs about our nature. Although there was no specific term in Hebrew for the abstraction that we call "nature," the authors succeeded in communicating their limited beliefs about our spiritual development. They did so by calling our attention to the concept of nature, which they materially associated with "soil" or *adamah* in Hebrew. "Man" or *adam* in Hebrew, comes from *adamah*. Here is where the author begins to focus our attention through his interplay of words. The "soil" is the mysterious substance from which all life comes. Into the soil, God breathes His *ruah* or "breath, wind, spirit," and man becomes a living being. We are immediately pointed to the primacy of the soil as the backdrop for our lessons about human nature. In the progression of the account, the soil finds a spokesperson in the voice of the serpent. "The serpent was the most astute of the creatures whom God had made" (Gen. 3:1). Of course he is! He lives closest to the soil. The voice of temptation is depicted as originating from within our nature, the soil. The serpent doesn't sound particularly threatening in and of himself does he? In the account the serpent is not depicted as some evil Satanic figure; those assumptions were an anachronistic throwback from later theological speculation and do not appear in the slightest in the language of the original account. From within our nature then comes a voice that Eve hears. While the account is written from the biases of a patriarchal society, we must acknowledge that women do seem to perceive the subtleties of emotion and body language more easily than their male counterparts, though this may be a matter of conditioning.

"Eve," *hawwah* in Hebrew, whose name is derived from the verb *hayah*, "to live," attends to the voice of the serpent and proffers Adam the apple, breaching the one commandment of God to not partake of the fruit of the tree of knowledge of good and evil. The language and tenor of the account partially reflects the predominant "moral failure" model and thinking of the time, seeing humankind's fragmentation as originating with a profound moral breach – violating the commandment of God and introducing duality: the knowledge of both good and evil. If we look more deeply into the language and metaphors of the account, however, we see depicted an interesting phenomenon. The key emotional response to this breach is not depicted in the language of moral failure at all. It may very well be that the older mythology carried a most ancient perception about our earthly struggle.

As Adam and Eve eat the apple, their "eyes are opened," and they realize that they are "naked." The "eyes are opened" imagery is an ancient metaphor for a sudden shift in consciousness of a profound nature. When startled or surprised, we do, indeed, open our eyes to take in the sensory overwhelm. The realization that follows is even more defining: they suddenly recognize that they are "naked." The tenor of this ancient metaphor is clearly a depiction of "shame" or "embarrassment," and not merely guilt over some moral breach. There is a shaming perception about their bodies, using one of the oldest subconscious metaphors for the expression of shame: nakedness! How many times has the image of shame appeared in our dreams where we find ourselves naked in an embarrassing situation or setting! What is most interesting is the fact that "shame" is the term that we use to describe the profound emotional impact of trauma and dissociation within the psyche. "Guilt" is the concept applied to moral failure and behavioral breaches of moral precepts. Even if the author was intending to teach us about a profound moral breach, he slips into the language of trauma, revealing a larger prehistory of shame than he was prepared to address. We often have difficulty distinguishing between the guilt of a behavioral breach and the shame that imprints at the core of our being.

Here resides the dilemma: shame induction is always subconscious and automatic. The internal freezing of overwhelming emotions is inherent to our design. It appears to have been part of our earliest genetic and physiological makeup. This automatic pausing of affect has allowed us to survive our primitive stages of evolution in order to increase our capacity for self-awareness and moral choice. It has magnificently shielded us from our preconscious traumas and allowed us to repress our pain until we were strong enough in our evolution to resolve it consciously. There is no longer any question that developmentally, we began dissociating long before we became very adept at responsible moral choice. This is true within our own personal development as well. Researchers find that most of us induced some feelings of shame long before we reached the age of moral development. John Bradshaw spoke of this in his book: *Healing the Shame that Binds You.*[18]

The implications of this knowledge about trauma induction are monumental on a spiritual and cultural level. Many of our most powerful religious systems have founded themselves on the concept that we must first be saved from our "sins" – our morally destructive choices and behaviors. Rituals and actions have been created to release us from the binds of our "Original Sin." All of their preaching and strategies have been directed at setting us on the path of righteous behaviors. I know this because I was trained to do so as a priest. The rituals of Baptism and purification, so common to the religious systems, however, did not release trauma encoded in the cells and fields of the body, but neither did they ever claim to do so; their focus was on sin. I have worked with thousands of clients, many of whom evidenced very early trauma that remained very much intact following such ritual interventions. My hands and the clear somatic indicators of trauma have never deceived me in this regard. Trauma, in its pre-moral nature remains largely untouched by the dictates of morality and the interventions that empower the conscious, rational, moral mind.

The problem that remains is simply this: all that we know about our knowledge of the protective act of trauma induction suggests that we were actually *protected* by this dissociative capacity through our most vulnerable stages of personal and evolutionary development. We were protected in our early preconscious, premoral, and precritical stages of development. In other words, there are clear indications that we were not thrown out of Eden due to a moral failure; *we were designed to evolve lovingly into it.* Until such time as we would learn to heal our traumatic experiences and master our disparate states of consciousness, we would continue to subconsciously and automatically encode any experience that overwhelmed or threatened our existence. Such protection was in place in our physiology years before moral development occurred within the psyche, and was present in our physiology at least 1.5 million years before the notion of an Original *Sin* was even conceived. *It appears that we were designed to be more than "moral;" we were intended to be "mystical" in nature.* And this mysticism is profoundly tied to our inherent mastery of our space-time perception – our influence over our states of consciousness.

Deterioration in moral decision-making occurs as a natural side effect of dissociation: the splitting of self from self. I knew this as a young child whose shame and shyness, induced through imitation of my father and his internalized traumas, restricted my choices and "moral" options – even at a young age. Like the little child that assumes that he/she did something wrong when a bad thing happens, we observed society at 1000 BC and concluded that we must have done a bad thing, for, most certainly, God would not create the world of moral decadence or degree of degradation that was visible at 1000 BC. Moral deterioration occurs as a natural consequence of deepening dissociation – the loss of self.

In later spiritual literature and theological evolution we began to realize that something more profound than moral indiscretion or a moral breach on our part had created the violence and social disorganization. In Catholic theology, they took the traditional moral failure model a step further and called it an "Original Sin" suggesting a primordial moral failure of an "ontological" nature to explain the degree of moral ineptitude and decadence in society.[19] A valiant attempt to address the fact that something was, indeed, missing from the original moral responsibility theory! What they succeeded in doing, however, was canonizing and overemphasizing the moral failure model when, instead, a new paradigm was preparing to emerge. At that point in history, theology itself seemed to become so intellectually dissociated from contact with our actual life experience that it is no wonder they missed the simplicity of the explanation. Try reading the mystics who were attempting to sort out their mystical experiences while using the moral failure model to control their thoughts, temptations, and trauma-induced emotional struggles! The seven percent moral mind has only limited impact on trauma-induced states of consciousness and such protective encoding. Religious behaviors become addictive and compulsive when they are used as attempts to force the subconscious mind which holds the trauma to conform to the will of the seven percent conscious, moral, rational mind. Mystical literature is filled with desperate attempts to reclaim possession of our intentionality or will power using moral cleansing and intellectual gymnastics.

Immediately before I formally moved into the new healing paradigm in my own life, I realized that religious systems' restrictive emphasis on the moral responsibility model put me in the position of being an enabler or abuser. Let me explain: With the misinterpretation of Genesis, the "moral responsibility" model became the exclusive vehicle for "salvation." It naturally placed an excessive emphasis on "sin" while the principal blockages resided in trauma – a pre-moral experience! I learned long ago from my addictions training that shaming an individual about his or her "failed behaviors" is one way to insure the intensification of the addictive cycle. By trying to use a morality model (based on the seven percent rational mind) to resolve pre-morally induced experiences, we were set up to fail – thereby inducing shame that the system was unprepared to address. Shaming an individual fosters compulsivity and addiction; it does not resolve it. With an "incomplete" theology, the system would induce spiritual trauma by its unconscious use of shaming language and demands for moral solutions over behaviors rooted in trauma. Before I shifted into my healing ministry, I deliberately stopped using morally shaming language around addicted and compulsive populations. I recognized that this included a notable percentage of my own congregation. At times it appeared that all of us had been shamed, to some degree, by the old language and its increasingly desperate attempts to give us back control of our "will power" – our diminished intentionality.

From what we now know about our origins, much more than an "Original Sin" occurred in our evolution. There was an earlier "breach" in the flow of consciousness itself on a profound level. We applaud the efforts of the early theorists and theologians who tried to provide some keys to management of our lives through their moral exhortations and precepts, but these speak primarily to the moral, rational mind and become downright abusive when imposed on a trauma survivor. I am afraid that it is quite clear from anthropology, physiology, psychology, and psychoneuroimmunology that we were dissociating long before we could have "sinned." There was much more going on than an "Original Sin" of the part of our seven percent moral, rational mind! There was a dissociative process that began subconsciously and automatically before "morality" could even exist for us. And this process evidences a *truly magnificent and loving wisdom,* certainly not a condemnation of our nature.[20] Such wisdom generates a theology of healing instead of one primarily focused on correct moral judgment.

This wise, protective system is exquisite in its inception and functioning. What I have found most interesting is the fact that the mythologies accurately reflect the impact of this original dissociation: Once Adam has eaten from the apple and gone through his eye-opening shame experience, he now knows the impact of the splitting of consciousness. As a result of his new duality, he will now have to "work the soil" to make it productive. In other words, his nature will not spontaneously offer up its fruit and sustain him any longer. His communication and harmony with the world around him has been disrupted at its core. This is the natural outcome of the split in intentionality that trauma induces. The proof of this resides in the fact that when we resolve the split in our intentionality, we manifest abundance and intimacy quite easily. As I resolve my traumas, I no longer have the voices of trauma contradicting my good intentions or subverting my efforts to create joy, beauty, and abundance. The more we resolve the fragmentation of our intentionality, the faster and more healthily we manifest our highest good.

The conclusion of these lessons is simple: We were not thrown out of Eden due to some primordial moral failure on our part, but were designed to evolve into a state of clear intentionality where we act in the creator's image and manifest as we intend. We already manifest as we intend: it is just that we manifest mostly unconsciously from unconscious intentionality, at this point in our evolution. Eden is most clearly not a remnant memory of a conscious primordial failure on our part! It is our destiny as a species, as we learn to master our states of consciousness and achieve singular intentionality. The Genesis account can be wholly appreciated within the magnificence of its literary integrity, but its mythology transcends the original context that was colored by the moral failure model through which it was interpreted. From my understanding of trauma induction, I have a profound respect for the devastating impact of shame on the spiritual psyche. And, from my own struggle to use my quantum creative potential responsibly, I am more appreciative of the depths of the human condition and our higher calling. In my heart, I know now that Edenic existence awaits us all if we embrace our power to heal the disparate states of consciousness that suggest otherwise.

CHAPTER 8

ℰᴑℂℜ

"THE RETURN TO INNOCENCE"

Innocence is a state of simplicity that we achieve as we release the fragmenting voices of trauma. Our intentions become singular and our walk with the Divine, continuous, when we are not diverted by attachment to the past or its fearful projection into the future.

For most of us, the loss of our emotional innocence occurred long before we were even very conscious. Many of us took on some shame from our parents simply in our natural imitation of their behaviors and responses to the world – a percentage of which were trauma-based. Parents, I have found, are always our perfect teachers: I mean this in the sense that they give us certain positive tools and resources while also modeling negative traits and behaviors that motivate us to "run" in the opposite direction! They are our teachers in and through trauma as well. I cannot tell you, for instance, which parent was more valuable to me: my mother who modeled her intuitive compassion and empathy, or my father who revealed the pain and consequences of holding such unresolved trauma within oneself. Both inspired a passion and a search which fuels my efforts to this day. We internalized our parents' traits, methods of coping, and speech patterns well before the age of moral reasoning at ages seven to eight. As a result of this process, our efforts to express ourselves were compromised long before conscious choice was even possible. In natural imitation of my own father, for example, I was "shy" by the age of four; this is a common phenomenon for many children. Through such parental conditioning our choices become restricted. The greater the trauma, the greater are the limitations imposed on our intentionality. Our capacity to fulfill our dreams and goals is limited by these early subconscious strictures placed on us before we had any say. These memory imprints profoundly influence our potential and the paths we subsequently tread.

Our power to manifest from a place of clear intention is usually disrupted by memory. Our capacity to manifest the Eden we are capable of is removed from us when the voice of trauma inserts itself into our creative process. Traumatic moments are instances when someone, something, a situation or event overwhelms us and causes us to freeze due to a sudden, overwhelming loss of power, integrity, or safety. As we freeze, a protective message is inserted informing us that we are on the verge of overwhelm and must immediately act to change the present circumstances. This signal is designed to warn us and, once encoded, to prevent the future recurrence of such a threatening event. Although this subconscious freezing process is protective in its intent, it heightens our sensitivity about similar events and creates a negative emotional response around potential "triggers." Over time this "response" affects our decision-making process and restricts our choices. This restriction in moral decision-making leaves us more reactive to reality, eventually replacing a sense of creative power with a sense of victimization.

All traumas are boundary violations. Our Edenic existence is compromised and we are thrown out of our place of integrity and safety. The truth is, however, from what we now understand about trauma, rather than being thrown out of the flow of life for eons, every trauma causes only a millisecond encoding of consciousness. For an instant we pause the internal act of perception that creates our reality. We "freeze-frame" and contain the pain, moving the scene out of the main flow of consciousness, repressing it into our subconscious mind to the degree of protection that we require. For the most intrusive events, we can move into "traumatic amnesia" afterwards. This is sometimes called "delayed recall," due to the length of time and depth of repression before the memory surfaces.

Held protectively in the subconscious mind, these scenes hold immense emotional power, since they were stored at profound moments of overwhelm. The younger the trance state, the more potent is its emotional charge. I have found that the most potent trances occur before the age of five, after which our moral reasoning often dampens the intensity of our emotional perceptions. These holonomic images hold a dense emotional charge – a static energy involving the absence of certain frequencies. Trauma scenes lack safety; they are missing certain frequencies of light. That is why they can be so easily felt or detected. In the absence of so many of the frequencies that constitute white light, their static density can be readily identified. Similarly, one of the simplest methods of healing ourselves is to restore the light and the emotional frequencies missing at the original moment of encoding.

Our problem with traumatic memories is that they are stored with an "incomplete charge" of some polarity. Missing the higher frequencies of safety, nurturing, and calm, the "frame" around such painful images exerts a "pull" or polarity. It draws us back into the image when first triggered, imposing its limited, incomplete perception on our senses, even though we are making every effort to stay in present time. In my first book, *The Healing Dimensions*,[21] I chronicled very dramatic cases of how the subconscious charge from the original trauma scene takes control of the system, dominating the efforts of the conscious mind and imposing its own protective responses. The resolution of these scenes, therefore, requires that we restore feelings of safety, integrity, and calm to those moments and scenes in which we have been compromised. I have found that the simplest way to do so is to send a signal to the subconscious, telling it that we have survived and have new options for safety and self-nurturing. When the subconscious accepts this signal, transmitted in its own language, it quickly relinquishes its hold on the old protective charge, accepting reprogramming. When we can demonstrate to our subconscious minds that we have new options for love, safety, and nurturing, it allows us to update our perception of the original event. We can then return to the main flow of consciousness and move out of our static state of defensiveness that holds us captive until it is safe to proceed.

The process I developed, called "Holographic Memory Resolution®," teaches us how to focus and identify the moment of encoding, visualize the scene as it should have occurred, and send this corrected emotional perception of safety through the system. This is most easily done by visualizing the corrected image and framing it, allowing your subconscious mind to reveal to you the missing emotional frequencies as colors. Inviting your mind to identify the colors of the frame around the corrected image permits your subconscious to use its knowledge and resources to show you the emotions that were absent during the original encoding. When you can demonstrate to the subconscious mind that you can now imagine or create safety and integrity in your life, it accepts your authority and relinquishes its protective hold on the scene. Custody of the memory is transferred to the conscious mind in present time – a mind possessing new options and solutions for creating safety. When the corrective feelings or colors are passed through the cells and fields of the body, we demonstrate to the subconscious that we now know exactly what should have occurred and that we are capable of feeling these emotions.

The subconscious mind does not know the difference between real imagery and creative imagery. Quantum physicists and scientists discussed this openly in the popular film: *What the #$*! Do We*

Know!? (referenced earlier). When we access a traumatic scene from our past, the image can seem as real as the day we stored it. The brain responds in the same manner that it did originally. Creative imagery, also originating with the subconscious mind, can be used to tap briefly into the original scene and its charge to determine exactly what occurred, thereby enabling us to create the precise image of what should have happened, building on the frequencies of the original trance. In this process, we learn that we do not need to change our memories themselves or our histories. We simply need to complete the emotional perceptions of pain that were frozen with the scene when we paused it to protect ourselves. When we complete the emotional charge of our stored image, adding the frequencies that were missing from the original event, we change our frame to "white light" so to speak. In physics, when we add all of the colors together, we experience white light or the completed visible spectrum. The same is true of the emotional spectrum of memory: when we can demonstrate to the subconscious mind that we possess the capacity to love ourselves, to complete what our mothers, fathers, teachers, peers, ministers, etc. could not give us at a certain moment of our existence, the subconscious surrenders its hold on the pain, acknowledging our capacity for self-love and seeing this as proof of true safety.

In the completion or reframing of our memories, competing intentions give rise to singular intentionality. The paralyzing fear of moving forward in time where we could be retraumatized gives way to the conscious mastery of our trance states, demonstrating that we can forge ahead while safely knowing, giving, and receiving love. As we reframe or complete each memory of our past, we return to living comfortably in the present without the triggers to remove us from the dynamic flow of life and love. Trauma is a static place of conflicting desires, and intentions, where our best efforts to create are diverted by the need to protect ourselves from triggers that remain unresolved in the subconscious. Once these triggers are resolved, we return to living fully in the present, where love, happiness, and abundance originate.

We now understand that our spiritual integrity has been protected over these past 1.5 million years of evolution. The assumed violation of our innocence at the instigation of a serpent gives way to an appreciation of the safeguards set in place in our earliest evolution. Though masked by the influence of trauma, our beauty, innocence, and nobility of spirit remain intact. In the resolution of our traumas, we return home to the pure white light that sustains us. We are welcomed home, not as some wayward prodigals returning, but as ones whose innocence and integrity were never truly interrupted. Not for an instant did the focus of the Divine Mind stray from the knowledge of our truth. In this abiding vision of our essential goodness, our innocence was never even lost.

Eden exists as a state of ever-renewed innocence, clarity, abundance and generosity of spirit. In the loss of our vision of personal integrity and truth, we are cast from the sacred place of spontaneous manifestation and abundance. There is no question, but that as our intentions are rendered singular – free of the distractions of conflicting voices and messages about our worth, identity, purpose, and potential, we instantaneously manifest the abundance that we conceive in our minds. Without the static interference of dense imprints in the emotional body, the thoughts that we generate from this enlightened state germinate before they pass our lips. Such is the creative potential we hold from our design. Eden is our destiny, not some tragic ruin waiting to be excavated from the layers of our prehistory!

CHAPTER 9

ഇൗൽ

"RECLAIMING OUR BODIES"

Trauma has imprinted and laid claim to our bodies for, at least, 1.5 million years. As we learn mastery of our states of consciousness, we begin to gain conscious control of our quantum creativity and discover our power to heal, love, create, and merge.

In the ancient Semitic languages of the Middle East, to have ones "eyes opened" is a metaphorical expression denoting a profound shift in consciousness. Borrowing from the Genesis account, we observe that Adam and Eve know a moment when their minds are jolted by the awareness of embarrassment or shame. From the tenor of the account we can easily feel the emotional split that occurs within when that which was good, innocent, and acceptable becomes an object of shame. Shame is at the heart of our spiritual struggle. It is probably our most binding affect, for it operates on the level of identity, undermining our very being. Though our religious systems have been preoccupied with the resolution of moral failure and guilt, recent insights into the power and impact of trauma suggest that the greater obstacle to our connection to All That Is resides in the barrier that shame introduces into our subconscious minds. The subconscious mind is the bridge between the conscious mind and the "Superconscious" mind or Divine Mind (the "Big Mind" of Buddhist teaching). Obstacles in the subconscious inhibit our access to the immense power of the Superconscious. Shame imprints in the subconscious.

The distinction is simple: Guilt is about behaviors and mistakes; shame is about identity and tries to negate our being. Such negative affect ties us to the persons, events, situations, and triggers of the original context. Trances bind us to the feelings and characteristics of the frozen scene. Once encoded, a trigger will draw us back into the trance in a mere millisecond of time. The simplest example of such affective binding is found in the example of anger.

When we trigger a memory of anger toward someone, it is as though we suddenly feel a hot burning rope connecting us to the individual with whom we are angry. As the anger intensifies, the rope is wound tighter and tighter, actually pulling us toward the very individual who is the object of our anger. Instead of pushing us away from the perpetrator, the more intense emotions actually draw us into relationship with that individual and the pain surrounding the original event. We proceed into a kind of "tug of war," spending more and more of our efforts to win the struggle. In the process, we engage the opposing individual or system more deeply and invest more and more of our life force in the relationship with our opponent. Sadness, fear, anger, shame, powerlessness, worthlessness, and hatred are all indicators that we are still struggling with an opposing force in the past. Emotions are a relational bridge capable of overwhelming the five senses and drawing us in an instant into perceptions encoded in another place and time. Such emotionally potent trances seize control of our perceptive process and pull us into their own powerful dynamics. The physiology of memory takes over and transmits its own signals to our senses, drawing most of our mind and its responses into the creative act of an earlier place and time. Such is the power of the trance. It is about the power of this psycho-physiological shift that we must reflect. Its power can terrorize the human spirit, restricting its choices and sense of integrity. In such cases, we act from survival mode with greatly diminished options. Our bodyminds no longer feel like our own! It is as though we are merely along for the ride. I understand the power that a trance holds. Over time I actually learned to manipulate some of my own trances. Until we're taught to resolve them, manipulation may be the best we can manage.

Addictions are examples of such self-manipulation. Being unable to resolve our pain, we use substances like alcohol or tobacco for purposes of "controlled dissociation." Once these substances assert their own addictive power, however, we lose our initial "control" and end up with additional trauma instead. Addictions create a "Level Two" trauma pattern by their prolonged emotional repression; they add further layers of trauma rather than resolve them. When we lack the resources to resolve our trances, we seek distracting or dissociative experiences, substances, and activities to reduce our pain, knowing of no other solutions. We have been reliving our traumatic experiences for almost 1.5 million years. But matters are about to change. We are becoming masters of those powerful states of consciousness which, until now, have dictated our choices and our evolution. My own experience in reclaiming my body from trauma, though painful, offers some valuable insights into the paths that are now opening up for us.

I was born into a body full of fear. My mother had six miscarriages and stillbirths before I was born. Sometimes if she merely moved suddenly with her RH blood sub-type she miscarried. I am certain that her anxiety about my safety during her pregnancy with me profoundly influenced my initial impressions of the world. I have found a number of clients over the years with accurate womb memories. My father was a gentle, but very shy, introverted man who had little formal education. He was gifted in the use of his hands with baking and electronics. I internalized his shyness at a young age, mostly through imitation and the impressions that I received in observing his interaction with the world. On the level of emotional lessons that I would eventually have to address as a result of my upbringing, I recall a vivid dream in which my mother was "fear" and my father was "shame and dependency."

As a child, I remember feeling wholly overwhelmed with fear. The fear seemed to override my good intentions and efforts to maneuver through life. In early childhood, my fear was so paralyzing that it was almost too frightening to ask the teacher for permission to go to the bathroom. Nuns were even more terrifying, though I later endeared myself to some for safety. Verbal communication with adults was overwhelming. Angry men terrorized me, being wholly unfamiliar with the phenomenon of intense emotion from a male. I was small in stature. But I could run fast! That compensated for quite a bit. Existence in the body, on the whole, seemed very challenging. I preferred the safety of the neighborhood tree house. Social settings unnerved me. I was often labeled as being "shy." The label hurt as much as it explained.

My greatest fear was in speaking publicly. Ultimately, I reclaimed control over this fear by identifying the memory that caused it. It was, in fact, a grade school trauma. We were instructed by our fifth grade teacher to go home and memorize a poem. I did the best I could in the time I had. When it came time to stand up and recite my poem, I froze in mid-sentence. I was advised by the teacher to return home and "have the poem memorized by tomorrow." I became quite anxious over the issue and did my best to learn the lines. When it came time to recite the poem in front of the class, I became nervous and "went blank." The teacher made a disparaging remark, embarrassing me in front of the class, whereupon I turned around and faced the chalkboard. I refused to turn around. I was overwhelmed with shame and self-consciousness, but also felt a rage begin to rise that resolved itself into: "No one will ever shame me about memorizing anything again." I do not recall the resolution of the scene that day – having numbed out from the adrenaline, but from that time forward, my life changed. I was mortally afraid of speaking in public! The approach of an exam requiring memorization triggered an immense anxiety/stress reaction. I eventually discovered, however, that I could tap into the fear induced in the fifth grade classroom scene, move from this feeling into the rage, and use the accompanying adrenaline to increase my performance under stress. By seventh grade I was a "straight A" student – mostly due to the fact that I had conditioned myself to feel memorization as a life or death struggle. I ended up valedictorian of my class in high school and even four-pointed my way through college. I learned that I could generate the steroid hormones and adrenaline that I needed to enhance performance by triggering a relive of the fifth grade trauma scene. After a time, the mere thought of an exam would result in the production of adrenaline and the ability to make myself stay awake to study for days without sleep. I learned of the power to manipulate my own trance states and use focused imagery to produce desired emotional and mental changes. The problem with this, of course, was that right after such periods I became ill. This was the natural by-product of overproducing adrenaline. When the body reacts to trauma and stress, it produces adrenaline to compensate. As adrenaline production increases, "T-cell" production decreases. This results in repression of the immune system and sets one up to ultimately become ill. We cannot manipulate ourselves using such trances without paying a price. When I resolved the memory, I could not manipulate my system in the same way, nor did I need to do so.

We are all the potential masters of our states of consciousness. Up to this point in our evolution, however, we have been more the victims of our trance states than their managers. Fantasy, daydreaming, creative visualization are all altered states of consciousness which we use to reduce our stress. These are states that we consciously manage. However, the more potent of our trance states – those subconsciously induced under stress or danger, reduce our conscious control of the body. Traumatic events and triggers seize control of our bodily responses, activating a protective reaction that takes precedence over the current activities and choices of the conscious mind. But how powerful is the control exerted by a trance state?

Some years ago, one of my trainees, a gifted body-worker and therapist experienced a remarkable change as a result of the reframing of her memories. She had been on fertility drugs to induce pregnancy due to the absence of a particular hormone. In successive testing over the years, this particular hormone was consistently absent. We reframed a series of abuse memories that permitted her to give herself permission to embrace her sexuality as a positive resource in her life rather than a burden and source of repeated emotional pain. Shortly after our session she had been scheduled for her routine hormonal monitoring and testing. Within a very brief window of time, the "missing" hormonal factor was completely evident, a fact which defied any rational explanation on the part of the specialists, given the window of time between tests for its manufacture within her system. Her understanding of these events was that the blockage in her belief system had been removed which permitted her to embrace her sexuality in its fullness, a factor that permitted her reproductive system to normalize in a very brief amount of time.

Sexual trauma or repression is profoundly disempowering in whatever form it takes. Though I had no overt sexual trauma growing up as a child, there was a subtle "Level Two" pattern of sexual repression in my family based on a trauma that occurred before I was born. I had an older brother, Jerry, who was born with some brain damage. They did not fully diagnose his condition until he was thirty-two. He was twenty-one years old when I was born. By the time that I hit puberty, there were some strong messages that had been generated in the family about controlling sexual feelings and expression. I later learned that he had started to "act out" in his teens and was found wandering around my sister's room one night. Stringent controls and expectations were placed over his potential sexual behavior, and, by the time I was born, a strong subconscious impulse toward a non-sexual lifestyle had been imprinted. This provided the backdrop for me to assume a celibate lifestyle by my "choice" of priesthood. While in the seminary, my spiritual director recommended the practice of yoga or Zen to help balance the energies of my body and to calm the intensity of my mind. I found it helpful. I still channeled much of this energy into the development of my intellect, losing touch at times with my emotional and affective needs. This intellectual dissociation made it easier to choose a celibate lifestyle, but the decision came from a restricted and somewhat deprived place in my being. In ministry I excelled professionally and intellectually, but found the profession rather workaholic. After six years of ordained ministry, I found myself burning out and needing to make a choice – either for parish ministry or full-time teaching. When I opted for a leave of absence and considered joining the Jesuits, my body went through a series of changes.

Under a "leave of absence," I was no longer strictly obligated to a celibate lifestyle – or at least that was my impression. What was more shocking and changed my whole decision-making process was the fact that giving myself permission to be sexual occurred at the same time that the healing potential in my hands became active. Was this coincidence? I think not. I think back on the case of my friend whose hormones normalized as soon as she gave herself permission to embrace her sexuality. The decision to make my life my own – to follow my own intuition, shifted many things for the better. I began to explore my feelings about my life decisions and identified a number of traumatic patterns from my family that had also been replicated in my choices in my religious system.

The energy centers of the body that govern sexuality are deeply connected to the core energy flow of the system. They govern our creativity and relate to the healthy expression of our core needs. When this center is in a state of trauma or imbalance, we deny our needs and move into sexual anorexia and deprivation or into a state of compulsivity and depletion. In order for healing to occur, the energies of the body must be balanced: the female and male principles referred to, as "yin" and "yang" in the oriental disciplines, must be in place. I know that these energies were not very balanced for me in traditional ministry. Immediately upon leaving formal ministry, however, a number of intuitive women entered my life that assisted me in the empowerment of the intuitive, feminine aspect or "yin" aspect of my life. With these energies in balance, I was able to facilitate the healing of others without engendering any sense of threat or unresolved polarity on the part of my clients. When the therapist holds unresolved trauma within his/her own field, these issues can find their way into the energy exchange and create a sense of imbalance and diminish the safety required for core release and resolution to occur. Similarly, we have seen that "wounded healers" have the capacity to be triggered by their client's issues and can even "act out" their issues when these memories are accessed. I have worked with many such individuals over these last years.

An important example, illustrating the need for self-care and healthy boundaries on the part of healers/facilitators comes from observing the struggles evidenced in recent years within the Catholic Church over issues surrounding inappropriate sexual behaviors and the handling of its clergy. I do so because there are important lessons here for all of us. My experience with thousands of trauma survivors over these last fifteen years has been most helpful. Any institution that supports the existence of a celibate lifestyle will automatically attract a certain percentage of individuals with problems. Looking back on the many priests and seminarians I knew during my seminary years, I can see that a number were struggling with their sexuality issues; some were restricted from having missed certain developmental opportunities from having entered a seminary at such a young age; a significant percentage were acting from subconscious family influences as in my own case; another portion of that population was developmentally inhibited due to some traumatic experience that may have been either conscious or unconscious; a final percentage seemed to be choosing celibacy from a conscious, more balanced place. Priesthood emerged as one of the highest professions for alcoholism due, in part, I believe, to the emotionally repressive influences cited above. A celibate lifestyle naturally poses a challenge to any healthy individual.

Based on a theology and ethic founded predominantly on a "moral failure" or "moral responsibility" model, there were few options offered by the church for the healing of sexual trauma. Given the Catholic Church's understanding of sexuality and its restrictive definition of "nature," many confused and traumatized individuals could imagine no solution other than abstinence or the redirection of this energy into a contained but meaningful lifestyle. A sacred vocation such as marriage or religious life can, under the influence of trauma, default into an attempt at containment of the behaviors that will-power alone cannot manage. Both priesthood and marriage are frequently used to contain or restrict wayward sexual impulses or "acting out" behaviors that arise from a trauma history. I have observed this pattern in the treatment of many with sexual addiction.

The "moral failure" model leaves the traumatized individual believing that s/he must learn to control the compulsivity induced from the shame of trauma by performing right actions. Offering no effective means for healing the trauma induced in the subconscious, this model offers the traumatized individual few choices other than abstinence from sexual behaviors or channeling the sexual energy into some meaningful occupation. Unfortunately, the mere repression of the emotions due to trauma usually leads to "acting out" or the turning these feelings inward on self as depression. For many of the wounded souls in ministry, a celibate lifestyle offered the hope of redirecting these repressed energies into a meaningful outlet while imposing abstinence from any sexually inappropriate behaviors. The priestly lifestyle was one that promised meaningful service.

A celibate lifestyle offered within a society, however, will inevitably attract a certain percentage of the population, both male and female, that is seeking to repress or resolve its traumatic pain. In John and Linda Friel's book, *Adult Children: The Secrets of*

Dysfunctional Families,[22] the authors add a role to the list of what I term Level Two, trauma-based subconscious role assignments. In their book they talk about the "Priest, Nun, Rabbi" role wherein a child from a religiously or morally rigid system experiences sexually repressive messages resulting in the subconscious choice of a celibate lifestyle.[23] This may not even be manifested in any formal celibate choice or ministry, but may appear as the individual in the family who seems to have an undeclared but permanent celibate lifestyle. For many individuals raised in more rigidly religious or controlled family systems, sexual shame is pronounced, resulting in higher levels of memory repression, denial, compulsivity, and even traumatic amnesia. There has been found a correlation between religious addiction or rigidity and sexual addiction. The former "sets up" the latter by its excessively shaming language and strategies. The problem is that, with all of our new knowledge and understanding of trauma induction, we know that a trauma cannot be resolved merely through a redirection or substitution of energies. Behavioral containment or redirection will not be adequate for resolution. To effectively address the specific frozen moment of a trauma's encoding, the mere substitution of a meaningful activity will not suffice. Even Freud stated that a traumatic event must be addressed if it is found to have a certain "determining quality" and "traumatic power" over an individual's life. The fear and shame induced by a traumatic experience must be addressed directly at the moment of induction, or the traumatic script will remain intact and capable of being "acted out" when triggered.

This is not an understanding that the hierarchy of the Catholic Church has grasped. The old "moral responsibility" model discussed above had no understanding of the implications of trauma on morality. One cannot simply "forgive" an abuse event in order to fully resolve it. One cannot "absolve" it in the confessional and expect it to be healed. That was the danger and limitation of the old "moral failure" model. This was also the principal reason I began my ministry in the field of trauma.

The "sacramental" rituals did not "heal" or resolve the encoded memories of the subconscious that bred shame and powerlessness. The confessional was established to address guilt and moral failure – behavioral breaches! It was not an appropriate place to take on the trance-induced shame profoundly imprinted in the ninety-three percent subconscious mind. In fact, simply allowing the individual to remain behind a screen so that her/his face would remain invisible frequently circumvented shame; in this way, s/he could overcome the shame enough to disclose the moral breach. Healing requires a safe interpersonal context for effective release. In fact, if one "forgives" a behavior rooted in trauma, it often enables the behavior to continue without even touching the shame core. This perpetuates the behavior and induces further shame when the behavior recurs upon triggering. Trauma cannot be simply "forgiven" and be resolved – particularly since forgiveness is often a rational act generated from the morally conscious mind. We find, however, that the emotional release that we attribute to forgiveness occurs almost spontaneously when we heal the originating trance. When we effectively remove ourselves from the dynamics of the abuse, we spontaneously begin to release our attachment to the perpetrating person or event.

The difficulty with the Catholic Church's position over the centuries is that it offers the impression of resolution through forgiveness and "absolution," without actually addressing the source of the behavior: the shame induced through subconscious trauma imprinting.[24] As a result, it sought to "forgive" the transgressions of its ministers and to create opportunities for better "behaviors," often reassigning them to a new parish for ministry, but without addressing the shame core underlying the issue. The blindness and limitations of the "moral responsibility model" underlie this grievous error. Just as theology was blind to the fact that early man (Adam) was the product of a profound split in consciousness itself, not merely a "moral transgression" or sin, the church's treatment of the wounded human spirit was inadequate to address the immensity of the task. The religious system did, in fact, become an enabler whose blindness allowed the abuse to continue. Such systems are being confronted with their limitations, and appropriately so! This pattern, however, probably began within family systems, where our spirituality actually originates.

One of the most common patterns in dysfunctional family systems – carried over into our educational systems, is to shame a child into modifying his/her behaviors. I cannot report to you the number of times that I heard accounts of parents shaming their children: "stop eating so much or you'll never find a husband;" "if you keep eating like that, you won't fit through the door;" etc. Shaming induces trauma and locks the feelings into the subconscious, anchoring into the subconscious creative process the very message and behavior that the parent is trying to stop! It guarantees its emergence and reappearance, as it becomes a belief imprinted in the subconscious mind.

It would appear that we have been under the influence of very potent altered states for many millennia. I first learned from some of my clients that the repetitive nature of their trauma created a slow, cumulative traumatization process, leading to a profound decrease in personal power and worth. These Level Two trauma patterns profoundly affect ones development and sense of self. Alcoholism, one of the most common Level Two trauma patterns, taught us this in the '50's. The majority of us have some negative Level Two patterning of this nature from our families and other caregivers. Applying a moral responsibility model to individuals who are already subconsciously restrained by the conditioning received from trauma proves limitedly effective at best. At worst, it abuses the traumatized individual by demanding a level of moral responsibility or forgiveness from one who is still frozen in an abuse scene or pattern of abuse. In such scenes, we are holding the perpetrator at bay – a millisecond away from the horror of the abuse! This is the protective function of the freezing of our trauma scenes – of our flashbacks! They are efforts to contain our perpetrators and our pain until we can deal with them. Premature demands on forgiveness or moral responsibility are abusive when the subconscious triggers are still left in place. We are asking the rational mind to forgive while the perpetrator is still abusing the majority of the mind.

As a result of technological advancements in global communication, we are offered "real time" experience of positive, negative, and even traumatic events. With this heightened exposure, we are being forced to recognize the power and presence of our personal and collective "trances." On September 11, 2001, millions of us witnessed the visible definition of trauma: the terrorism of the Twin Towers in New York and the Pentagon in Washington, D.C. The impact of this archetypal attack on America's cultural symbols of prosperity and defense triggered the unresolved terrorism in the collective subconscious mind. More specifically, any of us who held images of boundary violation, abuse, or histories of emotional or sexual terrorism were triggered when we watched the second plane hit. At that moment, millions of encoded trance states went active at the same millisecond. For the first time in human history, consciousness was riveted "live," triggering a massive encoding of fear and anger of a magnitude that we had never before witnessed. Though the terrorist acts had a huge impact in and of themselves, the greater force arose from the capacity of the images to trigger all of the unresolved violations stored in the subconscious minds of the global population. Whenever we hold an unresolved trance within our bodymind, we store feelings of powerlessness and fear on the one hand, along with anger and indignation on the other. In the hours that followed, I felt my bodymind fluctuating between my own repressed feelings of fear, and those of anger. I had all the symptoms that accompany the triggering of multiple trance states.

To demonstrate the power of a trance to seize control of the body, I will cite a couple of cases. One of my clients in her 20's, Jelaine we shall call her, who had experienced significant sexual abuse was instantly hypnotized to the screen upon seeing the second plane hit on Sept. 11th. In the subconscious mind's metaphorical language, buildings usually represent our bodies, our lives. A projectile object invading our home or place of business will always tap our fear of personal boundary violation. Jelaine stated that she could hardly tear herself away from the screen to eat or go to the bathroom once she witnessed the second plane's impact. When she finally fell asleep exhausted that night, she had a vivid nightmare in which her home was being broken into and two of her perpetrators were performing inappropriate sexual acts in front of her. She felt terrified and powerless to stop them. The images activated her already encoded images of personal boundary violation.

Another of my clients found herself wandering around the house for no apparent reason at regular intervals following her emotional trauma on Sept. 11th. When she heard my lecture mentioning the terrorists' attempts to target our societal and cultural archetypal symbols of defense (Pentagon), financial security (stock market), industrial achievement (the Twin Towers), government (the Capitol), and leadership (the White House) in order to instill fear, she recognized the source of one of her behaviors. Ever since 9-11 she had found herself periodically wandering around the house, but was unaware of the reason for this action. Finally she realized that she was perusing her security system: doors, windows, locks, etc. When we traced the actual source of the trigger, the memory was quite young: in her first years of life, she grew up within walking distance of the Pentagon. Knowledge of the proximity of the Pentagon had always reinforced her sense of security as a child. Similarly, its compromise impacted her profoundly on subconscious levels, instilling a primordial fear about her safety and security. She acted out this child-like fear by physically walking around checking her doors and windows. Such is the impact of terrorism on our subconscious minds. The child-mind, when triggered, often acts out its attempt at healing quite physically.

Traumas are all about the violation of boundaries. That is why September 11th resonates so powerfully in the minds and bodies of the populace. We witnessed the visual definition of trauma in the most important of our cultural contexts: defense, urban safety, industrial achievement, financial security, and the seat of government. The power of another person, event, or circumstance to instill fear, anger, shame, or powerlessness in us is directly related to the quality of our personal boundaries. As a child we are easily traumatized due to the fragility of our boundaries, but as we grow older, this capacity diminishes as we effectively resolve our early boundary breaches. As we learn to heal our memories, we complete the unresolved darkness of the scenes to create a sense of safety, love, and nurturing. Learning that we can complete our own boundary formation where our parents left off offers a great hope in dealing with future crises. Where, however, we have left unfinished breaches in our security system, archetypal invasions of the magnitude that we witnessed on Sept. 11th will always trigger the unresolved issues of violation in our histories. In the months that followed, all of our repressed, unresolved feelings about previous violations surfaced with a fury: our anger was directed back at some of our original perpetrators including financial institutions, religious systems, political bodies, and many other systems. Our individual and collective sense of overwhelm increased tremendously under the pressures added on September 11, 2001.

In speaking with educators and helping professionals after September 11th, what I found most interesting was the observation that, it was not the children that warranted their principal concern, but the number of parents "who became so stressed that they became physically ill" in the weeks that followed. We are unaccustomed to archetypal increases in stress levels. To those already stressed, the burden of this new level of trauma pushed the already repressed immune system into crisis. The rise in autoimmune disorders also attests to this. We cannot let such traumatic events usurp our focus for long without detriment to the bodymind. Traumatic images and events seize control of our quantum perception and redirect the flow of power to the site and image causing the feeling of overwhelm. These images seduce us through our fear and anger and have us engage our creativity in sustaining the imagery. At such times, we become co-creators of the very things we abhor. Focus is everything! Mindfulness is all.

It is a fact that we do not realize the power of the trances that we access, particularly those that seize control of the rational mind so quickly that we do not recognize their introduction. When triggered, I have seen trance states cause the adult to automatically revert back to the old (sometimes childhood) coping mechanisms whether they were functional or dysfunctional. Some survival reactions to trauma that I have seen include: hiding in closets, eating handfuls of raw flour or sugar, showering compulsively, surgically altering the body, making oneself pass out by holding the breath, leaving the body, becoming ill, inducing an anxiety attack, cutting on oneself, eating specific foods compulsively, choosing certain drugs that medicate the nerve center of pain, and acting out the original scripts of physical or sexual abuse on another, among many others.

To reclaim our bodies from the power of these trance states, we must first, identify and resolve our own triggers and scenes. Second, we should honor the sensitivity of our nervous systems and restrict our over-exposure to negative and violent images and information. Positive and negative information need to be balanced. Remember that both are holonomic and powerful in their influence. Third, we must learn to honor the power of our quantum creativity and make more conscious choices about what we "observe," since observation is no longer understood to be a passive process, but a creative one. We must ask ourselves what it is that we desire to consciously create as part of our daily lives. Fourth, if we have left negative memories unattended and unresolved in our bodies overlong, we may need to detoxify our systems or receive medical intervention if the negative encoding has resulted in illness or chronic conditions. Fifth, if the trance states and their incumbent negative belief systems have taken root in our lifestyle, we may need to place ourselves physically in new healing contexts and environments to initiate a significant shift in the direction of recovery.

When we cannot control our states of mind, we can sometimes calm the mind by relaxing the body. My spiritual director taught me this in Rome. This is also one of the basic principles behind yoga and the exercises of Zen. By going through a series of postures, we affect the endocrine system and balance the adrenaline flow in our bodies. The ancient postures of yoga create "attitudinal predispositions" which allow us to move into a different state of consciousness. Through these bodily manipulations, we predispose ourselves for balance and healing. In shifting the physiology of the body we can secondarily relax the mind. We can learn to use meditation, yoga, exercise, etc. as a means to calm the system and reinforce our security and integrity. We have many healing options available to us.

CHAPTER 10

෨෬

"LESSONS IN DUALITY"

Through breakthroughs in physics, psychology, cellular biology and anthropology, it is evident that our ultimate "duality" or capacity to split into diverse states of consciousness, preceded history, civilization, religion, and even language as we know it. Such fragmentation or splitting of consciousness occurred spontaneously in our earliest stages of evolution – at moments of physical or emotional overwhelm. This magnificent protective mechanism holds the map to our personal and collective reintegration. It bears an ancient invitation to spiritual intimacy and wholeness.

In the mythology of ancient man, "duality" or the split into good and bad were thought to be the result of a moral breach: the violation of a fundamental law or commandment. Knowing of no other explanation for the presence of such negativity in human life, ancient man assumed his own guilt: we must have violated the commandment and eaten of the forbidden tree of knowledge. This resulted, by his thinking, in the loss of Eden – a conscious violation of a commandment! Such was the restrictive thinking of the "moral failure" model and its effort to restore order to a decadent world.

In the original Genesis account, however, "shame" is the emotional response depicted in the ancient mythology, not merely guilt. This notion takes us beyond the "moral failure" model, for shame causes a splitting in the spiritual psyche, resulting in a loss of power. When we are shamed, we split into two separate states of consciousness. This is, in fact, the moment of trauma induction. Trauma causes an alienation of the self from the self. In this divisive experience, what was one becomes dual. Intentionality becomes split: one part of the self wishes to move forward in time, while another seeks to freeze to protect and prevent movement forward into pain or death. This mechanism, however, is less about anything conscious, and is more about subconscious and automatic protection of the system. We were designed to dissociate or split to survive and self-protect when overwhelmed. This protective system is inherent to our DNA, our physiology itself. It has been present since our earliest inception. We have been splitting into conscious and sub-conscious states of mind for at least 1.5 million years.

As we were evolving into conscious, sentient beings, we were easily frightened by the mysteries of nature. We knew little of "science" as we currently define it. Our limited knowledge made us vulnerable to the forces around us. We would have surely perished without the capacity to repress our fear and pain in order to survive. Strength was given to us in our moments of greatest fear by the protective responses rooted deeply within us. At moments of great crisis, as we witnessed with the inundation of New Orleans from Hurricane Katrina in August of 2005, many individuals were triggered and responded in keeping with older, embedded coping mechanisms: some became angry, aggressive and "fought" in response to the perceived threat to their lives and security, hearing in current events echoes of danger from the past. Others were moved and used the influx of adrenaline to affirm their core belief in the goodness of the human person and the value of human life. Traumatic events in our world will always serve as the gauge to determine the degree of personal and collective duality or "dissociation" that we hold within. At primordial moments of fear, at times of greatest overwhelm, we can find almost superhuman strength to lift fallen trees or vehicles off of our children, to pull injured persons from burning, flooding, and collapsing structures. In the immense traumas of this last decade, we have been flooded with enough adrenaline to perform the tasks needed to survive. This is our nature. This is our inherent design. When pushed to the limit, we have the capacity to shine. At moments of catastrophic tsunami, earthquake, hurricane, or the invasion of our space, as with the terrorist attacks in New York, London, and Washington, D.C., we frequently rise to the occasion.

One such courageous person was jogging near the Twin Towers on September 11, 2001. Upon hearing the impact of the first plane, she redirected her "run" toward the plaza. She began to help injured individuals make their way from the first tower when the second plane hit. She continued to do her best amid the chaos that ensued. With the impact of the second plane, all sound ceased: she could no longer handle the noise, the sounds of bodies and objects falling onto the plaza pavement around her. Her senses numbed, and she became temporarily deaf, allowing her to continue helping others who needed her desperately. As she became increasingly overwhelmed, she moved into a subconscious state of repression: eventually becoming amnesic about the entire day, forgetting the events she performed and witnessed. She did not even remember her heroics. Hours later, she found herself wandering around Manhattan – senses numbed and uncertain of how she had arrived there. She could not remember any of the earlier events. When I finally met her and helped to create enough safety to allow her to focus on her "body memories" of that day, she recalled the entire sequence of events. She remembered aiding others and a stranger who came to her aid. She was completely numbed out by this point. He helped her to leave the plaza as the towers fell and bodies fell onto the pavement around her. This stranger assisted her just as she had helped so many others – probably saving her life. What remarkable beings we are! I have found great strength and hope in witnessing the memories of so many thousands of people. We possess the capacity to become magnificent in crisis, not "failures." At such moments we may even surpass all of our previous "moral" conditioning. Though we may not all be official heroes, we are gifted with the capacity to contain our pain in order to survive the tragedies and moments of overwhelm. And sometimes we rise well above them in love and protection of others.

On the physiological level, the Genesis mythology is proving true. *There is a health consequence to the loss of Eden! Mortality does, indeed, follow.* As the adrenaline rises to help us deal with crisis, we note certain physiological changes to our system. The endocrine system increases its production of adrenaline while our immune system compensates, reducing our "T-cell" production to permit increased adrenal response. The long-term impact of this is notable, however, for with prolonged overproduction of adrenaline, we are left with weakened immune systems and, subsequently, become ill. Research is indicating that the average individual is in hyper-corticosteroid production: we are over-producing adrenaline, a steroid hormone, and responding as though we are in a constant state of trauma and stress. With live coverage of traumatic events, and television programs designed to produce an adrenaline "fear factor" response, we are overstressing our systems. These "reality" programs are tapping into our unresolved trances and, through our subconscious triggers, activating our encoded traumas: they trigger our adrenal response, and we become hypnotized to the scenes. Ratings rise for the media when a program can hypnotize us. As a result of tampering with and excessively triggering our altered states, I am convinced that we will witness an inevitable rise in autoimmune and stress/anxiety related disorders. Our health is compromised when we abuse the protective mechanisms of our physiology and psyche.

On the psychological level, trauma induces a conflict in intentionality. On the one hand, we wish to move forward, learn from our painful experiences and let go of the past; on the other hand, we want to freeze our pain, numb out, repress it, and prevent ourselves from ever returning to anything that even remotely resembles such a painful moment. For millennia we have been pausing, freezing, and repressing our pain. This does not bring resolution, however. It also adds to the body of pain that the subconscious has already accumulated from the past. These scenes are so sensitive with their negatively charged frames, that anything similar will produce the same protective reaction of adrenaline and muscular tension – all with the intention of preventing retraumatization. Unfortunately, we often end up reliving the original memory and can even reinjure ourselves as we reexperience the original trigger.

How many memories can we store in the subconscious without a profoundly damaging effect on our immune system? Perhaps the dissociation created by shame and trauma is the source of our loss of power and our conflicting intentionality. Illness and death can certainly result from over a million years of immune system repression. I am not sure that we would even recognize a trauma-free immune system after 1.5 million years of subconscious encoding. If we were to heal the breach in body, mind, and spirit that shame induces, would we not manifest from a place of clear intention? Could we not heal almost any illness with a stress-free, trauma-free immune system? Would we not retard the aging process if we lived without the stress of maintaining thousands of protective, stress-filled states of consciousness simultaneously? I don't think we have a clue as to how many programs we're running at the same time! And we wonder why we do not manifest our highest good more spontaneously! I believe that Eden awaits us. There is an open invitation here.

In exclusive adherence to the "moral responsibility" model, many persons and systems have shamed us into the same dissociative state that prevents singular intentionality. In other words, just like the parent that shames a child to try to prevent overeating – resulting in increased shame and compulsion about food, our religious systems have endorsed a "moral failure" model which shames us out of Eden! Shame causes us to split within our spiritual psyche. From such a place, spontaneous manifestation is lost. The reason is this: we lose our focus in the Eternal Present. When we begin to reside in both the past and the present; we are conflicted in our focus, our manifestation. We become lost in a trauma-based perception of the past as evidenced in our feelings of shame and anger, or we become preoccupied about the trauma's recurrence in our future, as revealed in our fear! So much energy is expended in this direction that we lose sight of the present moment.

The past and the future are illusions of the mind; Eden exists in the Eternal Present. We will not know its bliss until we learn to reside in the Eternal Present. "Abide in me, and I in you," is the invitation of the mysticism of the Gospel of John. To remain continuously in the eternal present, where all is answered, all is complete – where fullness, abundance, and authentic intimacy abide: that is Eden! As we approach singular intentionality, we spontaneously manifest our highest good. Even our thoughts are shaped less by trauma, less by shame about the past or fear about the future! We can learn to be present to another and really listen without the voices of our own trances interrupting this sacred encounter.

I do not know about you, but I am tired of this split in consciousness. I do not think that we will know real rest until our intentionality is one. It has been 1.5 million years in coming. For my part, I am committed to the journey. Who knows! In an Edenic state of mind, free of trauma and inner conflict, we might not even need to sleep – or, at the least, we could sleep without the exhaustive intrusions generated by our unresolved trances!

CHAPTER 11

ഇരു

"COMING OUT OF TRANCE"

Realizing that we move fluidly in and out of as many as fifty altered states of consciousness an hour, it is amazing we have ever heard or completed a conversation! What love and intimacy flow as we gain the capacity to listen and abide in "present time."

As many of us discovered as children, by the age of five I had learned how to escape emotional pain and stress through trancing. I have only heard of one other individual whose elementary school report card actually stated in the "conduct" section: "He daydreams too much in the classroom." That, of course, was during the second grade, with Mrs. Averil who was renowned for biting her knuckle and having quite a temper. I remember coming out of one of my "daydreams" in her classroom to find her calling my name and biting her knuckle right in front of my face. It was truly terrifying, for surely if she could bite herself she could do even worse to me! I remember very little of second grade besides that scene.

The eyes are one of the primary vehicles through which we receive our first messages about worth and value. Reflecting on my own history, I recall that my father did not ever make direct eye contact with me for very long periods of time; he was a very shy, shame-based individual, due to his trauma history. As a result, I was always very sensitive to intense eye contact. If overly engaged in direct eye contact, I often felt uncomfortable and averted my eyes. I have noticed that we usually avert our eyes when feelings of unworthiness or self-consciousness are triggered. We know that self-esteem is acquired through a "mirroring" process from the eyes of the primary caregivers. The eyes of our mothers and fathers were the principal source of our initial messages about worth and safety. If our parents were emotionally unavailable and could not engage us from a place of confidence or worthiness, we recorded the absence of love/light – a "void."

Researchers have found that the eyes are capable of sending and receiving photons of light – exchanging signals and communicating over notable distances. How often have we turned to find the eyes of another making contact with us from far across a room? Our earliest model of relationship was acquired through this visual imprinting and connection. Like my father, early on I internalized a certain discomfort associated with sustained eye contact. This process is subconscious and automatic due to a child's open and inquisitive natural disposition. Many of us internalized our first shame experiences through natural imitation of a traumatized or shame-based parent. Any embarrassment or disconnection on the part of our parents easily became our own discomfort. Though my father was a gentle and kind spirit, I saw the pain of his inability to benefit from the direct expression and reception of love. His shame isolated him within his own body, unable to become very comfortable with the affection, touch, and overtures of love offered by the radiant beings around him. To observe him was to witness the restrictive pain created by trance. It was through my observation of his pain that I made the commitment to find a different path. I could not imagine living my entire life within the emotional constraints of such trauma-induced trance states. I could not imagine surviving with such barriers to intimacy and love.

Before he died, during one of my visits to the hospital, I scanned his chest with my hands. I felt a pain in his upper right lung. I asked the doctor if that was the site of the cancer tumor in his lung. His physician looked at me with surprise and stated, "Yes, that's the location of the tumor … but how do you know that?" I simply stated that I could feel it with my hands, at which time he gave me a strange look and discontinued his enquiry. My own shock was the realization that I could feel the site – the reality being that I do not feel physiologically based conditions, but only those rooted in traumatic memory. I knew the moment that I felt his tumor site that he was dying from his unresolved trauma, which had manifested as cancer. I made the commitment at that time to do my best in this life to not die from my unresolved trauma history, but to do my best to leave this world from a conscious place, not a predominantly unconscious one. Acknowledging that we, as a species, have been living from a very subconsciously driven, trauma-based intentionality, I would prefer, instead, to transition from a conscious place. I do not wish to continue evolving unconsciously from my traumas and become the victim of diabetes, Parkinson's, colon cancer, lung cancer, heart conditions, head injuries, etc. in my body as my father had. I am not saying that all of these conditions were trauma-based, but our trauma histories most certainly influence our ability to heal and overcome illness. As my perfect "negative" teacher, my father inspired me to find a way out of my own trances. Witnessing in my father the sadness of being uncomfortable with open expressions of love or affection, the inability to accept compliments from his own children or to openly share his immense capacity for love – these emotional shackles inspired my passion for finding a way out of these altered states. Such trauma-induced limitations inhibit the relationship between father and son, parent and child, as well as our own sense of self-worth.

Shame and fear – the most potent by-products of trauma, isolate us and rob us of intimacy. They are moments when we become hypnotized and focused on the incompleteness of love in our lives. These emotions move us into a place of defense and withdrawal. Traumas rivet or capture our attention, holding us bound to emotional states that isolate and restrict our capacity for trust, our capacity to connect with another. In my work over the years with cancer patients and those with other serious pathologies, I have found no affect that binds one or fosters illness more than shame. The counterpart to shame, also stored at moments of trauma is anger, the "other side of the coin," so to speak. My father died under the influence of the shame induced from his unresolved traumas; of this I have no doubt. His actual pain I felt in my hands.

The second emotion that draws us away from the flow of light within us is fear. My mother, who transitioned in 1983, died from "breast cancer" – a least that is what the medical report read. In her care for others, my mother always placed others first, especially her children. Her way of finding meaning and value in her life was profoundly connected to her care of others. When she noticed a growth in her breast, she dealt with her fear and justified her delay in seeking medical care by focusing on her responsibilities to her family and others. In doing so, she hastened her departure from us. In the delay, her cancer metastasized and, over a period of nine years, killed her. Her fear of illness affected her judgment regarding medical intervention and led to her "early" departure. From the feelings of overwhelm caused by fear, we often cannot respond clearly to the messages of the rational, moral mind. Fear distorts the messages that could offer us assistance, coloring the communication with doubt and suspicion, often rendering unavailable to us the very help that we most need. At the time of her illness, I was unaware of the resources that we now employ which can help others heal such conditions. In the manner in which both of my parents transitioned, they offered me valuable lessons that I have shared with many others. These painful examples also shaped the evolution of my work and my own commitment to living a "fully conscious" existence. These precious teachers taught me that neither fear nor shame can remain within our systems without exercising a profound detrimental impact on our growth and evolution.

To really know love, health, and wholeness, we must step beyond the illusions, beyond the outdated images imposed on us individually and culturally. From the example of my own parent-teachers, there is a mandate to emerge from the trances that have so possessed us psycho-spiritually and physiologically. We must emerge from the trances of over a million years of encoding and risk redefinition: reexamining our very concepts of intimacy, health, and the original quality of goodness and love that underlies our nature. Such is our invitation and our greatest hope.

CHAPTER 12

ℒꝺ℘

"MYSTICAL INTIMACY"

There is a Wisdom which speaks continuously and beckons us to unparalleled intimacy. We hear it, finally, when the dissonant voice of trauma falls silent.

A physics of intimacy exists that bears a blueprint for awakening. We are at the advent of a great deepening of the human potential for relationship. As the "negative" voices and imprints of others are released from the cells and fields of our bodies, we become capable of remaining present to and attending to the voices of those around us. We also become more available to the voice of Wisdom that speaks from within us. We have gravely undervalued the impact of our words and gestures on the psycho-spiritual development of the individual and of our interpersonal relationships.

My first "baby steps" in this direction came at the invitation and need of those seeking help from their traumas. One of the first sensations I learned to recognize at the beginning of a session was the presence of anger in my clients, particularly if it was instilled from physical abuse. It always came as an uncomfortable burning sensation in my hands: the greater the burning, the deeper the anger. I began to notice a pattern, particularly when the burning in my hands was over one side of the face and not the other. If the intensity of this burning reached the point of becoming a physical pain, I knew immediately that this was created by a blow to the face. When the signal was particularly defined and quite physical to my hand, I simply asked if there had been trauma to the right side of the face. In most cases, it was due to someone "backhanding" my client in a moment of rage. It was irrelevant when the blow occurred, for the intensity seemed equal whether the trauma was encoded that morning or forty years prior. The cells and fields of the body presented the energy from the memory as though it was yesterday. This is not to say that all memories are stored in the cells and fields of the body with this same clarity, but the more traumatic memories certainly hold a strong charge long after the moment of encoding. Some small percentage of memories, I believe, release spontaneously or with a small amount of focusing, but the majority remain anchored protectively in the cells and fields of the bodymind.

The most dramatic cases involved violence. One evening, after a lecture that I presented on my work, I offered to "scan" those in attendance to demonstrate how the body is continuously broadcasting our history, especially our unresolved traumas. These areas of pain or tension in the body speak louder and louder to get our attention in order to heal. One man in attendance offered to step forward and to be scanned. As I began to move my hands over the left side of his head, I commented that something physical had surely happened to his head because my hands were experiencing a very physical pain whenever I passed over his left temple area. His eyes widened, and, in a very quiet voice he stated: "I was beaten up once by some boys, but I never told anyone about it." I gently responded that this trauma was still very much imprinted in the cells and fields of his body – especially around his head, and that it would be worth his while to reframe this at his earliest convenience. I knew that he was startled that someone could "pick up" on his pain without any prior disclosure on his part, but, as I explained to him, the body remembers all! It constantly speaks to us and tries to afford us opportunities to heal our energetic blockages.

It was a bit of a shock for this gentleman to discover that his traumatic memory was so "real" as to be recognizable by a total stranger at some distance from his body – in fact, without ever touching his body. He, as did so many of us on the journey to heal our memories, received a poignant lesson. We are capable of being imprinted in a deep and enduring manner with the violence of another, and that we are, likewise, capable of transferring our own consciousness and intentions – our traumas and violence to others. Emotions have a genuine physiology and a physics. We are capable of leaving a trace of our emotions identifiable in the cells and fields of the body of another. This was a level of intimacy and responsibility that my mother had hinted at through her experience of our pain. Most of my mother's experiences, to my knowledge, were mostly about physical danger, accidents, or medical crises; they were not usually traumas introduced through the intentionally violent acts of another. The recidivism[25] that is so high with cases of domestic violence in our society becomes totally comprehensible when we see how we have overlooked the powerful imprinting of such trauma in the cells and fields of the bodymind.

The most easily recognizable sensations of memory stored in the bodymind appear to be the darkest ones. In three cases I could barely approach the heads of my clients without feeling an excruciating pain in my hands. When asked what had created such pain, my clients identified very specific traumatic moments including two cases of gunshots to the head, and one case of "being kicked in the head by my husband during his cocaine usage – kicked until I ended up in the kitchen." Because she was on cocaine herself at the time, she had not thought that this was originally very traumatic for her, or had dismissed it due to her own guilt and involvement. Cases of domestic violence have this impact on the bodymind, encoding dense layers of energy that preempt our capacity to feel the higher, lighter frequencies of love, trust, and oneness. The dense energies of trauma create a protective, isolated environment that becomes heavier, more numbing with each additional layer. We have been "layering" and repressing such energies for over a million years.

I recall the case of one client where I kept feeling a truly violent and intense pain over her left ear – the location suggesting that the pain was somehow tied into criticism from her mother – that is, an auditory trauma on the left (feminine) side of her body. Though her mother was quite critical, which she readily admitted, the level of pain that I was feeling had only occurred in the most violent of traumas that I had ever found. To date, every case evidencing this degree of pain in my hands involved homicidal violence. She could provide no explanation beyond her mother's constant critical banter to explain the level of pain. Suddenly, however, just before the session concluded, she remembered that her grandfather had severely abused her mother. She added that he was an incredibly violent man who had served time in prison for a homicide. Her grandfather's abuse to her mother resulted in the transmission of this quality of violence to my client through the violent and abusive language of her mother. There was a degree of pain present in her body that was historically traceable. A quality of this homicidal violence was passed on to my client in the frequencies and outrage in her mother's voice, though her mother never laid a hand on her. I found this man's energetic imprint to be maintained in the body of my client, though he had not been directly abusive to her.

The capacity to feel the physical and emotional pain of another has led many healers and practitioners to a revised model of intimacy suggesting that there is only one flow of consciousness: there is only one Mind that connects us all. In the language of the physical body, it is as though there is only one spinal cord in the universe which we all share; we are that interconnected. There is only one point of reference, one "reference beam," as it is referred to in hologram theory, which handles all pain conversations in the bodymind. Scientists to this day cannot fully explain why we perceive all reality in the form of holograms. There have been various theories positing that this process is the result of right and left brain interaction, perhaps even front brain/back brain interaction, or even parallel processing systems. From my work, I suspect that our capacity to perceive reality holographically while in physical form is the result of right brain – left brain interaction which manifests in front and back as a holographic processing system: meaning that the frontal "object" beam and the rear spinal "reference" beams intersect to create our holographic images of reality. In other words, all three theories are partially correct, but incomplete without an understanding of the holographic nature of perception and the holographic properties of the universe itself. The "mind-body" link that is so heralded in contemporary medicine is based on the fact that memory in the physical body is "holonomic" and acts very much like a hologram, while consciousness itself is truly holographic in nature. My clients have described experiences of dissociation from the body during abuse, and their perceptions remain distinctly holographic in nature. Michael Talbot's work, *The Holographic Universe*, sheds much light on this subject.[26]

Access to the mind's holographic projection system is greatly enhanced through the dorsal channel of the spine. This portion of the spine handles all of our pain neurotransmissions. When I placed my hand on the dorsal horn of a client's spine for the first time and realized that I could feel the traumatic memory of another, my universe became much more intimate. For the first time I knew the truth of another's pain as well as felt his/her capacity to release such trauma. By uniting with the pain core of my client which was accessible through the dorsal portion of the spine, I knew another's pain as my own. I felt the moment the emotional charge of the memory released from the system, and I knew the ensuing joy and serenity as well. To this day, I routinely feel the sudden increase in calm – the lessening of physical and emotional pain as my clients move their "solutions" through their bodies. As they change their brainwave frequencies, I can feel my own shift as well. This is most noticeable when I am connected to the dorsal horn of the spine and all of the pain neurotransmissions in the bodymind.

Just as we can focus and feel pain in the extremities of our own bodies, so can we feel the pain of others as our own – as though they are truly extensions of ourselves. Likewise, we benefit whenever another heals or moves toward personal integration. As one part of the body heals, the whole body benefits. I physically feel my own field improve as another heals. This capacity for intimacy shifts us away from the notion that we should dissociate ourselves from the wounded parts. To deny our relationship to the wounded parts of our society no longer serves this larger, more realistic model of intimacy. We are bound to those in our criminal justice system. We are bound to the addicted and traumatized portions of our population. We are deeply connected to the children who reach out in search of unconditional love, to the adolescents in search of meaning and purpose.

We have hidden behind the density of the bodymind and its encoded traumas throughout the many millennia of our evolution. We can no longer afford to do so without grave consequences. The great intensification in interpersonal and cross-cultural communication has changed this. We will now participate in the live transmissions of global events as they occur. We will witness "live" as they occur, the September 11th events of our time, for we are now part of a great network of communication. We shall experience the blessings and the pain of this enhanced intimacy. We are all part of this enhanced network or "internet" of communication. Geographical separation becomes irrelevant in this time of spontaneous and immediate communication across the globe. Our capacity for being present to another is changing dramatically. The choice is in our own hands to determine the degree of vigilance when it comes to admitting imagery into our quantum projectors – the sacred space of the mind that participates in the singular flow of consciousness. To pollute one part of the river is to impact all; we are that interconnected.

Similarly, we have the capacity to become resources that deeply influence the collective flow of humankind. In our individual contemplation and greater participation in the one flow of consciousness, we bring our wisdom and ecstasy to the enrichment of the whole. To abide in the flow is to raise the frequency of this spiritual network. When we remain in the light, there is no lack of understanding, for we stand in the knowledge of All That Is. There is neither a need for sad retrospection about the past, nor fearful preoccupation about the future. Our highest good is most easily realized by bringing all of our finished and unfinished business into the pure flow of white light, into the singular flow of the One Mind that embraces all. Here abides our invitation to oneness and intimacy.

CHAPTER 13

ℰℭ

"RECLAIMING THE EMOTIONAL SPECTRUM"

*As we free ourselves from the dense energies of trauma, we open
to an unprecedented capacity for creativity, for never in our history
have we known or lived from the unencumbered flow of light with
the full spectrum of emotional possibility.*

One of the greatest advantages of healing our memories is the
restoration of our creativity and our capacity for relationship. When
we reclaim ourselves from these moments of pain and overwhelm,
restoring our sense of safety and integrity, we open new doors to
intimacy. Moments of stress and trauma activate a freezing process
that causes us to restrict ourselves emotionally in order to survive.
We freeze with the overwhelming feelings of the moment, leaving
ourselves excluded from other opportunities until this "primary affect"
is resolved. This is simply the protective nature of our system.

One way of understanding the limiting effect of trauma and
emotional repression is found in the expression of color. In many
cases of memory resolution with trauma survivors, I have witnessed
the same phenomenon: when the survivor seeks to change an
outdated scene of trauma from one of pain to one of safety, they hit a
blockage – an inability to visualize color. One particular case comes
to mind in this regard, with a woman whom we shall call Lauren.
When she attempted to reframe her memories of emotional abuse due
to the domestic violence witnessed between her father and mother,
she came upon an obstacle. When Lauren sought to change the old
outdated image of mom and dad quarreling and insert an image of
a healthier mom and dad after their treatment for alcoholism (which
occurred many years after the original abuse), she found that she
could only see mom and dad in "black and white." The emotional
and verbal abuse from mom and dad was extensive over many years.
Most puzzling, however, was the fact that Lauren's efforts at finding a
solution using "recovering" mom and dad could only produce black
imagery against a white/gray background. When asked about this
and whether anyone else could offer her safety and love instead, she
grinned and stated: "Grandma could make me safe; she has all the
colors." Briefly taken aback at her response, I suddenly realized that
for the many thousands of survivors I had assisted in the previous

years, the ability to visualize color in the inner mind was directly related to their ability to feel emotions safely.

Some years ago I observed that, for almost half of my clients, they were wearing the colors that they needed in the reframing of their trauma memories on a given day. This was predominantly an unconscious process, but it appeared routinely in my office. The subconscious mind speaks to us continuously through the body. Thinking back on the thousands of reframes I had witnessed, it became evident that there was a connection between color expression and safety. It made perfect sense that the capacity to visualize color was directly related to the individual's ability to feel safe, for color was the language of emotion to the child whose vocabulary for feelings was so limited. That was why art therapy seemed so effective for children who could draw or sculpt their expressions of pain but who lacked the vocabulary to express the complexity of their experiences.

One day I received two drawings from a teacher familiar with my work. One of her students, Sarah, had witnessed a gang-related shooting in which her brother was killed. She became despondent and lost much of her ability to stay focused in the classroom. Childhood depression due to trauma is sometimes mislabeled Attention Deficit Disorder or Hyperactivity. With significant trauma, trancing and losing focus in present time are not unusual reactions. In fact, this is common with such powerful negative imprinting. The teacher tried to comfort and to reassure her, to redirect her attention to more positive or meaningful activities, but Sarah could not maintain the redirection for very long. Finally, when the teacher recalled what she had learned from my adaptive use of color reframing, she tried the following instead: She had Sarah draw the trauma scene – of the gang members shooting her brother. The gang members were all depicted in red and black with sneering looks on their faces. The family members all wore tears. She then had Sarah redraw the picture the way she would like to have seen it. In the corrected scene, everyone is being nice to each other and having a good time. She then had Sarah close her eyes and move the colors of the corrected scene like water through her body. Immediately Sarah became calm and was able to continue her class involvement without any additional disruptive behaviors or distractions. Her re-visualization of the scene did not change history itself; it simply freed her subconscious mind from the scene in which she had been trapped where she was continuously reliving the moment of her brother's death. Sending the missing emotions to her subconscious through color freed her mind to complete the grieving process and return to focus in present time. Sounds almost too simple does it not? Dr. Jim Graham, an internationally known physician and addictionologist commented on my work once stating: "Brent, the difficulty with your approach is that people are accustomed to believing that healing has to be a painful and lengthy process; they are unaccustomed to healing quickly and easily." The process may appear simple, but the ease of its use comes from the amazing resources of your bodymind to capture states of consciousness in readily manageable forms. Let us take Sarah's case, for example.

The solution Sarah employed is simple: She first expressed her pain in the appropriate colors; she then visualized a solution and identified, through color, the emotions/feelings that were missing from the original scene. When she closed her eyes and moved her version of these colors through her body, she sent a (holographic) signal correction to her subconscious mind indicating that she now possessed the capacity to create safety, for one cannot move such colors/feelings (specific frequencies missing from the original moment) through the bodymind and still be trapped in the scene of trauma. The colors that appeared in association with the corrected image carried her unique spectral signature and were the exact complement to the limited, traumatizing frequencies she stored in the original trauma scene. When we add all of the colors together in the visible spectrum, we create "white light" – the completion and totality of all frequencies. Completing the deficiency or void created by the original encoding, we feel calm and complete about the original event. Resolving the polarity that was created, we feel balanced and whole instead. Freed from the moment of original encoding, Sarah could relax and continue the grieving process at a normal pace instead of feeling stuck in the horrific moment of her brother's death. *Color reframing does not alter our historical perception of traumatic events; it merely completes the emotional charge* that was left incomplete at the instant the scene was encoded. The difficulty with these altered states is that days and years after such events have passed, the subconscious mind is still responding protectively as though the danger is imminent. Color reframing eliminates the subconscious need to hold our pain indefinitely in order to protect us. By demonstrating our capacity to address this moment of encoding with the missing frequencies/colors, the subconscious relinquishes its need to maintain this scene as a separate state of consciousness. Once the emotional pain is neutralized, we can integrate these experiences as wisdom without any emotional attachment or polarity to return us to the scene.

In his "First Principle," described in *The Spiritual Exercises of St. Ignatius,* Ignatius Loyola states: "As far as we are concerned, we should not prefer health to sickness, riches to poverty, honor to dishonor, a long life to a short life … the same holds for all other things: Our one desire and choice should be what is more conducive to the end for which we are created." In the writings of the mystics, all experiences are valid paths to divinity. The totality of all emotional experiences – the sum of all of the frequencies of consciousness gives us white light. This would suggest that every experience has a value and a contribution to the whole – that we are incomplete unless we embrace all of our emotions: our anger and power (red), our sexuality and creativity (orange), our relationality (yellow), our hearts (rose and green), our voices (blue), our visions and intuitive guidance (violet), and our higher truth (white). When we close the visual center at the "third eye" to stop our abuse, we simultaneously restrict access to our visions and intuitive guidance. Trauma results in the restriction of emotional and spiritual experience. We freeze due to the absence of safety, love, nurturing, and protection. The less safe we are, the less white light we know at the time. The more violent the trauma, the darker is the "charge" that we encode. The greater the violence, the easier it is to feel and track within the energy field due to its heaviness, its density. That is why it is so easy to teach energy techniques using memories as the classroom. Love and safety return with the restoration of our power and integrity which manifest in the full spectrum of light. We are truly free to embrace all of our emotions when we assume our power as the luminous beings we are.

In my work, I am frequently asked about the values of colors. In truth, every image of consciousness has a unique set of frequencies or colors that are specific to our quantum projector: our mind. With our personal histories and individualized ways of interpreting our experiences, each scene we create, along with its emotional "charge," is singular and personal to our perception of life. Each emotional frame is unique in the production of our life history. However, I have noticed certain patterns over the many thousands of survivors who have demonstrated their inherent mastery of color. Every color that we know from our standard vocabulary can have both a "positive" or "negative" value, though all experience is merely lesson. Red, for instance, can reflect anger and push one toward fear and paralysis, though the true nature of red is power; its specific value is dependent upon its use – the intention behind it determines its morality and function. Anger can be used to protect and heal, or to abuse. It is the same with all colors and frequencies. There are no absolutely fixed values for any color. All colors can have varied meanings depending upon their context. A "golden scalpel" can express an abuse scene, while blackness can provide the calm and quiet needed at night in a household filled with domestic violence. Nonetheless, certain common patterns are prevalent in our cross-cultural employment of color.

The earth tones, particularly the earth and wood colors – brown, beige, tan, terracotta, walnut, mahogany, oak, etc., are always used to heal breaches in safety and security. Red, as I mentioned earlier, is commonly used to express anger or rage, but it can also express passion, love, joy, and power. Orange holds a wide range of values including creativity, sexuality, and calm. Yellow is used to express happiness, healthy relationship, and is commonly used to calm the nervous system and repair nerve damage; it is the second most common color used in the resolution of migraines. Green is used for physical healing, growth, and is a heart color; it is very broad in its applications. Pink is the feminine heart color and indicates our capacity to feel emotions safely. Blue is used for creating calm, easing stress, and is the color most commonly used to resolve migraines. Violet/purple is associated with spiritual awareness, insight, but also finds expression as wounding, bruising, and severe physical trauma.

A more common phenomenon when it comes to work with trauma survivors is the inability to visualize color or color solutions when trying to reframe. After my experience with Lauren and her "grandma who has all the colors," I began to notice that in the majority of cases when my clients were having trouble visualizing imagery or solutions, there was an emotional blockage present. I eventually learned to pause the process and ask: "How old might you be when it's no longer safe to feel emotions in your family?" The answer usually provided the trauma event or sequence of events that led to an emotional "shut-down." It was not uncommon to see this occur before the age of ten.

We are usually born with all of our sensory channels open to experience. The exceptions are, for instance, some of the clients that my sister Carole assists in her work. She heads one of the nation's leading programs for assisting deaf-blind individuals. The Cajun population of which I am a part has a genetic propensity for Usher's Syndrome, a disease that can produce both deafness and blindness. Most are born deaf as a result of this illness and, over time, also lose their vision. We have a number of families in Louisiana with this genetic illness. Even in the case of Usher's, however, there was usually a time when the client was visual and could see colors. When I visited my sister's office,

I had the opportunity to use the technique on one of her clients who was deaf-blind. Carole informed me that she had a migraine, and I was interested in seeing if the color reframing process would address her pain (assuming that the migraine was memory-based as I have found most to be). My sister explained my work to her by signing in her hands. Deaf-blind clients feel the words/letters being signed in their hands. She consented to let me try the technique. I placed my hands near her head to see if I could feel the migraine. When my hands can feel such a pain, I know immediately that at least part of the migraine is memory-based. I could, in fact, feel the pain and promptly proceeded with the process, asking her to describe the metaphorical form of the pain in her head. She did so and, indeed, tapped into the memory related to the trauma of her already having become deaf and subsequently losing her sight. Other relationship traumas followed as she became blind. She was able to use color language beautifully and even generated a burgundy color solution. Her migraine was gone at the end of the process. I didn't know until the end of the process that she had been suffering from the migraine for over a week. She was excited at the simplicity and power of the healing process. In our follow-up discussion, my sister mentioned that some of her visually impaired clients could pick color-coordinated clothing by feeling the color! Knowing my own kinesthetic awareness, this was a pleasant affirmation of our ability to feel the frequencies of color and emotion, to identify the low frequencies of unresolved "frames" of traumatic events.

As young children, our earliest messages are visual and felt. Lacking the cognitive resources to verbally articulate our experience, we imprint visually and kinesthetically: reality is largely what we see and feel. Here color becomes bound to emotion. When our sensory experience becomes overwhelming, we repress this imagery and its accompanying emotional charge. As we repress our imagery, we repress the frequencies that capture our inner vision and its emotional content. To the visually oriented mind, color frequencies are repressed to ease our pain. When we heal such memories, it is not uncommon to find a creative surge expressing itself in art and color. Our color expression is restored as safety is returned to the system. Similarly, since the capacity to feel emotion is profoundly tied to our experience of the spiritual (see my earlier book: The Healing Dimensions[27] on this subject), the repression of emotion restricts the range of spiritual experience, while its restoration enhances or restores spiritual intimacy. The totality of light is our potential, as is the ecstasy such integration can bring.

CHAPTER 14

ၵၢၼ

"OPENING TO TRUE SIGHT"

As we move beyond the limitations of "five sensory" perception and learn to "see" from the Higher Self or Holographic Mind, we find ourselves at play in a world of images – a world of our own Quantum creation! Quantum physics teaches us that the act of observation is not passive but creative: we actually create as we "observe." The universe itself becomes our playground.

By our very nature we are all mystics and visionaries. Our capacity to see multidimensionally, however, is impaired when emotional blockages are introduced. Shame is a primary affect and inhibits access to the higher frequencies of perception. Our spiritual growth will remain erratic when our path is obscured by unresolved traumas. We now understand that spiritual blindness is induced principally through emotional repression caused by trauma, not merely through moral failure. The most powerful side effect of the healing of our emotional traumas, therefore, is the resolution of the shame and energetic blockage that disrupts and distorts our connection to the Source. As we remove such static states of consciousness, our vision clears.

Ancient man articulated the impact of trauma perfectly in his earliest mythologies. Initially, in the Book of Genesis, it was assumed that Adam violated some primordial law regarding his nature; this was a natural assumption from the "moral failure" model operative at that time. The older mythology underlying the written text, however, managed to capture a more fundamental perception about human evolution when it described the impact of this early breach on our capacity for intimacy. As I mentioned previously, the original authors knew nothing of the subconscious mind and naturally assumed the "fall" to be conscious and moral in origin: hence, the later theological label of an "Original 'Sin'." In fact, however, we know that man was surely able to dissociate and freeze scenes of pain to protect himself before he was even capable of speech. The very design of his physiology protected him from overwhelm, but left warning signs when the body was holding unresolved trauma or stress.

In a language that seems to transcend the intention of the original author, Eve eats of the apple and gives some to Adam, whereupon "the eyes of both of them were opened and they realized that they were naked" (Genesis 3:7a). Note the role of the eyes or vision and its impact within the account. The emotional tenor of the mythological expression is one of shame/embarrassment, not guilt. Adam and Eve see shame; this shadow now obscures their vision of themselves as good, pure, and innocent in nature. As we noted earlier, shame is the emotional term for trauma: for a splitting on the level of self – of consciousness itself. It is a term reserved for trauma to the essential identity, not a judgment about a behavioral breach. "Guilt" is the term for a behavioral or moral violation. Shame inserts a false message about self and results in an alienation of the self from the self – it causes a split in self-perception. Shame impairs our vision of reality by making us "bifocal" – operating from more than one definition or perception of self. It is here that our vision of truth is lost or distorted. Trauma and shame rivet us in places and times that leave us feeling less than our true nature. They warp our self-perception and subsequently affect our experience of reality itself. When we no longer feel worthy or capable of power, we cease to visit or to seek out these experiences. More importantly, we fail to recognize them in others or in the world around us as well. Under the burden of shame, we may even hide or withdraw from life, perceiving ourselves as unworthy of any higher experience. In the Genesis account, God is depicted as "moving about in the Garden," looking for Adam and Eve, but due to their shame, they hide themselves from him. All levels of relationship are impacted by shame.

In truth, one of the most profound impacts of shame and trauma is upon our spiritual perception. One of my clients, Maureen, as a child had profound visual access to reality around her. When her grandfather died, for instance, she was taken to the wake. After viewing the body of her grandfather and offering a prayer for his soul, as she was encouraged to do, she wandered into the outside rose garden. While there, she suddenly could see and feel her grandfather's presence. He looked happy and peaceful and said to tell everyone that he was fine; she ran inside to tell her mother who promptly pulled her aside and scolded her severely "for making such things up." She was told never to do that again, whereupon she lost her ability to see and speak directly with her angels, guides, and loved ones. Prior to this trauma, she had a natural ability to see energy and color around people. The "third eye" opens once more when we cease trying to restrict our experience of reality to avoid condemnation or rejection from others.

My sister Carole was wonderful with her daughter Brittany when she began to demonstrate her natural intuitive abilities at an early age. When my niece Brittany was around ten years old, she greeted my sister early one morning and announced that her "angels" had come to her earlier and informed her that they had saved her mother and Aunt Margie from a car accident the night before. Apparently a drunk driver steered into my sister's lane, forcing her car off the road while they were driving home late from sign-language class. The car spun around, traversing several dangerous lanes of traffic on the interstate without hitting anything and without causing any bodily harm or whiplash to either of my sisters. Startled, they returned home safely, grateful for their miraculous escape. My niece had many experiences like this while talking with her "angels" and guides. Such perception, I believe, is normal when we remain emotionally open to our "inner vision." Routinely, however, with the induction of shame, we learn to repress our self-trust and inner sight. According to many researchers, we appear to have some degree of shame-induction by the time we are two and a half years old. Is it any surprise that we find our intuitive perception suffering in our development?

Once when I was visiting my sister Carole and her family, her daughter Brittany had a headache. Brittany was about nine years old at the time. Her pain prompted me to offer my assistance. After placing my hands near her head and working on her headache, I felt the pain leaving and moving through my hands. After a few minutes, the pain was gone. Smiling, she looked up at me and said, "Uncle Brent, do you know that you just did three types of healing with me: physical, mental, and emotional." Brittany was always sensitive to the movement of light and able to perceive the spiritual dimensions of reality.

As our traumas are resolved and the "density" created by encoded memories diminishes, we gain the ability to perceive certain subtle frequencies that we could not feel previously. Many of us are more "clairsentient" (feeling frequencies) than "clairvoyant" (seeing frequencies) around others. The advantage of being clairsentient is that we do not have to visually witness the graphic violence of an event, but can rely upon our senses to limit our personal experience of the trauma of another. For myself, I do not doubt that if I actually "saw" a third of what my ritually and systematically abused clients have experienced, I would not still be doing this work for a living. As clairsentients ("clear feeling"), we are more prone to feel frequencies than to see them; this restricts the potential for overwhelm and permits us to continue our work with more severely traumatized individuals.

The resolution of pain and trauma in the cells, meridians, and energy fields of the bodymind open us to higher levels of perception. When cleared of shame, we perceive reality less from the density and doubt of trauma and more from the luminosity that comprises all of creation. When we possess within ourselves white light: possessing all the colors of creation, we recognize our energetic connection to everything and everyone around us. When we live from a sense of deficiency or lack, we make our choices and move through life with the pull of the void and the unfinished, incompletely framed experiences that knock us off balance. Such knocks and falls often reveal to us that our decisions were influenced by the subconscious pull of the void rather than attraction borne of the light. We are learning to revision our memories and to transform our moments of pain to moments of love and completion. We possess the capacity to bring white light to all the moments of our history and to know that we were always deserving of love. To know all of our missing frequencies suggests that we, in fact, never fully lost touch with the river of white light that is the source of all consciousness. As we come to remember ourselves as borne of the light, we see in others the same reflection: the luminous being that we are. It is natural to feel the joy and pain of another in our transparency and without the density of trauma. This vision of our truth reveals the magnificence of the other as well. Such sight reveals the interconnectedness of all that is. It enables us to interact with our "angels" and guides, our departed loved ones who offer assistance. Without trauma's imposed darkness and illusion, our connection to the Source is immediate – our power to redirect the light is natural, and our ability to master our states of consciousness is unquestioned. We are far more capable of spiritual experience than we were led to believe. Fear and shame repress spiritual experience. Doing the work necessary to release the lessons of trauma brings its own spiritual rewards and vision. This vision has proven more authentic than we were traditionally led to believe, and it is reliable!

We may not all become immediately visionary, but "true sight" comes to us in many ways and degrees. I recall my sister finding Brittany crying when she was about five years old. When Carole asked her what was wrong, she muttered that she was having a very bad dream in which mommy and daddy were killed in a car accident occurring on a bridge in the rain. A few days later, my sister Carole and her husband found themselves on a bridge in a severe rainstorm. Carole suddenly remembered Brittany's dream and told her husband to slow down: "This looks just like the dream that Brittany described." In the news the following day, it was reported that hydroplaning on this same bridge resulted in a multi-vehicle accident that involved fatalities. My sister believes that the warning provided through Brittany's dream made the difference. Dreams are also altered states and can offer us truth and guidance. Our first stages of opening to "true sight" are often subtle and gentle, but capable of true vision we all are.

Though we, individually and as a culture, have oftentimes been frightened by and subsequently distrusted the visions and messages of intuition, the truth remains that we cannot know real safety until we do so. It is only the holographic or higher mind that can perceive multidimensionality accurately and communicate such complexity simply. This higher mind speaks through our intuition and those impulses that are beyond the constraints of the five senses. I have seen a well known intuitive and friend of mine, Mary Jo McCabe, tell her son to wait a few minutes before leaving the house because there is a drunk driver about five blocks away who is posing a danger to all the traffic in the area. Who of us would not embrace such information for our own safety and the safety of our loved ones? As we heal our memories and our bodies, we gain access to higher frequencies and more subtle information that were repressed with the freezing of our pain. With such ability, we navigate through life with healthier decisions and with a clearer sense of purpose.

CHAPTER 15

℘℘℘

"THE GATEWAY TO POWER"

Our deepest fear is not that we are inadequate. Our deepest fear is that we are powerful beyond measure. It is our light, not our darkness that most frightens us.

Excerpt from Nelson Mandela's Inaugural Address

Of the obstacles to healing, few are as inhibiting as our fear of anger. As children most of us were exposed to the misuse of anger. For many of us, our parents' aversion to this emotion due to their own traumas led to early avoidance on our part. My father, for example, repressed many of his emotions due to his own trauma history, but always managed to control his temper until he reached a breaking point and then exploded. As a result, the version of anger I did witness was a threatening and an uncomfortable one. This is an experience familiar to many of us. We recall many signals from both our families, educational, and religious systems that left us with the impression that anger was to be approached and treated with extreme caution. Herein resides the source of much of our diminished power to focus and heal our memories and our bodies.

In the language of the bodymind, the color red is associated with raw power. "I'm so angry that I see red" is a commonly heard declaration. Red is the frequency associated with the raw energy taken in at the base of the spine. In order to stay alive, this nerve plexus must remain open at all times to the core of the earth and in interaction with the light of our environment. Red is the color associated with this raw energy of survival; but, for some of us, the color red holds unpleasant associations. We have all, at one time or another, experienced the abuse of power – particularly anger and rage from another human being. In response to this overwhelming expression of force, we frequently encoded and repressed these images as we discussed previously. With the repression of this as trauma, the holonomic nature of our memories took over, numbed us out, and served to warn us if anything similar was about to occur. The "fight, flight, or freeze" response of the adrenal system kicked in and enabled survival. This protective mechanism is commonly evidenced in the survivor's description of life in an alcoholic or dysfunctional household. The problem with such repression of anger is this: using our holographic ability to reduce overwhelming emotion to a manageable fragment, any portion of a stored scene can trigger the original trance state and its accompanying flight/fight/freeze response. For many of us, fighting back was not a viable option when we were so young or powerless. Anything resembling anger, therefore, was met with a response of terror or "freezing," and prevented us from tapping into our own power at such moments. In some cases where the expression of anger was an ongoing danger, a Level Two trauma pattern was induced which presented anger as a continuous threat to our safety and survival. Such Level Two metaphors carry immense power through their accumulation of energy over time and can easily overwhelm the singular efforts of the survivor.

As anger accumulates over time, it becomes internalized as part of a larger container – an earlier pattern of repression. Since such emotional overwhelm is routinely contained in a holographic metaphor; any taste of anger – even the smallest fragment is similar enough in content to trigger the larger body of stored frustration. This is the nature of holographic triggers: the whole can be accessed by any fragment similar enough in content or feeling to tap into the larger body of pain. When we have a "temper," we are actually admitting to the existence of repressed anger from our past – left unresolved but contained in the bodymind. In reality, the amount of anger that we hold directly correlates to the amount of trauma that we carry unresolved within us. As we build up pressure at the site(s) of containment, we risk venting the entire content on the next trigger or instigator that comes our way. We abuse others in present time when we "dump" our whole body of frustration – usually accumulated in the past, onto our current relationships or circumstances. It is inappropriate to seek current-day resolution of the traumas of our past by downloading them onto an offender in present time.

In some cases, as with the repression of women, cultural trauma is induced by merely being born into or inheriting the system. We have seen such culturally repressive traumas manifest in familial, educational, societal, political, and religious systems. With regard to the latter, I remember many times while as a priest, individuals would come for confession and confess the sin of "being angry" with someone. Though I tried to instruct them that feelings are pre-moral – that they are simply forms of energy, a spontaneous emotional response to a situation, somehow these individuals had associated anger with its inappropriate expression. This bias usually originated in their trauma histories. Sometimes I reminded them that even Jesus became angry when the Temple was violated.

The repression of anger, which can occur in the body anywhere that we can store memory, is of great significance. Observing the locations in the body where anger is stored and correlating these sites to the occurrence of serious illness, we can readily see how the repression of such powerful affect impairs our immune system and contributes to illness. I have seen this commonly with arthritis, cancer, tumors, fibroids, fibromyalgia, and countless other "inflammatory" conditions. Anger, guilt, and shame, often portrayed in the color red, lock pathologies into the bodymind. If we are convinced that we are powerless, undeserving of wholeness or healing, we have difficulty resolving these pathologies. It is as though we are uncertain of the origin of the pain and the trauma within our systems: does it originate with me or did it come from someone on the outside? When we are frozen in this uncertainty, the pathology is maintained. The "white light" of wholeness is kept at a distance – dissociated from us by our own traumas and the subsequent repression of our power.

If we look at the electromagnetic spectrum – particularly the visible spectrum, we see that anger (red) forms the base color or first in the spectrum. It is the foundation color of the spectrum and, in a sense, is also the foundation color of the body's energy system. In the spiritual and cross-cultural traditions of many nations, the color red is associated with the nerve plexus located at the base of the spine where energy from the earth, moving up through the legs, is accumulated to support the rest of the system. The impact of trauma to the feet or legs can often be felt at the "root chakra" or nerve plexus located at the base of the spine.

The gateway to the nervous system, so to speak, is this root chakra that processes the "red" core energy required by the rest of the system for survival. The repression of this system impacts the whole of the bodymind in profound ways. Without a profound sense of safety or grounding, without sufficient reassurances of support and survival, the higher needs and abilities – intimacy and sexuality (sacrum), interpersonal communication (solar plexus), love and commitment (heart), self-expression (throat), intuitive vision and decision-making (third eye), and spiritual interconnectedness (crown), are compromised. How, for instance, can we possess the vision needed to make wise decisions if we are uncertain whether we will make it safely through the day: how can violet light (red plus blue) be appreciated when the "red" frequencies are repressed at the level of core survival? Such early survival traumas leave us so preoccupied with safety issues that we cannot progress to the meeting of our "higher" needs in the emotional spectrum. Though our seven percent conscious mind may have many spiritual reassurances about our connection to the spiritual, our ninety-three percent subconscious mind may still be trapped in a life-threatening image, waiting for safety and resolution to occur. I will discuss this much further in our chapter on "Healing and Forgiveness" along with the abuses that can occur in the name of "forgiveness."

We are finally learning as our own healers to resolve our pain with what actually completes the void left by trauma. For example, with an unresolved trauma relating to our core survival (root plexus – red), we cannot simply use sex (sacrum plexus – orange) to fill the void left in the absence of power; we cannot replace this personal power loss by filling it with an interpersonal relationship (solar plexus – yellow, and heart plexus – green/pink; these chakras are actually considered as one in Hindu culture), though such relationships can empower us to find our own solution; we cannot resolve our blockage at the root plexus by repeatedly verbalizing our pain without addressing its moment of inception (throat plexus -- blue); nor can we substitute mystical visions or religious experience (third eye – indigo/violet) while avoiding our primal fear concerning our survival. As a priest, armed with the tools that I had, I attempted to resolve the traumas that had occurred to me from the death of my mother, the death of the Bishop who supported my choices, and my best friend who left ministry – all occurring within nine months around 1983. In the process, I became quite workaholic and overwhelmed without immediately addressing the traumas and the pain. Such busy-ness did little more than to distract me from the dissatisfaction of my life's direction. As soon as I made the decision to pursue my own healing and follow my truth, my talents and direction presented themselves spontaneously. When we address our grief, traumas, and anger at their source, our lives begin to align immediately.

When I left ministry, I was trying to choose one of three options: to approach a full-time teaching position with a university, based on my degree experience; to join the Jesuits, who had invited me to consider the possibility based on my interdisciplinary expertise in archaeology and scripture; or to pursue my interest in counseling which I had always enjoyed. In order to clarify my own thoughts and decision-making, I deemed it wise to address the traumas of the previous years. In order to do so, I attended a "Quality of Life" workshop based on the work of

Sharon Wegscheider-Cruse, whom I now consider a dear friend. At that workshop, I got in touch with the grief of my past traumas, including the profound feelings of aloneness and abandonment that had been triggered. There was a critical moment when I remember asking myself: "If I were to resolve all of these substantial trauma patterns from my family, culture, religious system, etc., would 'I' still exist – would I be recognizable to myself?" In other words, "Who would I be?" I had apparently spent much of my life reacting to profound subconscious influences from my history. The traumas were considerable, but I came to believe that, despite the fears and powerlessness instilled by these experiences, they could not have occurred without an equal force that promised the possibility of healing. I came to recognize that, with each trauma I had experienced, (black) feelings of fear and powerlessness were instilled; but I was also surprised at the quantity of anger that had been stored – anger exactly proportionate for each event. When accessed, the anger provided the strength I needed to enter the overwhelming memories of myself as a young boy whose safety was profoundly compromised in his relationship with his father. This was more of a Level Two pattern than merely a single moment or traumatic event. The anger was proportionate to the abandonment, however, and the metaphor resolved easily. We always possess exactly enough anger to address our trauma patterns!

It was humbling to realize that, as a priest, I had subconsciously chosen celibacy as a protection from the risks of intimacy and in reaction to the shyness instilled from my father. I had used my workaholic twenty-four hour a day ministerial lifestyle as a screen for my insecurities, and religion as a substitute for the fear of societal rejection. This gave rise to the melancholy and grief that preceded my decision to trust my own inner wisdom for guidance. Reclaiming and effectively utilizing the sadness and anger that I had repressed over many years, gave me the strength to find my true spiritual path and become more authentic with myself. My path has been clear ever since.

Our attempts to resolve our traumas by using something "outside" of us that does not address the original breach will prove addictive and ineffective in the long run. We cannot medicate, rationalize, repress, substitute, or ignore the raw power that is repressed when trauma is stored in the bodymind. Oh, we can do so for a time, but the repression of such force only increases its potency and gives rise to additional problems and even illness. I do not judge people who have survived through some addictive behavior, for such substitution can keep one alive until an effective healing solution can be found. But if left repressed and unresolved overlong, such addictions create great spiritual trauma and can even kill.

Anger is one aspect of the raw power that can heal us. We possess exactly enough anger to resolve our traumatic memories. Our anger, in fact, is directly proportionate to our trauma history. In working with the most "victimized" survivors, anger is the key to empowerment. When there is a terror or fear of anger, we must often address this trauma first, for this resistance, of all obstacles, impairs the capacity to reclaim our power from a perpetrator that may still be exacting his/her abuse on us in our subconsciously stored scenes. Our anger can be used to heal and protect, to declare how perfect our presence is in this lifetime in spite of our negative teachers and their messages to the contrary. We can do so from a place of calm and certainty. Our expertise with anger becomes akin to the lessons of the martial arts: once we reclaim and realize that we have the power to defend, maim, or even kill, we no longer need to do so. We subsequently find a confidence, stability and peace that ushers us into a whole new realm of intimacy and transformation. This red, raw energy is the gateway to whole new possibilities.

CHAPTER 16

ಐಖ

"THE HEALER WE HOLD WITHIN"

Each of us holds a surplus of light in the palms of our hands. As we heal ourselves and emerge from the burdens and density of our history, we discover an ease and facility in focusing this light for the healing of self or others.

You are a remarkable healer. You hold within your hands and in your consciousness, an immense power to influence the dynamic flow of energy which we define as the bodymind. I use this term freely in this text because the mind has a profound influence over the body and its moment-to-moment manifestation. Quantum physics has created a bridge between the mind that observes and the matter that subsequently manifests. This new physics teaches us that the act of observation is creative and that the body is the resulting creation of our states of consciousness – our minds! The mind manifests the body from its conscious and unconscious influences. Since trauma imprints in the subconscious mind, thereby affecting the flow of this creative power, it is not surprising that our power to heal was first disclosed to me in the context of my struggles to help individuals heal their memories.

One of the most shocking results of my work with trauma survivors over these last fifteen years was the realization that a significant percentage of what was labeled disease, chronic pain, or illness simply vanished when certain memories were resolved. Initially, I believed as most of us do, that the aches and pains of our everyday existence have their origins in our physiology. Even when the first migraine sufferers walked into my office in Louisiana, I was doubtful that the resolution of their memories would even impact these overwhelming states of pain that had been labeled "hormonal" by their physicians. The most startling outcome of these sessions was the fact that well over ninety percent of these women did not leave with their migraines. In the early stages of my work, I was unaware that adrenaline was, in fact, a steroid hormone. When memories of trauma are triggered, the subconscious mind becomes active, resurrecting the original scene and its accompanying affect. As this occurs, adrenaline rushes through our system to provide the strength to resolve the crisis now surfacing in the bodymind. With the increase in adrenaline comes a decrease in immunity through a reduction in T-cell production. This is the bodymind's way of devoting its energy to the crisis at hand. When we are overly stressed for prolonged periods of time or endure some traumatic experience, the weakening of our immunity, contingent upon the duration of this stress and pain, can give rise to illness. We have known of this connection between stress and illness since Hans Selye's "General Adaptation Syndrome,"[28] where he demonstrated how the increase in steroid hormone production resulted in weakened immunity. Since that time, we know much more about the physiology of this process, and the work of David Cheek and Ernest Rossi documented how we have mapped this dynamic down to the cellular and molecular levels.[29] Our studies of trauma and dissociation and their impact on the bodymind have greatly enlightened us in this regard.

We now understand that with the triggering of our memories comes the trance or altered state. If this state is a positive one, the need for adrenaline is minimal or non-existent, for there is no crisis! We find this to be the case with meditation, fantasy, and daydreaming – all of which represent positive altered states that we utilize to enhance our daily life and functioning. If, however, we trigger an encoded traumatic memory, the body again responds with a rush of adrenaline and moves back into the original state of crisis and its accompanying physiology, just as it experienced at the initial moment of encoding. I became acutely aware of this truth when my hands would feel the specific pain that accompanied my client's original traumatic experience.

At the beginning of chapter six, I briefly mentioned the case of the family friend who came to my office seeking my help with her migraine. I will elaborate upon this experience, for it was this case that, initially, taught me about the ability in my hands to feel memory and its impact on the bodymind. It occurred shortly after I had discovered my ability to use the energy in my hands to heal simple skin ailments: warts, fever blisters, etc. I had already healed my own warts when friends and family found out and asked me to use this ability for their benefit as well. I soon discovered that I could influence my own headaches as well and facilitate their release through the movements of my hands in and around my head. The pivotal event that integrated "talk therapy" with "energy work" occurred one day when a friend of my oldest sister entered my office at the outpatient center. She had been referred to me for trauma resolution therapy. I was using the verbal color reframing process that I had developed to help her resolve some traumatic memories, but was not employing my hands or the energy application along the spine at that time in my evolution. She entered the office that day and promptly stated that she was having a migraine. Before we even began the formal session, she asked whether I would be willing to use the energy in my hands to resolve her migraine as I had done for friends and family. "Unless you resolve my migraine, I'm probably going to have to leave because I'm too light and sound sensitive when the migraine is coming on," she declared. I mentioned to her that I normally did not use the energy technique in the treatment center because the protocols for the energy work were not fully in place yet. (They were instituted a short time later at that Catholic hospital, but I had moved on to a position in New Mexico by that time.) She stated that unless I diminished the intense pain of the migraine, she would probably have to leave due to her sound sensitivity. I agreed to try applying the energy from my hands – with no contact on the body, before the session began, in hopes of getting her to a calmer place so we could address her abuse memories. When I placed my hands near her head, I immediately felt pain. I now know that this indicates the presence of traumatic memory. If such migraines or headaches are purely physiological in origin, I feel little or nothing. After placing my hands on the sides of her head, I felt the pain begin to subside, but shortly thereafter, it returned even stronger. I had been quite successful with the resolution of stress-induced headaches and migraines, but was surprised when the pain returned more intensely. I commented on the return of the pain and told her that her migraine appeared to be resisting my intervention, whereupon she stated: "I was afraid of that – I've been having a flashback about an abuse scene from my father for three days and was afraid the migraine was about that." When she mentioned the abuse memory, I reverted to the verbal reframing technique that I employed to access and resolve traumatic memory. This was achieved by revisualizing the scene the way it should have occurred and then sending this feeling of safety to the subconscious mind to demonstrate that we can now, in present time, create such safety; once the bodymind realizes that safety is possible, it releases its protective hold on the memory tension and the pain resolves. This process is usually done through color reframing; the color frame of the corrected image captures the feeling of safety in a holographic, frequency form and allows us to send it quickly through the bodymind to reprogram the subconscious.

I had forgotten to put my hands down from beside her head when she mentioned the flashback, and I had begun the verbal reframing technique with my hands still in place. As she began to access the memory of sexual abuse from her intoxicated father, my hands went into significant pain. As she identified the specific moment when he "touched" her in the dark, the pain became very sharp in my hands. As she visualized her solution – her father in rehabilitation for alcoholism seventeen years sooner, she pictured her five-year old self peacefully asleep, free of any possible abuse. While she visualized this solution, I felt her migraine waves pass through my hands as they exited her system. After about three minutes, the pain was completely gone. She thanked me for using my hands to help her resolve her migraine, failing to realize that she had actually resolved her own migraine by sending her personal colors for safety which she identified in the frame of her corrected image. I was privileged to witness her healing process and was able to feel the transaction through the sensitivity in my hands. Some weeks later, I used that same sensitivity to identify a point of pain near Cervical Vertebra 7 that provides ready access to the dorsal horn of the spine. The dorsal horn of the spine handles all of the pain neurotransmitters. This same pain was evident in the spine of all of my clients. When I actually placed my hand on this location and sent energy in through the aperture near C-7, my clients suddenly found it easier to access and reframe their traumatic memories. Moreover, they began to spontaneously map complex sequences and histories of illness or pathology through the changes that occurred with the resolution of each memory. With the knowledge given to me through my hands, the reframing process that I call "HMR" or "Holographic Memory Resolution©" was born.

The lessons of my hands, however, are not unique to me. We all hold the capacity to channel white light for the healing of consciousness. Our hands interact continuously with the fields of the planet and all of the electromagnetic fields upon it. While the whole of the bodymind is capable of channeling this light, the hands and the human heart are among the most powerful. These centers are the most interactive with the fields of energy that constitute our reality. The dense energies of trauma encoded in the other nerve centers of the bodymind reduce our access to this white light. Given the amount of stress and trauma that the average body holds, it is no wonder that the healers of ancient times first discovered our capacity to channel light through their hands. The hands release easily and are the most interactive fields – constantly in physical motion – interfacing with the fields of the environment and the core of the planet. As we heal the traumatic memories encoded in the principal nerve centers of the body, our capacity to perceive the subtle energies of trauma increases proportionately. When we free the energy processing centers of the bodymind to channel white light, we become sensitive to any contrasting energies that pass through those same nerve plexes. When I teach HMR, I inform all of the trainees that, due to our accumulated traumas in the bodymind, most of us are only able to consistently access and maintain white light in our hands. By using our hands in close proximity to the body of another, we support that individual's healing process; we merge the white light of our hands with the holographic projection system that manifests as consciousness. By doing so we amplify the individual's sensory access to memory by increasing the light within his/her own holographic projection system. Scientists have long hypothesized why we see imagery in a multi-dimensional or 3-D manner. My understanding is that this way of perceiving is the result of right-brain and left-brain interaction that presents in front and back of the body as a holographic projection system. Holograms require two beams of light: a reference beam and an object beam. By supporting the energy flow along the dorsal horn of the spine we amplify the "reference beam" function as it is referred to in hologram theory, and by placing the other hand over the site of the memory fragment encoding, we amplify the object beam function. When I first began doing this around 1995, I noticed that the pain of the trauma memory equalized in both hands when they were correctly positioned in the front and back of the body of my client. I could tell when memory access was optimal due to the pain levels in my hands. As soon as I positioned my hands correctly – front and back, even the clients who normally had difficulty visualizing were able to do so. Their access to memory and capacity for healing were enhanced.

We enhance the healing of others by merging our white light fields with theirs. As we support or raise their light and energy fields, they perceive the body as "less dense." This enables them to access the information, imagery, and frequencies that they need to heal themselves. As we begin to perceive ourselves as less "solid" and more holographic, we become more comfortable scanning ourselves and locating the holonomic memory fragments that store our joy and our pain. We are able to meditate more easily, and we are able to access and heal our memories more readily. We are able to move more fluidly in this holographic universe when we surrender the notion of self that was defined by the weight, density, and lower frequencies of trauma. It was Albert Einstein who observed that matter is nothing more than slowed down or crystallized energy. In a manner of speaking, it is traumatized energy! As we move away from the Source, our light diminishes and we lose touch with the higher frequencies we knew as home. This "slowing down" of light or consciousness that occurs upon incarnation is, therefore, a kind of trauma for us. The truth is that, while we are on earth, we are at play in the trauma school – at least the earth we know in its current state! It is good to know that we have options for advancing or accelerating our lessons and the healing of memory and trauma in the bodymind.

We support the healing process of others when we simply move into close proximity to them. We also accomplish this in prayer. If there is, in fact, only one river of consciousness, we can focus our attention on another part of this living body of consciousness and move there immediately. It is not at all unlike how I focus my mind into my hands as I do this work. I move my mind into my hands and become highly conscious from this place. Mind is not bound to one site in the body or to the body at all for that matter. As we heal our own blockages and traumatic memories, we move more strongly into the river and bring more light to our interaction with others. As I cleared the traumas encoded in my head and stomach, for example, I was available to feel both the pain of the head injury and the nausea that accompanied the concussion that my client had experienced. These two sensations, in combination, cued me to ask about a concussion in my client's history. When we resolve our traumas, there remains only white light, and in that unified field of light, we are simply clarified aspects of the singular consciousness that unites all.

What then, we may ask, would be the impact of clearing all of the subconscious imprints inserted in the bodymind through trauma? Were we to resolve all of the altered states and their dense presentations in the nerve centers of the bodymind, could disease even exist in such a white light field? I began my healing path with the realization that I could use the energy at the tips of my fingers to resolve the herpes virus manifesting as warts and fever blisters. By raising these sites to white light, the virus ceased to exist. Many naturopathic physicians posit the possibility that, were we to raise all of the fields of the bodymind to a true state of balance or white light, a virus could not even exist within the system! In this perspective, we may have the cure for AIDS and other autoimmune disorders. Such a cure would require the mastery of our encoded altered states of consciousness.

When we reframe our trauma memories and "complete" our states of consciousness by inserting the missing emotional frequencies, we learn to love and heal ourselves. The subconscious mind that knows neither past nor future accepts reprogramming easily. In your unique knowledge of your experiences, emotional states, and moments of traumatic encoding, you possess the wisdom to heal yourself. With precise knowledge of the emotional frequencies absent at these milliseconds of overwhelm, we gain the capacity to complete our past. In this mastery of our states of consciousness, we discover the innate wisdom of the bodymind to identify exactly what we were missing at each moment of our existence and to insert the emotional perceptions that were lacking at such instances.

The difficulty remains, however, that within seven years of a trauma's induction, all of the cells of our body have now replicated within this distorted energy field. Every seven years, this pattern is amplified as the cellular memory and its requisite receptors adapt to the continuing presence of this dark, dense field of energy. Cell adaptation and mutation occurs in response to this distorted field, serving as a warning that something is amiss within the system and providing the opportunity to correct the problem. If ignored or discounted, the distortion will gain intensity with each seven-year cycle. Depending upon the degree of distortion, this energetic anomaly could result in illness as the cellular replication continues over these seven-year periods. On the other hand, with the resolution of such distortions in the fields of the bodymind, these imprints begin to reverse themselves. Disease and pathology ensue when the distortions are left unattended overlong. Conventional medical intervention and even surgery may be required, depending on the progression of the illness. When the distorted states of consciousness underlying illness are resolved, a disease pattern may, at times, be reversed and even alleviated. Just as a disease may be amplified over a seven-year cycle if the precipitating states of consciousness are ignored, such illness can often be reversed over time.

By attending to our memory triggers, resolving those already encoded, and avoiding over-stimulation of our memories through media, we can slow the progression of our negative subconscious imprints, and give ourselves the time needed to clear the cells and fields of the bodymind. The holographic mind or Higher Self affords us the capacity to view our memories and to reframe them promptly. The sooner the imprints of traumatic memory are resolved, the less likely they are to foster additional pathology or to become amplified in the cell mitosis of the bodymind. By attending more promptly to the cues of the bodymind, we can preempt the need for "healing crises" and learn to live from the optimal health afforded us through mindful living.

CHAPTER 17

෫ාග

"TANTRA, TOUCH, AND HEALING"

Sexual intimacy was not intended as a substitute for authentic union with the other. However, in the course of our evolution, the density of our traumas has prevented us from merging with each other as light to light or spirit to spirit. In ancient Hebrew, the word "ruah" meant "breath, wind, or spirit."

As we release the numbing energies of trauma stored in the bodymind, we open to heightened sensitivity and intimacy. There is no question that the densities of trauma, when resolved, enable heightened communication and exchange of energy. Looking at history, it would appear that we have attempted to use physical intimacy, touch, and sexuality as a substitute for the capacity to truly merge with another. The concept of "tantra," even in ancient cultures, included integration of the spiritual capacity for intimacy with the physical. And when I speak of this I am not speaking symbolically or abstractly. As I began resolving the density of my own trauma memories, my capacity for intimacy – to be receptive to the emotional signals and energetic transmissions of others, increased proportionately. My mother taught me that the physical body is not merely the repository of my own feelings, but is actually a nexus of consciousness that has a capacity for expansion, connection, and transfer of energy – even over unlimited distances. What is our true capacity for intimacy? How much trauma does the bodymind hold?

Cultural and societal traumas leave an imprint upon our development before we are conscious enough to make alternative choices. From a historical perspective, we see our earliest perceptions of self being affected by the influences of the powerful systems around us. The majority of our current systems were born of cultural and moral influences largely based on our ancient mythologies and sacred texts. The power of the biblical influence alone gives reason to pause for reflection. Those interpreting the early creation mythology mistook the shame of "nakedness" as relating to the physical body, rather than a reflection of the internal dissociation that it was. The serpent was often interpreted in phallic and threatening ways rather than being the spokesperson for the soil of human nature and "the most astute of the creatures whom God had made."(Gen. 3:1a) Physiological misinformation also took its toll on our history as well. In the primitive thinking of humankind, even up through the Middle Ages, the male was thought to hold all that was needed for pregnancy, while the female was merely the repository. This demeaned the role of women and elevated the patriarchy and the role of the male to exaggerated importance. Excessive guilt and shame naturally accompanied sexual acts such as masturbation, since actual lives were believed to be lost! A language of categorizing behaviors as "mortal" (deadly) and "venial" (of lesser import) developed which clearly exaggerated the emotional, moral, and physiological reality of sexual actions. Such language, excessive and fear-based in its intent, served to induce feelings of shame that, in an ironic and abusive twist of intent, caused spiritual trauma by alienating the self from the self. That which was healthy and normal became the object of suspicion and self-doubt. During my six years of study in Rome, I noted that the leading Catholic theologians were becoming aware of the inherently shaming nature of the traditional moral failure model and were seeking to change the language to one that honored the individual's fundamental commitment to a spiritual life. Within the context of an authentically spiritual life, a single self-damning action or mortal sin did not seem possible in the minds of these theologians or those of us with common sense. My mother was great about this: while my father lived in fear that he would go to hell if he did not attend Mass on Sunday, my mother would indicate that she had a rough week health-wise and that God understood her pain and weakness, particularly when she had faced the challenge of her cancer treatments. My mother knew that spirituality began within and was celebrated with others in community. She had no doubt about her salvation when she lived a daily spiritual life.

We are finally, as a culture, beginning to learn that we cannot shame an individual or population into "right moral behavior," for the use of shame induces dissociation, which generates compulsion and addiction. Moral capability is actually diminished through shame and trauma. Fear-based morality is trauma inducing and cancels out the possibility of a fully positive outcome. In utilizing language and tools for moral assessment that were excessive and threatening, the religious systems instilled fear of consequences, but in doing so, shame was induced. While thinking that they were acting on the side of excessive caution when certain moral or ethical issues were ambiguous or uncertain, the conservative arm of the religious systems induced shame and thereby initiated a traumatization process that created preoccupation which locked in the very behavior that was undesirable into the subconscious. In layman's terms, trauma hypnotizes us or rivets our attention, preserving in the subconscious the images and feelings that overwhelm us. From this position, recurrence of the behavior is far more likely. In shaming people about their behaviors, it is far more likely that the behavior will recur. In using excessive fear tactics, our family, educational, religious, and political systems induce trauma in us that actually fosters compulsivity and addiction.

Aside from learning of the detrimental influence of the old approaches to behavioral management, another factor is now emerging to challenge us to expand our traditional understanding of the moral capacity of each individual. The entire discussion about right moral behavior in religion has hinged on the understanding of what constitutes "nature." The agreement on how we define "nature" makes or breaks the argument concerning morality. "Grace builds on nature" is the moral building block upon which all subsequent theology flows and has for centuries. Hence, the theologians argue, based on their accepted definition of nature, that we have an obligation to shape our moral teachings to effectively support the manifestation of Divine Love that manifests itself in the diversity of all creation. The moral theologians in Rome recognized, for instance, that the issue with homosexuality hinged on the fundamental assumption that such actions were "against nature." In reality, such behaviors occur spontaneously in nature, even in the animal population, though they are not the majority occurrence. For many average observers, as I have found for myself after working with thousands of trauma survivors, a percentage of whom were gay or lesbian, we have no further doubts. How do we explain the resemblance of physical features, gestures, speech patterns, mannerisms, etc., in so many individuals raised in entirely separate cultures and environments? Though many do not display such overt indicators, I believe that a natural phenomenon exists in most cases. So does a majority of the current population. I have no doubt about a physiological or genetic contributor to this occurrence in nature. I suspect that soon we will prove such as a result of our dedication to the complete mapping of the human genome. The Episcopal Church is to be lauded for its strides in integrating this intuitive and practical wisdom into its structures when the conservatism of Rome continues its shaming language in spite of our expanding scientific and social understanding of nature. When we deny the rights of a population to exist on an equal footing, we shame that population and induce the very dissociation and addiction that we are seeking to discourage in our society. The "gay marriage" issue captures much of this discussion.

Given the shame induction and subsequent sexual dissociation that society has poured upon the homosexual population, it is no wonder that committed gay relationships have had to struggle for their existence. To normalize the option is not to admit that "gay" is the norm for our definition of marriage, or even that one has to agree that it is "natural," but it is to admit that it is natural for a percentage of the population that deserves more than shame and traumatization from the rest of society as it struggles for healthy moral self-expression. Does the exclusion and shaming of this population assist in its overall integration, or does making this population accountable for committed relationships, material property, legal rights and obligations, etc., help to stabilize and ground this minority within society? When given proper attention and affection, for example, the traumatized child or teen tends to calm down and cease his/her "acting out" behaviors – thereby enabling integration into the family system. Do we want to empower and embrace the creativity and contribution that these individuals offer to our evolution? Those who wish to "act out" same-sex sexual behaviors addictively and without consequence abhor the idea of legal recognition or commitment.

Dissociation does not work long-term for the healing of individuals or memories. We cannot exclude without shaming in this case. Shame is the principal vehicle for spiritual abuse. It is more spiritually impacting than moral judgment because it fosters actual dissociation within the psyche. One must be very careful claiming authority over the right to define nature, for even the Bible was written primarily from the limitations of the moral responsibility model and had little language or capacity to address the mechanisms of trauma induction that are inherent to our genetics and physiology. As such, the innate mechanisms to help us avoid self-destruction from shame experiences were set in place 1.5 million years before the first attempts at morality or the Bible were even written. There are clear indications that our very nature holds a magnificent wisdom and intent to help us avoid experiences of dissociation and self-destruction. If grace builds upon nature, then the divine mandate of our nature is clearly laid out in its design to prevent dissociation and spiritual fragmentation of the psyche! Perhaps we need to reexamine our tendencies to wield morality as the principal tool of discernment while we are still blind to our propensity to dissociate entire populations and contradict the natural order of our physiology that sought so earnestly to prevent us from spiritual disintegration. There is a great and divine wisdom in our nature and physiology that reveals a mandate to protect the spiritual psyche from shame and dissociation. Perhaps we should reexamine our definition of human nature while holding this divine wisdom in mind.

Our understanding of "marriage" is changing because our comprehension of the complexity of human nature is evolving. The social phenomenon of "gay marriage" triggers both a civil and a religious issue. Given the predominance of the old fear-based "moral failure" model so central in the thinking of most religious systems, the notion of gay marriage triggers a huge controversy which can only be resolved as each religious system matures in its understanding of nature as we are disclosing it within this text. As leading systems such as the Episcopal Church teach us how to integrate our spiritual beliefs with the practical wisdom of human nature, a working spirituality will emerge that honors all populations and minorities. Gay marriage will never be the norm in our society because the population itself is a minority occurrence in nature. But it should be normalized for this population because it is a documented minority occurrence in nature and because the argument to the contrary is based on an outdated model that is inherently shaming and abusive in nature. Given the polarization that has occurred recently in our societal and political upheaval, civil union would provide a starting point, given the reticence of the religious systems to change. But homeostasis[30] has always been a sustaining principle for dysfunctional systems. By deepening our understanding of the mechanisms that cause spiritual dissociation, we may begin to bridge the huge gaps that we have inherited from the old "moral failure" model. There is no question when we examine the histories of most religious systems, particularly after our recent experiences of terrorism, that we can be spiritually dissociative and unable to love – while we believe we are being religiously fervent! Christianity, Judaism, and Islam have all been notorious in warring between themselves and within their own factions; such is possible only with significant separation and dissociation. Here we see the spiritual damage of dissociation and of failing to understand the subtle forms of trauma that creep into and create imbalance within a system. There have been powerful and subtle layers of traumatization that have occurred to nearly every religious system by their lack of knowledge and education concerning trauma and the profound spiritual impact of dissociation. The religiously righteous individual who is acting from a spiritually dissociative place is a frightening phenomenon! How long can we go on dissociating and abusing individuals in the name of God? An example of how our religiosity can be tainted by our trauma history and can impair the fulfillment of the divine mandate to love can be seen in the case below.

In one particular instance, I recall a mother whose son was in treatment for depression and suicidal ideation. Her son was clearly homosexual and, at the age of seventeen, was coming to accept this reality within him. His mother, a religiously rigid individual with little knowledge of homosexuality, indicated that she would rather disown her son than accept his orientation. It was, initially heartbreaking to him and to staff to see how this mother was capable of rejecting her own son. In addition, he had never even acted on any of his sexual impulses. There was no behavior to judge! The sensation in his heart that this young man felt at the rejection by his own mother was heart-rending. The emotional rigidity such as that which his mother evidenced is common in the dysfunctional or addicted family system. Such rigidity will even twist religious precepts to its own ends. When insecurity and trauma are present, it is not uncommon to hold onto religious precepts in an addictive manner – even to the point of the exclusion of love and intimacy. This, for all practical purposes, is religious addiction: when your religious precepts prevent you from offering unconditional love to your own son. When religious precepts are used to justify prejudice, harm and even violence to others, we are witnessing a type of "spiritual dissociation." The lessons of September 11, 2001, made this abundantly clear. After such a long history of evolution without effectively healing our traumas and memories, such spiritual dissociation is frequently in evidence in the systems and in the world around us. Exclusion and prejudice are indicators of trauma and should be addressed within a model that seeks to heal these abusive attitudes at their moments and places of inception.

A sense of belonging is essential for the healthy expression of affect and sexuality; otherwise, addiction and compulsivity are fostered. I witnessed this phenomenon in ministry with many of my fellow priests. Celibacy will always attract a percentage of the population that possesses sexual trauma. By its intolerance of homosexuality, for example, the Catholic Church restricted the options for healthy expression of this orientation. Many of my fellow priests were confused about this issue and were attempting to find a morally compatible solution to the feelings that their church labeled "unnatural." There was no option provided for resolution besides right moral behavior and abstinence from homosexual behaviors. Hence, both those trying to control their homosexual impulses and those who were sexually abused and whose memories inhibited healthy sexual expression were particularly attracted to a celibate option – having no other. They desired to spend their lives productively and in good spiritual grace. However, as we discussed above, substitution may sustain the trauma survivor for a time, but to embrace the system that is traumatizing one at the same time is not likely to bring resolution. In fact, those who had severe sexual abuse found themselves acting out their abuse histories. In a smaller percentage of cases where severe abuse had occurred to them as a young child, they became capable of acting out their own abuse on children, particularly when they encountered a child of the age at which they were abused and their development arrested. At such times, the subconscious script of the original abuse is triggered and "acted out" with diminished awareness of moral consequence due to the powerful repressed nature of the trance. This acting out phenomenon has led to the crisis in the Catholic Church where we have witnessed the absolute ineffectiveness of a "moral responsibility" model in trying to treat a condition that is subconsciously encoded and empowered. The seven percent "moral mind," in place at age seven to eight, cannot resolve memories that are encoded in the ninety-three percent subconscious layers of the mind. Severe abuse histories usually underlie the acting out behaviors of those who abuse children; I have treated many during my work at inpatient treatment centers. In fostering shame and failing to address the root of the trauma histories of those they ordain, the Catholic Church is morally responsible for its enabling behaviors and the abuse that resulted. Increasing its moral rigidity and control over its priests or disassociating them from the system will not resolve the traumas they hold. This is a lesson that the church will come to learn by necessity. They cannot continue to maintain an inherently shaming model and emerge gracefully from this crisis.

Trauma, whether a single event or a pattern of emotional repression, has left a noticeable impact upon a huge percentage of the general population. Our touch and our ability to express love through physical intimacy have been greatly affected. For many survivors, the tactile triggers induced from specific abuse moments have restricted their range of affect and potential for sexual expression. A subtler trauma occurs when we grow up with parents whose expression of emotion is very repressed. We may subsequently find ourselves clueless about appropriate affective expression. Since the majority of our sexual interaction with society is through healthy affectivity and touch, repressive family messages constrict our primary affective channel and can foster excessive emphasis on sex or genital stimulation. Such sexual behaviors become addictive or compulsive when affective channels are closed or absent.

With the resolution of our traumas, our bodies become once again our own. In fact, for the first time in human history, we approach an intimacy freed from the blockages in the nerve centers of the bodymind.

Our breathing can be freed from the original restriction induced from a traumatic moment so that we can truly be present to the one with whom we seek to connect. The physical, sexual, emotional, mental, and spiritual dimensions of our lives are not separately compartmentalized experiences but can converge as a composite experience. Our affect, our words, our touch, and our genitality all carry more potential for connection and bonding. We become less preoccupied with genital interaction when our other channels offer more potent exchanges. The true sexual potential of human nature emerges when our most intimate expressions bear the totality of our presence rather than only those aspects not compartmentalized by trauma.

Sexuality and affectivity bear with them a potential and a mandate regarding healing. I have seen this repeatedly when I have shared space with guests. An example of this occurred in one case that I referenced earlier in this work. It occurred during the Tucson Gem and Mineral Show when I was flooded with visitors and allowed a colleague from out of town to share my bed. As I started to fall asleep, I felt an intense pain unlike anything that I have ever felt pass through my right side. I managed to release the pain through meditation and knew it was not my own. The next morning I asked my friend about the pain and enquired whether he had ever experienced such pain centered in his head, neck and left side. At that time he shared the abuse experience that occurred when he was only a few months old, during which he received a beating from an alcoholic father in which he incurred a fractured skull and, from the bruising and the swelling, was virtually unrecognizable. There are profound implications for our partners, our friends, and us as we heal our traumas and increase our capacity for intimacy. Though this case only involved a visiting friend, such ability can be used to sense compatibility, unresolved trauma, or an opportunity for healing and growth – thereby deepening a relationship. We will attract compatible individuals more easily and more readily discern the presence of true friends and "soul-mates" without the distractions of our traumas.

A true psychosexual awakening (the term psyche in the Greek includes the spiritual aspect of being) will bring the merger of body, mind, and spirit. Intimacy beyond our current imagining lies before us if we commit to the path of healing. The inherent exigency of our nature is to explore our true potential for intimacy and love.

CHAPTER 18

℘☯℘

"THE BODY AS MIRROR"

Our bodies are the maps to our enlightenment; they mirror our unfinished states of consciousness and provide the perfect invitation for our emergence as the conscious creators of our reality.

In light of the findings of quantum physics, we are learning that our bodies are recreated anew each millisecond through our act of perception. This creative act is largely unconscious and automatic at this point in our evolution. Our bodies are the expression of both our conscious and unconscious belief systems. As such, they mirror to us both the conscious and unconscious imprinting that occurs as we move through life. Both the outer world of relationships and the more intimate world we know as body are reflections of this powerful internal creative act. As such, the body, with all of its aches and pains, can be used to confirm the direction that our intentionality is taking us as we navigate our path on the earth plane.

Oriental medicine has contributed significantly to our understanding of the body's wisdom in this regard. The right side of our body reflects issues that relate largely to the masculine aspect of self, while the left side mirrors the feminine. In working with so many survivors, this principle has proven consistently, though not exclusively valid. Sometimes, for instance, a physical injury or a sports injury might fall to one side or another without providing any specific point of reference in the realm of male-female balance within the psyche. As we learn more about quantum physics and the power of perception, the manner in which we view our bodies becomes most important. After working with the physical and emotional pain of so many survivors, certain trauma patterns have emerged revealing themes that manifest in our physiology. Here we build upon the foundation set by Louise Hay in her observation of many themes that present as illness, pain, and trauma in the bodymind.[31]

In the structure of the bodymind, for instance, the legs represent our support in life: they sustain us. Right leg represents masculine support, while the left represents the feminine. The mapping of thousands of survivors' memories suggests, additionally, a chronology: ranging from infancy at the base of the foot, to the transfer of power at

127

the hips where we begin to become self-directive. Developmentally, the knees often relate to support during adolescence and the teen years, while the top of the knee to the upper hip reflects the transfer of power from parent to child occurring from the late teens (top of the knees) to early or mid twenties (hips). The transfer of power from mom to us occurs in the left hip, while the transfer of power from dad to us occurs on the right. The spine represents our "core support" in life. A general chronology is often in evidence here, beginning with infancy and early childhood support at the base of the spine, rising all the way up to the shoulders where we initiate the movement to lift objects and, as adults, choose what we "take on" or relinquish in terms of responsibility. Most of us have knots of tension concentrated in our *right* neck and shoulder areas – a combination of the following influences: 1) being in a predominantly male-oriented, performance-based society, 2) being more inclined to initiate movement from a left-brain, right side masculine, linear orientation (often reinforced through the educational systems), and 3) from the association of responsibility with feelings of guilt and shame. The emotional by-product of trauma – shame, is frequently mistaken as something for which we feel responsible, thereby resulting in an encoding in the neck and shoulder areas where personal responsibility is initiated.

The arms are the vehicles through which we "reach out and touch" external reality. Hence, the arms express "relationality." The right arm is the expression of relationship to male peers, siblings, and current relationships, while the left arm expresses the same for female relationships. A chronology with respect to this is uncertain at present, though certain patterns do present themselves. In one case, I could distinctly feel a pain that stopped abruptly at this woman's rotator cuff. My impression was that she was taking on but limiting trauma and responsibility regarding a female relationship in present time. When I commented about this but asked about why the pain would cut itself off so abruptly in her shoulder, she stated that her stepdaughter wanted to move back home, but had manic-depressive illness and was unwilling to commit to taking her medications. At this point, the woman stated: "I just had to cut her off in order for us to not be traumatized by her unwillingness to take care of herself." The pain, its location and intensity made perfect sense with her explanation. At the rotator cuff we initiate the decision to enter, maintain or withdraw from a relationship. Our physiology accurately mirrors the creative power of our consciousness and its choices.

The heart as the principal emotional processing center deserves some attention. In more recent years, a notable pattern has emerged from observation. On the right side of the heart runs a meridian that reflects male relationship, while the left side reflects its female counterpart. There is a chronology in evidence that begins with the lower part of the meridian at birth and moves up into present time. I know this because deaths, losses, and abandonment appear as distinctive sensations of pain at their appropriate chronological points along the meridian. If, however, there is equal abandonment from both parents, the coolness of the abandonment sensation will appear perfectly centered over the heart area – with no advantage given to either the male or female meridians. The position reflects the exact chronology of the abandonment and the degree of frigidity will reveal much about the depth of this trauma. It appears that all of the core emotional traumas of the bodymind find their central processing in and around the heart center. This makes sense from the standpoint that the electrical amplitude of the heart is reported to be over sixty times stronger than the electrical impulses of the brain.[32] It is no wonder that there is vast repository of data to be found in and around the heart plexus. The heart truly is our primary emotional processing center. I believe that it was from here that my mother was able to connect and feel our traumas at such vast distances. There appears to be no limit or edge to the heart's electromagnetic field.

With respect to the senses of hearing and sight, each of these follows its respective left and right orientations. The right eye reflects visual imprints from males or visual trauma on the right side of the body, while the left eye reflects visual imprints from females or trauma witnessed on the left side of the body. Similarly, the right ear holds traumatic verbal messages from males or events occurring on the right side of the body, while the left ear holds the female counterpart or trauma on the left. There can be abuse from a male of such severity that it imprints on the left side of the body, however, and vice versa for an abusive female. On some occasions, the abuse from the mother, for instance, may present as more masculine and aggressive than the messages from the more passive father. A "single parent" situation that leaves mom as both mother and father may cloud the values of the sites of encoding.

In this lifetime, many of us have come to learn healthy expression of our emotions. These issues appear in the jaw, throat, and neck area. One of the most common sensations that I experience in an initial scan of a client is the repression of emotion that is encoded in these areas. When we are not permitted or able to verbalize our feelings during a transaction, they become trapped in the jaw, throat, or neck area. The right side frequently reflects the repression of emotion or self-expression related to a male figure in past or present time, while the left side reflects the same relationship to a female figure. When memories of emotional repression or abuse surface in our dreams or sleep states, we grind our teeth in response and develop jaw and joint problems such as "TMJ" (Temporal Mandibular Joint). Many dentists are employing "cranio-sacral" manipulation of the musculature of the body to help resolve this tension in the jaw and neck areas. Frequently, when a client begins to discuss an abusive relationship with a male, for instance, I will feel the sudden pain and tightening in the jaw, neck muscles, and throat areas where s/he has begun constricting to protect from further emotional repression or abuse.

The body is continuously speaking to us and revealing the presence of stress and trauma as it is encoded in our everyday journey through life. In our tendencies toward dissociation, we have not always attended to its messages or their urgency – thereby missing an opportunity to restore health and reduce stress. The repeated accumulation of such stress in the nerve centers of the bodymind will mandate our attention and will direct us to the source of the discomfort if we but listen. The body offers us a map to wholeness and health if we attend to it. The wisdom of the bodymind is speaking continuously to enhance our opportunities for happiness and creativity. If we ignore this wisdom and our ability to store these painful states of consciousness, the bodymind will eventually demand our attention through healing crises – particularly when we have become overloaded. This is the magnificent wisdom of our design. These are the lessons offered us in the interactive field we call the bodymind. As we learn to master the states of consciousness that precipitate crisis and illness, we discover our ability to transform and heal the physical body. But as Barbara Brennan reminds us in *Hands of Light,* "Enlightenment is the goal; healing is a by-product."[33] Let us remember that the body is a precious expression of the soul. We are spiritual beings having a corporeal adventure!

CHAPTER 19

ഋരു

"FORGIVENESS AND HEALING"

Sometimes we forgive, not because the offender has done anything to warrant our forgiveness, but because we deserve better than to remain bound to them so intimately through the power of our own emotions. Under the shackles of anger and hatred we lose power and are drawn closer through the weight of these emotions. The stronger the emotion, the greater the attachment. Unaware of this bind, we often wonder why we are not more available for relationship in present time.

Given the opportunity, all of us would like to be freed from the emotional constraints of the past. Traumas bind us to persons, places, and events that continue to exact a toll on our energy and concentration. We are unable to be fully present to the person we are with when we continue to be pulled into the adverse scenes, emotions, and memories of the past. The unresolved polarities of trauma: fear (sadness) and anger are like restrictive chains that tie us to the past. They bear weight and drain our energy. When we are triggered, we engage this old connection to the past in a kind of "tug-of-war" – once again struggling with this individual or situation to find resolution. As we step back in time into the feelings and affect of the situation, we deepen the trance and tighten our hold on the chain that connects us to them. As this link tightens, *we are pulled deeper into relationship* with this individual. In other words, when we engage our anger about a past trauma or memory, we actually reconnect with the object of our anger, thereby intensifying our relationship and returning to that exact moment where we left off. The anger, instead of freeing us from the past, actually recreates the situation and the original brainwave patterns usurping our current energy. While the anger initially feeds us with adrenaline and provides a temporary source of strength or power, the irresolution of the situation continues to drain our power. Our emotional attachments to the past need to be released, not necessarily because the offending individual has done anything to merit our "forgiveness" or release, but because we deserve better than to continue being restrained or diminished by our attachment to this individual. We will be held in check or "leashed" by our own anger, hatred or resentment until we release the affect that binds us to them. If we are waiting until they repent, apologize, or make restitution for their actions, we might find ourselves waiting a very long time and still be disappointed that, at the end of these individuals' lives, they "didn't see the error of their ways." Their souls' timetable of healing rarely corresponds to our own. The truth of the matter is: as long as we hold onto our sadness, fear, or anger, we consent to maintain the old static quality of relationship that we held at the moment of trauma or abuse. We then wonder why we have difficulty being more present in our current relationships or manifesting a more nurturing lifestyle.

In our religious traditions, many of us were trained in the old moral responsibility model. We were taught the value of forgiveness of others. However, we were not taught the relationship between forgiveness of a moral violation and the healing of a trauma. As human beings we all make mistakes. That is part and parcel of how we learn and evolve as human beings. It is laudable that we seek to forgive others just as we ourselves need to be forgiven when we err. The Twelve Step programs based on Alcoholics Anonymous have proven quite effective in helping us to "make amends" when we have identified the "exact nature of our wrongs" (Fifth Step). This healing of moral wrongs is to be encouraged and supports our growth – reducing our fear of taking risks and moving us into new areas of growth and exploration. However, this notion of forgiveness is predominantly a matter of the moral, rational mind that is capable of recognizing error and making changes. Trauma is a different bird altogether!

Trauma is a subconscious, pre-moral reaction that automatically engages at moments of overwhelm. It is a reaction of the ninety-three percent portion of the mind that is below ("sub") the conscious threshold. This process, as we have already discussed, pauses perception and all that the perceptive act contains until we are able to return to the scene and provide resolution. This encoding warns us of its presence by presenting certain triggers and impulses that can be traced back to the moment of encoding. This natural backtracking feature enables us to recognize a memory trigger when it surfaces. When the affective charge of the present is disproportionate to current circumstances, we are inevitably dealing with memory!

A difficulty arises for most of us when we attempt to use the moral failure model to resolve a traumatic event. A common example is the one that follows: When someone encourages us to "forgive" the individual who abused us, we will often seek to understand and release the feelings of violation that were perpetrated by this person. We may even make a moral, rational choice at this point to forgive our offender. This decision to forgive helps to individuate us from our enmeshment in the trauma scene and predisposes us for healing in many cases; but, in other cases, such an effort only deepens the impact of the trauma. This phenomenon warrants closer examination.

When the offender is "captured" in the scene at the moment of encoding – a moment of emotional overwhelm, our subconscious mind kicks in to protect and pause our perception in order to survive. All of the pain, fear, and anger surfacing at our violation are captured and stored in the image as it moves into our subconscious mind. Adrenaline, endorphins and encephalins hit our system to sustain it in order to make it through the event. We survive the experience, but now hold the perpetrator contained in the only place where we could take control of the pain: inside the imagery that is now encoded in the cells and fields of our bodymind. The ninety-three percent subconscious devotes all its energy to protecting us proportionate to our degree of overwhelm. In the most dramatic of cases, we can move quickly into traumatic amnesia and may not even remember the event within moments of its occurrence. Our bodies, however, will always remember. This is the magnificent protective function of the subconscious and the "fight, flight, freeze" response to overwhelm. This system has served us perfectly in our 1.5 million years on this planet.

When, as a priest, I was trained only in the moral responsibility model and knew nothing of the power of traumatic encoding, I only knew "forgiveness" as an option to offer the trauma survivor. Even before I left ministry, however, I realized that to encourage an individual who was caught in a trauma-based or addictive cycle to forgive, frequently generated shame and only worsened his/her condition. I did not initially understand why asking someone to forgive resulted in lower self-esteem and profound feelings of failure and shame. But that is exactly what my moral exhortations generated. Even before I left ministry I stopped using morally shaming language, realizing that a significant percentage of my congregation had issues with addictive behaviors and compulsivity. This I knew to be the product of trauma and codependency (unmet developmental needs that left us looking outward for a solution). *I now know that codependency is the child of trauma.* Traumatic moments and patterns arrest our development and generate compulsivity and depression.

To ask an individual to forgive a perpetrator using the seven percent moral mind can create a hideous bind in which one part of the mind (conscious, rational, moral) is trying to do the "right thing," while the other portion of the mind remains trapped in the scene with the abuser with no one to come and rescue. As priests, we were not trained in trauma resolution. In fact, I had only one formal three-hour lecture on addiction before I was told that eighty-five percent of my marriage counseling cases would be alcohol and drug-related. This did not make sense to me. I chose on my own to spend a summer studying addictions treatment and the Twelve Step programs in order to provide more effective spiritual counseling. I also wanted to understand why we, in my family, found ourselves sometimes attracted to addicted or emotionally repressed individuals or systems. Once I began to realize the power of a traumatic moment of encoding, I understood exactly why the encouragement to "forgive" was shaming to the survivor.

After making an effort to "forgive" a perpetrator, the survivor would think of the scene of the abuse and would once again trigger the unresolved emotional charge of the event. Moving back into this pain, the survivor would chide him/herself for not having truly "forgiven" this person, for s/he is still feeling the shame, fear, and anger of the scene as though it was untouched. At this point, the minister might intensify his moral harangue about the importance of forgiveness, chiding the survivor for not really forgiving her/his perpetrator. The vicious cycle that ensued was a more determined effort on the part of the moral, rational mind to release the affective charge of the scene. As many therapists, psychologists, psychiatrists, etc., now know, resolution for a traumatic event can only come with the resolution of the *affective charge instilled at the moment of encoding*. To put it simply, we must address and heal the right part of the mind to get closure and resolution. Even the best attempt on the part of the rational mind will meet with only limited success when the original trance is ignored. Believing that s/he was once again doing something wrong, the survivor moved into deeper shame and guilt when s/he once again found the scene intact and the fear and anger still in place. Fear, shame, sadness, and anger are all valued indicators declaring that a trance remains unresolved. The presence of these emotions is actually a testament to the ineffectiveness of the moral failure model in the treatment of trauma.

The proof of what I say here is publicly available in reviewing the cases of how the Catholic hierarchy believed that it had "healed" the traumas of its wounded priests by "forgiving" and then reassigning them to another parish. When its only model for healing was the moral responsibility model, and after witnessing the guilt, shame, and remorse of those priests who acted out with children, the hierarchy made the erroneous assumption that this sincere desire to change and "forgive self" would resolve the source of the compulsive, abusive behavior. It did not. In fact, just as the moral harangue deepened the shame of the individual who failed utterly in releasing the emotional pain of trauma, those priests spiraled into deeper shame, thereby fostering and often insuring the recurrence of the abusive behaviors, for if there is one thing that we have learned in the addiction field, it is this: shame only accelerates an addictive, compulsive cycle. In limiting itself to the moral responsibility model, the Catholic Church enabled the abuse to continue and even accelerated it! This is a typical pattern in dysfunctional family systems: Shame the child to change a behavior, and watch the behavior accelerate! Shame the child whose weight you want to change, and watch her eat more as a result! Family systems, educational systems, religious systems, societal systems, political systems, health care systems (chemical dependency treatment centers), have all in their histories, at one time or another, shamed individuals or populations to reduce their destructive behaviors. The problem is this: if the majority of the destructive behaviors originate with trauma and not with "moral failure," the dysfunctional and addictive behaviors will accelerate and not be reduced at all.

Moral responsibility and forgiveness are virtually spontaneous when traumas are resolved. When we fully release the emotional chains that hold us bound to persons, places, and events that are not of our conscious volition, we find ourselves free to make healthy moral choices – to forgive and release from a conscious, rational, participative place, rather than a place inaccessible to us while we are trapped in scenes of pain and overwhelm. I cannot even venture to guess at how gravely our moral judgment has been impacted after over a million years of memory repression and traumatic encoding. We must learn to love, embrace, and actually heal the wounded parts of ourselves as individuals and as a society if we are to evolve upward.

Forgiveness is an immensely powerful act of release when it is enacted from a mind free to make such choices – freed from the skewed influences of one's trauma history. Forgiveness is also a natural and spontaneous occurrence when we are no longer trapped in scenes that tell us that we are powerless, shameful, worthless, and defective. Every trauma scene, small or large, has left us with an impression that has restricted our breadth and our power. The restricted applicability of the old moral responsibility model has impacted us in ways that we can hardly imagine. Even the Twelve Steps of Alcoholics Anonymous were at least partly framed in the language of this model. Although the Twelve Steps capture the inherent definition of spirituality (a tripartite relationship between self, others, and a Higher Power), they also focus on "moral inventory" and "our wrongs." In the treatment of addictions, there is a place for moral amends, but the immensity of the trauma that usually underlies the compulsivity and addiction is largely un-addressed even in contemporary treatment settings. I know this, because I developed my work in the inpatient treatment settings in response to such a need. Did I ever meet an active addict without a trauma history? Not yet!

We have been so wholly focused on talking ourselves into being responsible for our behaviors that we have overlooked the power of the protective mechanism of trauma induction. As a shy, shame-based child who simply mirrored my father's behaviors and disposition long before the age of moral responsibility, I always knew that my choices were restricted by the power of my fear and shame. I did not know their sources, since my traumas were subtle patterns and secondary influences rather than single moments of encoding. I only knew my fear and shyness, and these emotions gravely restricted my choices when it came to social interaction, personal growth, and spiritual awareness. Shame is a primary affect; it prevents other emotions from being internalized until it is resolved.

In my work with survivors, I rarely use the "forgiveness" word unless I am explaining the above. The reason is this: In shifting the direction of my ministry from that of the conscious, moral mind to the subconscious, traumatized mind, I prefer to speak of healing first. When we heal our traumatic memories, forgiveness and conscious release of the chains that bind us are a fairly simple matter. Once we are no longer under the life-threatening burden of shame, powerlessness, and fear, we experience such freedom and truth that we have no need to remain attached to those persons and events that abuse. We spontaneously release, admitting that shame always begins outside the self and is not our nature. To realize the essential goodness within oneself enables its recognition in all spiritual beings. We are not born with shame. We acquire it through experience. Guilt is a simple matter: I make a mistake – I apologize and make amends. Shame is another matter: I "am" a mistake. And such a feeling, I assure you, is the by-product of trauma and not the natural result of a moral failure. Shame generates the most opposition to the natural forward momentum of spiritual beings. I believe that we must "get serious" about our efforts to address trauma and its induction in the various populations of our society and stop the "just say no" tactics that have such a very limited effect. We are in an age where sensory stimulation has so increased that we are trancing far more frequently and overstressing our immune systems. Media has discovered that its ratings rise when our adrenaline is stimulated. Given the number of encoded pain memories that the average person holds, we are at risk from the standpoint of addictions and autoimmune disorders. The approach presented here holds much hope, and it is timely indeed.

CHAPTER 20

✂✁

"THE SCIENCE OF MANIFESTATION"

Quantum physics has confirmed that we create the reality around us. That this process has been predominantly unconscious for most of our evolution is little surprise. As we learn to manage the states that once mastered us, we begin to manifest from a conscious place.

Never before in our evolution have we been closer to understanding our true nature and power as cocreators of our world and all that it holds. With the advent of quantum physics and the clarification that it has offered us, we have been thrust into a stewardship so vast that we are still reeling from its implications: What we observe we create! Texts such as *The Dancing Wu Li Masters*, by Gary Zukav, offer the uninitiated a guide to understanding the power of quantum physics.[34] The act of observation is not passive, but, rather, transforms probability into reality. Such is the lesson of quantum physics. The power of the mind is brought to the forefront in this understanding of our power over particle and wave. We come to the conclusion that we create our reality through the act of perception that is influenced by the movements of both our conscious and unconscious minds. What we intend we create. But there is a complication: intention must take into account the focusing of will through both our conscious and unconscious minds. This includes the imprinting that is imposed on us by stress and trauma and is stored in the subconscious mind.

With the demise of the old "moral failure" model comes a revised model that incorporates the role of both conscious and subconscious intention. Responsibility takes on a whole new meaning when it incorporates the subconscious mind and its protective function. Trauma inserts a subconscious bias or distortion that profoundly affects our "intentionality" as it is called. We may consciously intend to be unafraid of water, but the unresolved near-drowning experience we had will not allow our phobia to subside. The subconscious protects us by triggering a defensive physiological and emotional reaction when we approach anything similar to the encoded traumatic event. Such programming routinely overrides conscious choice. The subconscious intent appears totally rational within its original context, but may appear excessive and foolish when removed from the event that precipitated it. In reality, there is nothing irrational about a subconscious imprint of this nature.

One of the naturopathic physicians that I have trained, Dr. Tim Frank, shares the story of a young man who was sent to him by one of the leading specialists working with individuals exposed to environmental toxins. The specialist was baffled by the case of a young man around the age of nine who had a consistent allergic reaction to water if it touched his skin. Hydrotherapies, etc., could not be used in efforts to detoxify this young man from environmental exposure to certain chemicals. He was referred to Dr. Frank who did an HMR session using my reframing process. He accessed a memory around the age of three when this young boy was placed in the bathtub for his daily bath. He immediately felt a burning all over his body and began to itch all over. This was his first allergic reaction to water and it encoded as a protective trance. In retrospect, there was probably the residue of a chemical cleaner or other substance remaining in the tub. With his severe allergic reaction, however, a trance was created spontaneously to protect him from the fear and overwhelm. Subsequently, whenever he approached water, he would begin to itch and feel burning all over his skin – later resulting in severe eczema and skin rashes. When Dr. Frank tracked the memory to its point of origin and reframed it, the young man had no further reaction to water and was able to utilize hydrotherapies and begin resolving his eczema condition. This is the power of subconscious intentionality to dominate our most powerful logic and conscious intent. As dramatic in nature as the above case may be, it is most instructive and identifies for us the impact that subconscious blockages often exert over our conscious efforts to find health and happiness.

With the resolution of our traumas comes a clearer sense of our true nature and potential. The focus of responsibility shifts in light of the power that is revealed as we resolve the blockages to our fundamental identity and innate creativity. Quantum physics has redefined responsibility in light of its findings. We are not merely the passive observers of a reality created for us, but instead, have been endowed with the ability to create reality as we "observe." This new physics suggests that the body itself at each moment is the creative expression of our combined conscious and subconscious intentions and beliefs. This also applies to the world we perceive "around us." We are more truly stewards of creation than we ever imagined possible. In an oversimplified summary of quantum physics: the act of observation collapses the quantum probability wave into reality. What we observe we create and cocreate with others. As Gary Zukav pointed out in The Seat of the Soul, however, we have mainly been creating unconsciously from our "unconscious intentions."[35] This means that we have grown accustomed to observing reality and creating reality from the subconscious imprints of our trauma histories and our inherited definitions of reality.

On a simpler and more personal note, I have observed that, as I resolve my traumas, my positive intentions manifest much more quickly. Instead of having to ask or pray for something to an outside Provider, I discover that my thoughts and choices, freed from the distorting influence of traumatic messages, manifest spontaneously. Perhaps this inner power was the gift referred to by so many of our spiritual teachers. As our traumas are resolved, our inner guidance and intuition improves. The need to be concerned about the future dissolves in the face of the absolute confidence that emerges from living fully empowered in the present moment.

Unresolved traumatic imprints leave a dark profile or shadow which is projected outward as our inner light seeks to express itself. In the physics of brainwaves, we would describe our connection to the light source in the range of the Delta waves (0.01-4 Hertz) – the stage reached during profound meditation or dreamless sleep during which individuals have been found to emit low frequency sound waves, photons of light, and vibration. Traumatic memory and its imprints appear to encode in the Theta (4-7 Hertz) and Alpha (7-14 Hertz) ranges. Conscious awareness and intent appear to manifest in the Beta (14-21 Hertz) range. I believe that at some profound level within the mind, probably at Delta, we reconnect with All That Is – an ultimate Source and river of light. Our incomplete or traumatic memories leave an imprint in the Alpha-Theta range, as brainwave measurement of my work with survivors has revealed. The conscious mind bears witness to these deeper interactions.

To the hands of many energy workers, trauma appears as a dense, heavy form of energy. The density or slowed energies of trauma redirect or modify the purity of our creative light and manifest exactly what we carry within the "emotional body" of our Alpha-Theta brainwave range. If what we intend consciously is able to tap our power source and move outward without any interruptions or distortions from the subconscious (Alpha-Theta range), we manifest this intention as reality. If there is trauma from our past that contradicts our good intention, the subconscious imprint will alter our intent and dictate its own modified version – usually a lot less than what we intended, perhaps even its opposite. This is the physics of intentionality and manifestation as affected by trauma. In my lectures, I jokingly call this phenomenon the "bat signal" and share several life experiences where my unresolved traumas attracted the same dark profile that I had failed to resolve. If you want to summon "Batman," paint a black bat over a white light. Into the night sky your light shines forth – everywhere except where the light is blocked by the dark imprint upon it. This creates a vacuum or void in the form of a beautifully outlined bat that will summon to you every batman within a hundred miles. Substitute this bat signal with the emotionally unavailable profile of a parent, stepparent, or one of your past caregivers, and you will see exactly why you may have manifested your past over and over again in relationships. Those who fit the trauma-based profile feel a magnetic attraction as strongly as you do; it is often mistaken for love. The difficulty is that this magnetic attraction comes from the void or vacuum created by the dark imprinting, not from wholeness or abundance. And the person answering the void holds the same or complementary profile as that of the individual who first precipitated the trauma. Even the void can hold two faces, however. Many women, for instance, in their determination to not repeat the pattern of marrying their aggressive alcoholic father over again end up choosing an individual who is so passive and codependent that they are equally frustrated – only this time it is from lack of emotion and passivity instead of violence and excess. Neither of these versions is capable of healing the original wounded ego state anyway. We must resolve our memories from within their original context of encoding. This scene has been preserved precisely for this purpose – a statically held image maintained to provide the opportunity to resolve this unhealthy profile. We must resolve these profiles at their place and moment of inception. Over time, we come to learn that all of the occurrences in our outside world act as mirrors, revealing the clarity or obscurity present in our subconscious "lens." The "emotional body" or the "pain body" – as Eckhart Tolle calls it, stores our memories and functions as the lens through which all of our intentions pass. As we learn about the creations we are projecting and inviting, we learn to heal the old outdated profiles and manifest our highest good.

In the language of spirituality, that which we call "karma" is none other than the unresolved emotional frames or profiles of our memories and our histories. These images and events of the past bear a polarity or charge until they are fully resolved. They are invitations, as are all traumas, to learn to love others and ourselves – to complete those moments where we received or delivered less than love. As we learn to complete these moments of quantum perception where we manifest less than white light or love, we heal these energetic breaches within our field and no longer attract this pattern.

Another aspect to the discussion of manifestation relates to the deeper influences of the "unconscious mind" (what we associate with the Delta brainwave level) beyond the realm of memory-induced trauma. This relates to spiritual purpose and deeper patterns that affect the whole of our lives. Manifestation can occur from a profound level of intention that seems to wholly defy rational explanation. This form of manifestation in a lifetime appears as a distortion from the level of the "blueprint" – a profound spiritual plane. Certain souls seem to enter life with a specific limitation, disease, handicap, or timetable. These immense patterns are much greater than any single moment or externally induced trauma. The spiritual function of these patterns frequently finds no recognizable point of reference in the experience of the conscious mind. In addition, trauma resolution seems to have little or no significant effect on these conditions but can release the stress and trauma that results from the world's mistreatment of these individuals and their challenges. Such life experiences and events do not seem to have a direct relationship to any subconscious memory encoding, but manifest intense pain nonetheless. Besides this unconscious source of trauma, there are also environmental and genetic sources of trauma that cause pain in our everyday lives. In this treatise, however, we are focusing on the patterns that originate in memory and learned experience. These patterns we can learn to master, for they are simply states of consciousness. Such is our invitation and challenge in this lifetime.

CHAPTER 21

ℰᴑℭℛ

"THE KEY TO THE MYSTERIES"

The traumas in our evolution first revealed to us our innate capacity to pause consciousness itself. This capacity to arrest Consciousness suggests a remarkable and intimate connection to Source. We are only now beginning to fathom the implications of what it means to be "light from light" and to have influence over this primordial creative act.

If we are to grasp the depths of our mystical potential, we must fully attend to the movements of consciousness. We pay lip service to spirituality if we attempt to speak of consciousness while ignoring the lessons of trauma: the bodymind's mastery of its own states of consciousness. You have, undoubtedly noticed by this time that many of the spiritual insights that I share are intimately bound to lessons of trauma. How strange, I initially thought, that each effort that I made to articulate the beauty and mystery of human life was connected to an epiphany borne in darkness. Perhaps this path refers us back to that same mysterious journey which the mystics alluded to when they spoke of their passage through the "dark night of the soul." In one of my Spanish courses in college I had the opportunity to translate the poem of St. John of the Cross that tells of the mystic's spiritual encounter with Divine love on a "dark night." This same darkness frequently forms the backdrop for our flashes of insight and illumination.

Wisdom accompanies us as we emerge from the "dark nights" of our lives. As I began to resolve my own "trances" and awakened from my own unconsciousness, I realized that the experiences shared in this work mapped for me an interpretational key or "hermeneutic principle" that offered a profound and startling picture of the spiritual psyche and its workings. A great mystery and order was revealed in witnessing over twelve thousand trauma survivors tapping their inner wisdom to heal their states of consciousness. Perhaps the *Celestine Prophecy*[36] was not so much fiction after all. Is there a hidden codex of truth within the very fabric of our being – perhaps within our DNA itself? Is there a path to enlightenment mapped for us in our very design? Were we immersed in the human condition without the means for transforming it? Apparently not!

Since the beginning of history, we assumed our capacity to exercise free will to be our means to fulfillment and enlightenment. Our mythologies clearly reflect this. We have been exhorted, cajoled, and inspired by the works and teachings of masters and mystics, the majority of whose influence came from the influences of the old "moral responsibility" model. Our self-help and inspirational books to this day carry this bias. The key to unlocking the power of our nature, however, comes from embracing the whole of our mind in its full creative power. This includes the potent capacity to create and store imagery – and even more, to pause consciousness itself. This power is revealed to us in the understanding of trauma induction. It is in the experience of darkness that true appreciation of the light is born.[37] Earth is the path of the *via negativa*. It is the school of learning via trauma. Perhaps this appears so because man is, indeed, a "fallen god," or, as I affectionately phrase it, "traumatized divinity." This is true in the sense that matter itself is nothing more than slowed down or crystallized energy, according to Einstein. Imagine a Mind so perfect that its purest realization is the truth of its nature as love. The exigency of such love is the sharing or expression of itself in natural expansion. Hence, creation occurs as the natural outpouring of love. The "big bang" generates an unfathomable creative movement outward, and as the energy slows, it crystallizes into matter – into the universe we know. In this great flash of light, a holographic universe is borne or projected. From this understanding, a new physics is also generated: matter is not so much something as it is the absence of something. Matter is the slowing down or crystallization of energy. On the microcosmic scale, this occurs as the soul enters into the body as well. The purest light moves into forgetfulness and a kind of unconscious slumber as it slows and binds itself to the current vibration of our DNA. Suddenly, we are at play in the land of illusion and holographic perception. If we imagine all of the universe, its galaxies, the solar system, our planet, its inhabitants, even this body or ours – all as the projections generated by a single, all encompassing holographic projector and the singular, sentient Light Source that emanates it, we would have a more accurate understanding of our position in a holographic universe. We are playing with images! We are moving within the expansive consciousness that embraces all: the Divine Mind. This affords us a unique experience and the opportunity to explore life as individuals. In essence, we move closer to the Divine Mind in knowing ourselves as unique and individual, for so also is the One Mind!

How powerful, we may ask, is this experience of Mind that we come to identify as "self"? Years ago, researchers noticed some startling features in some of the most severe trauma survivors. Individuals with "Multiple Personality Disorder" frequently demonstrated incredible power or ability. In his book, *Quantum Healing,* Deepak Chopra cited cases where individuals would slip into one personality and evidence an allergic reaction, and "lose" the allergy as they shifted to another personality.[38] I have witnessed this type of shift many times. Within the dissociative client could exist a personality that studied anatomy twenty-four hours a day. Some individuals evidenced personalities that possessed different speech patterns, vocabularies, genders, ideologies, and physiologies. One personality might be alcoholic, while another was allergic to alcohol. When they switched into another "alter" or personality, they showed no evidence of these illnesses or symptoms. Another personality could meditate and speak as though it was in continuous contact with the Divine Mind or "God" as so many phrased it. One of my colleagues, Dr. Owen Scott, shared some reflections concerning conversations that he held with the most mystically aware or spiritually connected aspects of some of his dissociative clients. I could tell that the virtually unlimited resources and information that were revealed had profoundly touched him.

One of the most significant lessons from our study of trauma is the realization that we possess the capacity for unlimited multitasking within our own psyche. We are so remarkably multidimensional. But this model has even greater implications. Just as there can exist multiple personalities within the mind of a single individual, likewise, we exist as unique articulations or individual expressions within the One Mind or flow of consciousness. It is simply a matter of recognizing the degree of dissociation from Source or the "Host." It is not at all uncommon for one personality in the dissociative client to be completely unaware of the existence of the other personalities. In our collective spiritual dissociation, we have not proven much different from these individuals. Our society has largely failed to recognize its interconnectedness to its own respective personalities. One of my dissociative clients, a mother of several children, had a gay teenager personality, a Jewish male personality, an actress, a nun, a prostitute, and many others – all aspects of herself used to contain various trauma experiences of rejection and abuse. Imagine your one mind simultaneously containing all of these diverse expressions. This is not so far removed from the self-expression of the Divine Mind, I suspect. And in reviewing spiritual texts such as the Gospel of Mark, it is not surprising to see spiritual teachers such as Jesus making a concerted and highly visible effort to reach out to the most dissociated or rejected elements of society. In our evolution, we have become spiritually dissociative. Prisoners or criminals, prostitutes and Samaritans you see, are "not like us." "We're different." This false reasoning makes it possible to repress these individuals just as we have repressed our own memories in the past. In this conveniently dissociative state, we do not have to know the pain of our other personalities – those more wounded than ourselves. It is time to recognize that, given the tripartite nature of spirituality, any personal movement toward enlightenment impacts the whole if we are all interconnected. If I become dissociative, I reduce society's overall connection to the Source. In reintegrating myself into the whole after trauma, I increase the capacity for spiritual intimacy and relationality. We grow and bear fruit as part of the larger tree, the larger mind in which we live, move, and have our being.

Our individual and collective traumas reveal to us our degree of dissociation from Spirit and from our power. In learning to address these states of consciousness, we find a powerful key for unlocking our potential and embracing our true nature as creators. Many of those "confusing" experiences of our lives make perfect sense when we view them from our "observer" stance – utilizing the capacity of our multidimensional minds to traverse time and to observe the patterns. From this larger perspective we are able to heal any single moment or intention, learning our mastery of love and light. Through the invitation of trauma, therefore, we discover that we hold the key to resolving the confusion and blindness imparted by our individual and collective moments of overwhelm. In this mystery school of trauma, much is revealed.

CHAPTER 22

෨ඁ

"THE NEW HEALING PARADIGM"

To be in physical form is to dwell within a continuous summons to enlightenment. Physical healing, the alleviation of pain and illness, is a natural by-product of the enlightenment which comes with the mastery of consciousness. The ultimate healing transcends physicality itself.

In learning to master and integrate our states of consciousness, we discover our ability to direct light and energy to create *consciously*. We become the masters of our imagery and consciousness rather than remain its victims. We no longer evolve as the overwhelmed recipients of our daily experience, but become more spontaneously directive in its manifestation. We move from powerlessness to our innate power. This power does not require the continuous monitoring of the rational moral mind, however, as we are accustomed to think. The capacity to manifest our highest good arises spontaneously when we are freed of the negative messages and intentionality inserted by trauma. Aligned with our emotional and intuitive center, we spontaneously render up our highest good. We discover the capacity to "answer" our prayers before we have had to rationally articulate them. Jesus assured us of our inner light in his life message; the Light of the World now resides within.

It is our nature, our natural exigency to manifest love, intimacy, abundance, and health. In a trauma-based mindset filled with conflicting intentions, we have trouble making decisions; we doubt our own inner guidance and codependently look outward for everything: spirituality, success, love, abundance, etc. As we release the attachments induced through trauma, we move smoothly through complex and even dangerous pathways. We spontaneously make the right turn and avoid the pitfalls of our world when we are aligned with our truth. Without the interference of shame as a primary affect, our intuitive guidance easily navigates our way through the apparent obstacles of daily life. This inner voice speaks primarily through a channel akin to emotion. It is an intuitive knowledge, seeming more felt than rational, that transcends the logical moral mind and provides wisdom and direction that is immediate and clear. As we resolve our traumas and release the conflicting voices that confused our decision-making, we create and manifest with simplicity.

When conflicting voices arise within us and usurp our focus and power, the challenge is typically one involving a triggered memory and less that of rational confusion. One simple exercise that I developed to resolve the confusion that occurs through trauma is the following: Take some time to visualize the individual that traumatized you. Ask permission to "see" all of the wounded selves or "ego states" that were created within him/her through trauma. See how many of these dysfunctional states were evident in your interaction with this individual – perhaps are still active to this day. Take a moment to explain to all of the wounded ego states within yourself, that this individual was frequently operating from these trances when s/he acted abusively toward you. Explain to your "traumatized selves" that, without the resources to resolve this fragmentation, your offender had little opportunity to act differently. While s/he is still responsible for her/his actions, you now understand how such behaviors occurred. A lack of understanding over the apparent insanity enacted by our abusers often leaves us stuck and unable to release our attachment to the abuse scene. Our rational minds are fully capable of understanding the abuse when we witness the source and complexity of another's trances. This, however, requires the multidimensional thinking of the adult, and cannot come from the unilateral vision of the child-mind. How many times have I heard my clients repeat: "But it just isn't fair!" "Fairness" in games and social interaction is the processing of the child mind and the rules of play. Fairness is dismissed in a millisecond when morality gives way to the imposition of trauma and its oppression. The child-mind has difficulty overcoming this concept without the intervention of the adult's multidimensional perception.

By learning to recognize the presence of trauma-induced altered states within us and in those around us, the digressions along our spiritual journey become shorter. I always loved the spirituality of the Twelve Steps, particularly the paradoxical manner in which the admission of powerlessness reconnected us to our higher resources for healing. In stepping back and admitting the powerlessness manifest in the trauma pattern of addiction, for instance, we become enough of an observer to manifest differently. Eckhart Tolle speaks much of this observer stance that allowed him to transform his own life experience. If we cannot step back far enough to even recognize the trance, we cannot reframe it. Once we do so, however, and gain some perspective, we have choices. We cannot resolve the trance that has so taken possession of us when we are unaware of its existence. If we cannot extricate ourselves from the trance itself, we most certainly cannot observe it. The act of observing originates with our multidimensional nature and affords the capacity to detach from those states of consciousness that previously defined us; they are states of consciousness, and no one state can fully capture us.

We are moving into a new phase of our spiritual evolution. The child mind, so bound to the material and physical solutions of a concrete world cannot think multidimensionally. Our compulsive and addictive attempts at coping with encoded pain are frequently the product of this early need-driven mind. In moving into the holographic mind or higher self, we learn to think in multiple dimensions. In doing so, we gain the capacity to observe and master our states of consciousness rather than to become overwhelmed and bound by them. We come to recognize our quantum ability to create our world and its perceptions. Over time, we gain mastery of our intentions by resolving those conflicting messages that usurped our will long before morality was even an option. This usurpation of power occurred in both our personal history and our collective evolution long before we understood the precepts of morality. The reclamation of our lost intentionality has occurred in stages, providing spiritual insights into our loss of willpower and offering unexpected hope.

The birth of this new paradigm of healing and hope occurred in stages, accelerating over the last fifty years. With the recognition of alcoholism as a disease in the '50's we discovered the inadequacy of the "moral responsibility" model. The "just stop drinking" exhortation fell on deaf ears. Willpower alone could not resolve such a problem. We discovered that a potent pathology underlies addiction and is non-responsive to moral exhortation or condemnation. This pathology is also evident in the partner and children of the addicted family system: low self-esteem, difficulty making decisions, compulsivity, and an excessive outward orientation to get ones needs met. In the 1960's we recognized this pathology in the partner of the addicted individual, and by the 1970's, found this same pattern in the children or "adult children of alcoholics" – ACOA's as we termed them. By the '80's we realized that this pattern was present not only in the alcoholic system, but was also present in any system where there was significant emotional repression. This pattern created an "arrested state of development" and was termed "codependency." In the 90's we realized that "codependency is the child of trauma," as I phrase it. The ability to "freeze" our development derived from our innate protective capacity to pause consciousness itself when it became overwhelming. Emphasis shifted in the treatment center to addressing the memory triggers that fostered addiction. We learned that without prompt address of these triggers, relapse was likely. Addiction Relapse Prevention Specialists like Terry Gorski called this "backtracking," and even cited approaches like HMR when discussing effective strategies for resolving these triggers.

The actual source of our arrested development is our protective mechanism that freezes consciousness to protect us at moments of overwhelm. The understanding of trauma induction became the hermeneutic key allowing us to reexamine our use of language and to stop shaming individuals. We began revising our treatment models, trying to eliminate shaming language and practices. We progressed. The increasingly potent voice of trauma in our day and time has eliminated the option for us to dismiss it or repress it. We are witnessing a significant increase in addictions and autoimmune disorders as a direct result of our struggle to cope with the unparalleled manifestations of trauma in our country and in our world. With the current state of media and technology, events like September 11, 2001, and hurricane Katrina in 2005 reach deeply into our homes and our everyday lives.

The gift of the addictions field to the medical profession resides in this newfound emphasis on the power of memory and its capacity to create and sustain pathology. The mechanisms of trauma induction result in adrenaline overproduction, reduced immunity, and initiate the first stage of addiction: psychological attachment to medicating or addictive behaviors and substances. A traumatic event hypnotizes us and captures our pain as an altered state, repressing its content into the subconscious to prevent overwhelm. When triggered, the emotional pain that was bound to this potent protective state of consciousness re-surfaces. With the advent of this pain, and without the tools to resolve such a powerful state of consciousness, the search for an appropriate medicating substance or experience ensues. Much of this process is subconscious, but it results in the selection of drugs and experiences that medicate the specific pain of memory. We are even discovering correlations between which nerve center holds the memory and the "drug of choice." The medication or medicating experience is often chosen because it precisely addresses the pain found in the nerve plexus that holds the memory. Teenagers exposed to domestic violence or quarreling, for example, might choose marijuana because it induces "black sleep" and blocks the nightmares surfacing from the abuse. This same marijuana, used to calm the stomach and digestive tracts of cancer patients on chemotherapy, will also calm the stomach that has encoded the fear and anxiety of the chaotic or violent household.

An individual with Attention Deficit Disorder (ADD) might choose cocaine, for instance, which initially leaves him feeling normal for the first time in his life due to its effects as a stimulant. Alcohol is a depressant and depresses ones inhibitors, resulting in a euphoric feeling, but numbing nearly all of the major nerve centers of the body. Tobacco, one of our most addictive substances, is frequently locked into the psyche around the age of seventeen, when some life transition occurred, at which time the only immediate comfort available to deal with the stress, fear, and aloneness was a cigarette. Hence, the choice of a particular substance is often profoundly related to the stress or trauma history that induced the pain.

Given the holonomic nature of memory in the body, a single fragment of an encoded memory moves us into an altered state with all of the original symptoms and pain. The potency of such altered states became evident to me when I first realized that I felt in my hands the same pain that my client felt. I later recognized that the ability to feel this pain was the same experience that my mother felt in her own body when her children were traumatized; the difference was that my mother felt the pain at the moment of trauma to her children, whereas I was able to feel the pain as it surfaced from memory. To the subconscious mind, apparently, there is no distinction between present and past. When we focus on our bodies and trigger a memory, we resurrect the original pain bound to the stored imagery and move into an altered state where our minds and physiology respond as we did originally.

The discovery that the physiology of the body so closely follows the cues of the mind led to modifications in the treatment model for individuals with addictions and various disorders. These changes have affected not only the recovery community, but also many educational and religious systems that have found their rational and moral appeals ineffective in modifying the behaviors of addicted and compulsive individuals. The ineffectiveness of the moral responsibility model in addressing compulsivity became evident and mandated changes when approaching these individuals. We discovered that we could not use methodologies that were shaming without triggering the pain that fostered relapse and accelerated the compulsive cycle. Intrusive or overly aggressive approaches resembled the boundary violations of trauma and caused the client to withdraw from treatment and "shut down." Similarly, when shamed by accusations of moral failure, particularly common in the efforts of the religious systems to treat addiction, the compulsive individual moved deeper into compulsivity.

We learned to change our language and operate from a place of non-judgment in order to address the trauma core of the individual. While abstinence from any destructive behaviors remained the first priority, our attention in treatment centers shifted to the need to address the source of the compulsivity. When the psychological triggers and subconscious attachments to the compulsive behaviors diminished through resolution of the scenes of trauma, conscious intentionality was, we discovered, at least partially, restored. Moral awareness and responsibility increased spontaneously with the resolution of the traumas occupying the ninety-three percent subconscious mind. The limits of the moral responsibility model became apparent with a greater understanding of the power of our minds to alter and store states of consciousness.

For thousands of years we have judged and berated ourselves for our misuse of willpower. Many contemporary authors and esteemed teachers continue to do so to this day. The language of self-blame arises instantaneously in response to many situations and conditions that we now know are firmly rooted in trauma. In my counseling work, I routinely experience the negative self-talk and "fallen will" perception in the language and belief systems of my clients. This negative self-referencing fostered by our culture inhibits recovery and healing. Shame is the one emotional perception that locks in pathology, whether it is emotional or physical. The mythologies written in the last five thousand years of history reflected this bias as well. In the interpretation of these mythologies, this bias was often amplified. Religious systems have been notorious for their excessive emphasis on moral control of behaviors while missing the subconscious influences that can compromise morality in a millisecond – but this is a millisecond of paused consciousness, not merely an errant thought or a deliberate misuse of will. The spiritual obstacle presented here is much larger than morality. It poses an invitation and a challenge that clearly predates societal, personal, and religious morality. We were dissociating long before we could articulate moral principles in our evolution. The challenge here comes from a quantum level. Hence, we come to the articulation of the new paradigm. This is no abstraction or unfounded optimism. It is grounded in quantum physics and our capacity to change our reality as we master our states of consciousness, and it is eminently practical.

In training over one hundred and twenty naturopathic physicians in this approach to trauma resolution, for instance, they have come to the realization that new protocols must be introduced if we are to most efficiently address our pain. Before the patient is even provided medication to alleviate a pain, the naturopath assesses the client to determine if the pain is memory-based or if it originates from the physical level. Do not misunderstand me: there is a physiology to memory as well as illness. Using memory reframing, in twenty minutes I have helped a client to fully resolve a pain that was labeled "nerve damage" for seventeen years and treated with narcotics. This particular pain, the by-product of a car accident, left her with chronic pain in her legs of such intensity that it was assessed and treated as nerve damage. In resolving the scene of the car accident and visualizing help arriving promptly, the accident-induced trance was resolved as was the pain in her legs. When her mind captured the fearful image that no one was coming to her family's aid while she alone remained conscious with her legs crushed, the intense pain sensations from the accident were contained and captured by the trance. By addressing this state of consciousness, the resolution of her memory-based pain was immediate.

There remains a profound bias in approaching our personal and cultural experience of pain. We continue to think from the "child-mind" and assume pain to be purely physical or somatic at first (that is—originating purely from the physiology of the body), and only after traditional medical assessments have failed, do we consider an explanation that originates in the power of memory. In my work as a trauma therapist, I assume the pain to simply be memory-based; if the simple reframing of the pain metaphor fails to resolve or significantly reduce the discomfort, I refer the client for further naturopathic, allopathic (traditional medicine), or pharmacological intervention. Much of our migraine pain, PMS, depression, anxiety, panic, and chronic pain is sustained by unresolved traumatic memory.

In this new paradigm, we honor the physiology of emotion and view pathology as an expression of consciousness. We dare not treat the body without honoring the mind that manifests it. We speak to our clients with the respect due such intricate wisdom and design and do not impose our findings from a place devoid of compassion. In a presentation that I made to each of the three major hospitals in Reno, Nevada, I mentioned the importance of doing our best to not present information to a client in a traumatizing manner. If we traumatize our clients by how we present a diagnosis or test result, we see their adrenaline rise in response and their T-Cell production decrease – thereby reducing their immunity to deal with illness. One of the physicians at my presentation stated that they were already being trained or retrained in how to communicate with clients. "We are now aware of the importance of communicating properly with the client – in part," he stated, "due to the fact that if the surgery does not go well in spite of our best efforts, and we have made some personal connection with the client, he or she is less likely to sue us if they know that we have tried our best." Certainly this is a less than ideal motive for change, from my standpoint, but it will prove valuable to help shift the paradigm.

Trauma, I have discovered, is frequently not what it appears to be. For instance, with September 11, 2001, the event itself certainly held a traumatic value, but trauma is encoded with direct proportion to the strength of your own boundaries and within your own frame of reference. For instance, though the event itself posed a vast potential for inducing trauma, exactly as the terrorists intended, the degree of traumatization was very much related to how the information was received. Those who received the news from a caring, concerned loved one, for instance, seemed to imprint less strongly than one who received the information live with no mediation. Those who witnessed the events directly, in other words, "took more of a hit." In a great percentage of traumatic events, one factor that determines the degree of imprinting is related to how we receive the information or in how the event is processed with us by those around us, particularly our caregivers. With grief issues, for instance, there is no way to prevent the death itself, but with death often comes the triggering of any previous unresolved losses or grief – a factor which will amplify the intensity and even impair the normal grieving process. A parent, for instance, whose childhood traumas were largely unresolved, may pour him/herself into caring for this child and investing much of his/her self-esteem in the rearing of this child. Should anything happen to the child, the grief issue is amplified beyond reasoning – capturing all of the unresolved feelings of emptiness, not only from the child's actual death, but from all of the accumulated sadness predating this relationship.

I have seen in many trauma cases, individuals who initially appeared quite healthy with no significant pain history. After experiencing some particular event, however, such as a car accident, injury, or loss, they found themselves triggered and suddenly felt an immense body of subconscious repressed emotional and physical pain that became chronic and overwhelming. All it takes is one catalytic event to pull together all associated pain symptoms for the holonomic memory of the body to consolidate the accumulated trauma into a single pain metaphor. Suddenly we have chronic and even acute pain levels that the doctor cannot fully explain. This has been particularly evident in the cases of fibromyalgia and our other autoimmune disorders. Without grasping the trauma induction mechanisms that are generating such immune system repression, the medical profession is generously dispensing labels for the autoimmune problems now rampant in our society. In a physician's office at an HMO, a relatively young physician was trying to label me with Irritable Bowel Syndrome after a four-minute conversation without any testing or detailed history. He was already writing out prescriptions before he had completed an assessment. He was proven wrong over a short period of time; I also declined further services from him.

Many of our autoimmune disorders are diagnoses or labels that are used deductively to provide a vehicle or mechanism for treatment. Given the intricacy of memory encoding, we will eventually have to wed our capacity to track and resolve the complexity of memory with the assessments that we make of the pain in our bodies. In the new paradigm, the sentient awareness of the client is honored as fully as the symptoms of the physical body. The latter is greatly diminished when the technologies to address the pain of memory are wedded to those used to resolve the pathology now manifest on the physical level. The addictions model has already shifted to realize that we cannot give you relief from your addiction by merely detoxifying your body. According to Alcoholics Anonymous, abstinence from the substance constitutes only about five percent of the recovery process at best. The other ninety-five percent relates to the emotional and psychological processes that attach one to the substance and medicating behaviors. How much of this do you think relates to memory and encoded trauma?

Whether it is the medical system, the addictions treatment model, the religious or educational systems, we witness the acceleration of healing when we embrace the inherent wisdom of the bodymind and its states of consciousness, and we see adverse consequences when we treat only one aspect of self. The medical model can no longer treat only the body. The addictions model learned this in the 1950's. Treatment centers for addictions have proven ineffective when they fail to address the first stage of addiction: the psychological dependency fostered by memory and trauma. Religious systems are learning that the moral failure model which only addresses the conscious management of will is largely ineffective when dealing with the potent intentions imprinted by trauma in the ninety-three percent subconscious mind. They learned this the hard way in their failure at treating their own addicted ministers.

The emerging model is clear: we cannot optimally treat the body without fully honoring the mind; we cannot dissociate into our physiology. Neither can we dissociate into our rational minds or intellects and disregard the power of the subconscious imprinting that speaks through the body. The needs and drives of the body, when left in a state of trauma or imbalance will surely manifest in the physical world. The religious systems cannot deny the natural exigency of the body and believe that some realignment of our conscious willpower or "act of confession" will resolve the subconscious imprinting. It will most surely be "acted out" or internalized as illness if left intact and unresolved. There are no moral principles strong enough to address the potency of the memories held protectively in the bodymind. Our moral responsibility is to honor the primacy of that which holds the capacity to undermine our morality in a millisecond of encoding by inserting its own survival message. This is the nature and potency of consciousness. *This is the divine wisdom of our design that has ever accompanied us protectively, watching over us at every millisecond of our evolution.* Trauma is and has ever been premoral in its induction. We are protected before the conscious mind can even reason it out. Trauma resolution and the healing of the disparate states of consciousness, therefore, must be our starting point. This understanding offers a hermeneutic key for us to reexamine our approach to the treatment of body, mind, and spirit. The Greek concept of the psyche included the "inner life – one's inmost being" and embraced the whole of the person. Morality disassociated from the power of subconscious intentionality is handicapped at best. At worst, it is reperpetrating. Medicine must embrace the mind; psychology must embrace the psyche; spirituality must embrace the whole of the mind, particularly as expressed through the body. There is no "incarnation" unless we embrace the whole of what it means to be human, and earth is currently a trauma school.

Creativity, health, and abundance flow when all aspects of self are in balance and aligned. But are we prepared to embrace the power and responsibility that come with the integration of these anciently disparate aspects of consciousness? As Bernie Siegel stated in *Love, Medicine, and Miracles,* people are addicted to their beliefs.[39] In any case, the anchors that hold us back are located in body memory. The invitation to wholeness and health has stood from our earliest evolution; it merely awaits our embrace.

CHAPTER 23

℘℩

"FROM DARKNESS TO LIGHT"

The Ego is the archetypal composite of our unresolved traumas. Its influence has clouded our choices, health, and relationships for over 1.5 million years. As we commit to our own healing and resolve the influence of this shadow self, we discover the light and wisdom that arises spontaneously from within. Our nature is one of light, not shadow.

Our most profound level of healing is not that of the physical body, but that of the spiritual psyche. Here again, we are moving away from the monolithic and outdated moral failure model to a developmental model that promptly addresses the shame that has already compromised our intentionality. John Bradshaw suggested in his book, Healing the Shame That Binds You,[40] that most of us have experienced some degree of shame induction by the time that we are two and a half years old. We do not even reach the age of moral development until we are seven or eight years old. Hence, the degree of unresolved trauma and accompanying shame that we carry has a profound impact on our intentionality, our subsequent development, and our capacity to follow moral precepts. Compulsivity and the loss of willpower increase proportionately as shame is induced. Obviously, therefore, strategies and systems that use shame or fear-inducing tactics to elicit proper moral responses have already, in part, sabotaged the desired outcome by their faulty approach. We cannot afford to overlook the power of the static states of consciousness imposed by trauma.

The new paradigm respects the power and integrity of the individual in a new way. It recognizes the inherent power of the bodymind to map and resolve its trauma history. It honors each moment of perception as the creative expression that it is – mirroring to us our inner state of evolution and the subsequent balance or imbalance. While it is true that we have evolved both individually and collectively, the collective patterns of trauma will manifest as more potent at times than our personal history can justify or explain. For those of us with fewer traumas or who are father along in the healing process, we are presented with an opportunity to support those who are still so deeply immersed in the lessons of the pain body. Our spiritual and intuitive resources come into play when we are no longer distracted by our inner voices of pain. We come to find a capacity for authentic intimacy that profoundly impacts the whole body. The ability to truly attend to and empathically relate to another without internalizing his/her pain becomes possible. If authentic love is the ability to "stand in the shoes" of another, we gain the capacity for such purity of presence without the manipulations of our own trauma-laden intentions.

Trauma is the source of the "ego." This pseudo-I is the composite of all of our fear-based illusions created from moments of deficiency, abuse, and abandonment. It is the gauge and measure of our progress in healing and integration of memory. In originating from trauma, the ego possesses a number of false messages:

1. The ego lives with a distorted perception of time. If I proceed forward in time, even a millisecond, I will die. The ego, therefore, is interested in maintaining the status quo at all times. Its existence is dependent upon a static and stationary existence. It was created at a moment of overwhelm to pause consciousness until someone came along to heal or reintegrate this wounded state back into the whole, but no one has yet returned. We were not taught how to do so or that we even needed to do so. There is no moral fault or failure in this, but there are consequences. The principle of "dynamic homeostasis" – of trying to maintain the system as it is in order to survive is at work from an ego perspective.

2. The ego lives from an ethic of deficiency. This ego believes that, if I give of myself to another, I shall lose what little I have and cease to exist. When we are truly loved and valued by another, we are never diminished; we are enhanced through the closeness. Our light is enhanced, not lessened when we merge in love with another. The fear-based ethic of the ego is founded on a misperception of inadequacy that sees the outsider as competition and threat – largely due to the fact that the system was not made to feel secure in the first place. When we are secure with ourselves, we do not see the overtures of others as threat or rivalry, but are free to engage the other from a sure knowledge that we can offer authentic love and intimacy should we choose to do so; such relationships are not compulsive in nature. The ego-based relationship is compulsive and imbalanced: often seeking security from the other since it is not already present in self. Others become used addictively – simply to make me feel better, in this ethic. It is an ethic of inadequacy.

3. The ego lives from the "child mind." The ego functions largely from the frozen developmental position of the "child mind" that is bound to a physical and material perception of reality. Since the ego is the child of trauma, it possesses a developmental "glitch" – namely, it froze at a level of perception that was very bound to the physical and material world for its sense of security. The child's world is very physical. I am hungry; you feed me. I am wet; you change me. Need is interpreted physically and materially. As we grow and become more multidimensional, we realize that some of the emptiness we feel may not be physical, but may, in fact, be emotional. To the child mind, the similarity between the emotional need and the physical need leads to an error. We see this most frequently with the eating disordered individual. The child mind makes the assumption that the empty feeling is hunger, though it is caused by emotional abandonment from mom or dad. In response to the feeling, the child assumes that food will alleviate the emptiness. In reality, there is no quantity of food that will ever fill the void created by such emotional encoding. It is like trying to put the wrong key in the lock. Trauma is encoded energetically in the nerve cells, synapses, muscles, tissues, and meridians of the bodymind. There is no quantity or type of food that will address the specific deficiency created by a trauma; trauma must be addressed within its own language and physiology. Substitution may tide us over until authentic healing can occur, but, oftentimes, we end up with a second problem, addiction or disorder in our efforts to substitute or medicate the pain until the right solution comes to us. We cannot judge or fault individuals who have used an addictive behavior or substance to survive, but when this behavior begins to cause even greater harm to self or others, we must find a new way of coping. Sometimes the use of an addictive substance prevented an individual from moving into even deeper levels of trauma, but the use of such substances can only be temporary at best without creating additional complications and worsening one's circumstances.

In working with eating disordered clients, the child mind evidences what I refer to as a "reverse physics." As young infants, we felt loved when the concrete sensory experience of food was provided to ease our pain. As this material of weight was added to our bodies, we were comforted and reassured. The traumatized adult, still acting from the precepts of the child mind, will try to fill the emotional void with the material substance that possesses this weight. In doing so as adults, however, the pain is not fully alleviated and we now have weight gain. When the proper physics is applied to a trauma trigger or impulse, the addition of the right emotional solution resolves the impulse quickly, and the standard reply issues forth: "Wow, I feel so much lighter!" Only with trauma resolution do we add energy to the system and become noticeably lighter. The physics of trauma resolution works inversely to that of the child mind. We cannot eat and resolve the burden of our traumatic memory: we will not become lighter employing the solution of the child mind. In fact, as I observed with one of my anorexic clients, when the "three thousand pound weight" of the years of emotional abuse from her mother's perfectionism was felt, she would begin to work out frantically to alleviate this overpowering weight sensation. Even if she dropped below ninety pounds in weight, the three thousand pound weight remained. If she ate the smallest amount of actual food, the weight of the food triggered the (holonomic) memory of the larger burden encoded, and she would panic – again returning to the treadmill to diminish the panic and the oppressive mountain of weight on her chest. Only this weight did not resolve with the treadmill. Only when we place in the system the feelings of love, safety and nurturing that should have been present, do we move closer in frequency to "white light" or love, and become "lighter." This lightness registers on both physical and energetic levels, and it is more lasting in its effect. Such is the reverse physics of the multidimensional mind. The higher in frequency we rise in the resolution of our traumas, the lighter and less burdened does the physical body become.

4. The ego is shame-based. From an emotional standpoint, the ego spends much of its time cycling between fear, shame, powerlessness, and anger. This negative perception of self is totally comprehensible when we see:

• That our physiology was designed to protect us through a psycho-physiological splitting process that would protect us in our personal and collective evolution until we could handle overwhelming circumstances; the sign of such encoding was a sense of wrongness or shame that followed the storage of our pain. Our difficulty arises when we interpret such feelings as defectiveness rather than see these emotions as the warning beacons that they are. They alert us to the encoding of that which is less than love within the bodymind.

• That our culture and our religious systems began our education by interpreting or maintaining the ancient mythology as moral failure or Original Sin rather than the protective dissociation that it was. The real obstacle to spiritual intimacy is not that of the mistake or moral transgression for which we apologize, make amends, and from which we learn as human beings. The true challenge to singular consciousness is the mechanism that splits the white light entrusted to us into separate channels, each bearing its own intention and agenda. In the conflict that arises between conscious and subconscious intentionality, we are virtually immobilized and manifest the state of conflict instead. There is something insidious about religious systems fostering shame induction and doing so in the name of God. I know from my seminary training that the moral responsibility model was very well intentioned in its efforts and its belief that this was the true path to spiritual liberation. The failure of this model in treating its own most wounded souls is an opportunity for humble recognition of the need for growth and change. I see this humility in the recovering individuals such as alcoholics who have faced the truth about the failure of willpower in healing such traumas and who have admitted their powerlessness over the subconsciously induced compulsivity of addiction and trauma. It was very humbling for me, having had one of the best educations that the Catholic church had to offer, to realize that I had enabled and fostered addictions and compulsivity in my parishioners by my strict adherence to a moral failure model which largely ignored the power of trauma and subconscious intentionality. The old moral failure model was inherently shaming, in many respects, as we have discussed earlier in this text. The additional tool of trauma resolution is the perfect complement to empower the resources that return management of the bodymind to conscious intentionality.

5. The ego has an imbalanced spirituality. The spirituality of the ego is distorted by the influence of trauma. The principal polarities induced by trauma are fear and anger. Shame induces this splitting and results in the polarization of the spiritual psyche. Such distorted spirituality is frequently manifested in our world in a systemic form or in our attraction to fear-based or anger-based systems. The study of dysfunctional systems has revealed to us that trauma generates two patterns of relationship: one pattern we call "codependent"; the other we call "counterdependent."[41] The codependent type of spirituality is fear-based and is characterized by reinforced feelings of inferiority, dependency, excessive other-centeredness, and over-receptivity (boundary weakness). The counterdependent form is anger-based and evidences grandiosity (an exaggerated or excessive sense of worth), independence, narcissism, self-centeredness, and intrusiveness. In looking at many of our religious systems, we recognize the presence of these trauma-based polarities. In manipulating us through fear, religious systems foster codependency and prey upon our trauma-induced vulnerability. Since the religious system's boundaries and the political system's boundaries have been blurring of late, you may note that some of the same observations are applicable to strategies now at work in the political arena.

In their anger and frustration, some of these systems become highly grandiose and distorted in their thinking. Anger reflects the polarity where power is reserved during a trauma. Such repressed anger, however, is often the vehicle that the psyche uses to make itself feel safe through its sense of power and its ability to enforce isolation. I recall one specific case in my office at the treatment center in Tucson. I was about to resume a group process with one of the clients in the room when another group member interrupted to announce that he could not continue the process. When I asked why, he stated that it was because this could not possibly be an effective process for memory resolution. When I asked him for clarification, he explained that the only persons who could truly help people heal their memories were the anointed ministers from his church in Arkansas. I asked if this was only true of his church in Arkansas or if this was part of a larger group of churches; he indicated that it was "pretty much just (his) church in Arkansas." Honestly, I was speechless for a moment. I sensed his fear of participation in the process, but saw the withdrawal into his distorted religious beliefs as part of his overall addictive cycle that had brought him to treatment. His excessive religiosity made sense later on when I met with him individually and discovered his efforts to deny his sexual addiction and alcoholism – both of which were highly condemned by the morally rigid system to which he was so earnestly trying to conform. There is a huge correlation between religious compulsivity and sexual addiction – the shaming methodology of the rigid religious system accelerates the progress of the sexual addiction. His attraction to such a rigid religious system had a great deal to do with his efforts to find something "outside" of himself that would impose some control over his areas of compulsivity that he could not exact for himself. I suspect that many of us have tried to use religious systems, institutions, and even marriages to get our psyches to conform in areas of conflict or struggle that we could not control from within.

Our understanding of the manner in which our spiritual, political, relational, and career choices are impacted by trauma is of paramount importance. The distortion created by trauma profoundly influences our intentionality and frequently corrupts our intended outcome. The client from Arkansas had no way of knowing that his sincere efforts to follow the God presented by his religious community were actually fostering his addictions and accelerating his path to inpatient treatment.

Dysfunctional systems manipulate through incitement of fear and anger. In the induction of fear, they draw upon our prehistories of fear and foster our dependency upon them: fear of hellfire and damnation will do the trick! So it has been with many systems for centuries. Others incite us to righteous anger and lead us to believe that they alone hold the truth and the only truth: grandiose to say the least! The more insular such systems become, the more removed from the mystical connection to all they are. Such systems will foster religious addiction and prey upon the vulnerable individual who, like the codependent personality, "needs" the counterdependent to worship. The insecurity of the ego results in a spiritual vulnerability: failing to recognize the power that resides within. The "locus" of all spirituality is the self. This Divinity is then shared in community with others. To think that Divinity is principally located outside of oneself or that only one system possesses it is the antithesis of the message of Jesus. His message was particularly directed to the "fringe" persons and those who did not fit into the traditional systems of his day. He was particularly interested in those who were sick and traumatized: the outcasts and rejects of his day. His was not an exclusive club!

The emphasis under this new paradigm is healing and the creation of safe, loving contexts for healing, instead of the moral judgment and polarities of the old moral failure model. Our priority must be the healing of the substantial breaches that undermine our flow of power: our intentionality. This paradigm begins, therefore, with an accurate understanding of our power to shift, store, create, alter, and resolve our states of consciousness. The moral responsibility model is woefully inadequate, though abstinence from ones destructive behaviors must occur early, utilizing all social and personal resources available, if authentic healing is to occur. The old fear-based moral failure model afforded some a respite from their own self-destructive behaviors and tendencies, though it could not resolve them. How many of my clients avoided suicide because they were terrified that they would "go to hell" if they did so! Though a fearful and traumatizing moral approach, it provided for many people the temporal pause needed until an effective path to healing could be found. Through patience and necessity, many gained the time they needed to find the resources that could resolve their pain and free them from their triggers in a more effective manner. With at least some limited abstinence from the addictive substance or destructive behavior, the emotional cues that permitted the mapping and resolution of memory promptly surfaced. I recall one of my clients in the treatment center who was still detoxifying from alcohol when his flashbacks from Vietnam surfaced and began to completely overwhelm him. Although the alcohol remaining in his system limitedly affected his mental tracking ability, he was coherent enough to follow my voice and find the visual solution that resolved the flashbacks surfacing at that time.

Without the knowledge to resolve the sources that corrupt our intentionality and foster violence, addiction, compulsivity, depression, and illness, we have resigned ourselves to the containment and biochemical numbing of these somatic cues. In doing so, we lose the opportunity and invitation to embrace our power as the masters of our states of consciousness. There are times when the prolonged exposure to the physiology of trauma in our systems depletes our neurotransmitters and damages our physiology. Traditional medicine and drug (psychopharmacological) intervention, I suspect, will always have a place in our world as a result of the depth of trauma now imprinted in the cells and fields of our bodies. But we have far more influence over the bodymind than we were ever led to believe, particularly when our bodies have not yet progressed to the final level of warning: physical illness.

In my work with so many trauma survivors over these last years, I have noticed that when we address an encoded trauma in a timely manner, it does not become reinforced in the physiology of the body. Dr. Soram Khalsa, one of the earliest physicians to introduce "Integrative Medicine" to Los Angeles, mentioned to me that one of the first questions that he asks his newly referred breast cancer patients when they come to him is: "Have you experienced trauma from a male in the last seven years of your life?" He stated that in a huge percentage of cases, his client immediately identifies with the question and provides an answer. The reason for this is simple: Seven years from the induction of a trauma in the cells and fields of the body, all the cells in that part of the body have replicated. This phenomenon was visually depicted in the movie, *What the #$*! Do We Know!?* (referenced earlier in this work). Over the next seven-year cycle, beginning at the moment that the millisecond of pain is stored, all of the cells of the body begin replicating within this "black" or "red" distortion (using the language of frequency and metaphor). Imagine what this energy has the capacity to do when left unattended over a long period of time! The body as repository, protector, and teacher will speak more and more loudly to remind the bearer of the encoding. Try tracing a traumatic experience backward in time, noting the seven-year cycles. Recently I worked with an individual who underwent a terrible trauma at age three when her grandfather "ran over her leg" accidentally with the car; fourteen years later, almost to the day, she was involved in another car accident and actually fractured her spine. It is not uncommon to see an unresolved trauma remanifest itself even more loudly as the cells of the body cry out for resolution. When left unattended on the emotional and mental levels, the body simply amplifies the signal until it captures the attention of the conscious mind. This last stage of effort to get our attention is that of the physical body and the "healing crisis" or "accident" that manifests quite physically. I believe that the body cues us frequently as to the unresolved trances that we have encoded. I know, however, that many of us go to painstaking lengths to avoid hearing the memory-cues of the bodymind. Much of this avoidance is ego-based; some is simply misinformation.

We were not taught how to master our states of consciousness. There is no blame in this, however, for most of our parents had no skills in this regard either. In fact, it is amazing that they accomplished what they did with the level of pain that they had to endure. My father, I know for a fact, in not knowing how to resolve his traumas, ended up containing all this pain in his body – then manifested it through the many illnesses he bore until his death: colon cancer, lung cancer, Parkinson's, diabetes, head injuries, heart attacks, and others. I knew this when I realized that I could feel the site of his lung tumor before he died. I do not feel illnesses or sites that are purely physiological in origin. I feel memories! At that moment I resolved to do my best to not die from my memories; I realized the power of memory at that time. I would like to depart this world consciously, not as a victim of my unresolved subconscious pain. I do not wish to die from my memories or my unfinished states of consciousness.

Trauma, in my mind, is nothing more than a moment of overwhelm when we were forced to pause reality with "less than love" present. It is simply an incomplete state of consciousness. Now, it would be nice if, while here on earth, we had only received love and understanding – only "white light," but earth is not that kind of school – it is, at least for now, the trauma school! We learn of our inherent light and power by discovering our ability to dispel the darkness – to master our states of consciousness and the darkness that is imposed at moments of overwhelm. When we courageously return to those milliseconds of pain and discover that we possess the capacity to complete them, we remember the Source. In Hebrew, the verb zakar, "to remember," is actually sacramental: it truly "makes present" beyond the limits of space and time and is infinitely more than some fond recollection.

For we cannot know the missing colors or frequencies of each of our states of consciousness unless we are still in touch with that river of White Light – the main flow of consciousness, or "the Divine Mind" as I refer to it. Wasn't that the message of Jesus some two thousand years ago anyway: "I am the way, the truth, and the life" (John 14:5)? "I am the Light of the World" (John 8:12), and he departed so that this light would be forever recognized as "within." This precious body of ours is the Temple of Divine Consciousness, and it speaks to us continuously. The message of his life was more than moral salvation from an Original Sin, it was to enable us to feel and complete within us those "eddies" of consciousness that have left us feeling estranged from our oneness with the Divine. The invitation is that of healing and mystical oneness; and these concepts are inseparable. We have been entrusted with the gift and capacity to love – to "complete" consciousness itself at each moment where it was lacking in our individual and collective history. In embracing this power, if only one millisecond at a time, we discover our capacity to transcend the limits and pain of space and time; we discover our quantum ability to create our reality and to create a reality of love. I have never known a client who could not, ultimately, return to this Totality and identify exactly the feelings and emotions that were absent at a particular moment in his/her life. What does this imply?

In truth, we have never left the river of White Light – the Source of All. We may have been distracted by the "eddies" of our traumas, addictions, relational struggles, physical and emotional pain, but we have never fully lost this connection. On earth, we may move into the illusions offered by five-sensory awareness and become so hypnotized by our experiences that we find it difficult to feel or remember our connection to the One Mind. There are no obstacles to mystical oneness imposed by the Divine Mind. The impediments to union are held in existence, both individually and collectively, by our subconscious imprinting. And they have long been in place in the human race.

We approach a privileged time of healing and awakening. A new paradigm approaches that is fully supported by science and is inherently "integrative." "Integrative medicine" and "holistic healing" are the catch phrases of our day. Are we surprised that all truths, regardless of the disciplines that generate them, are now converging? Quantum physics and spirituality converge in agreement about the power of consciousness: the act of observation is creative! In fact, science is teaching us heightened respect for our creative power; our stewardship of creation is very real and immediate in light of quantum physics. It is time that we use the tools now offered us to master our states of consciousness. There is no question that there was an inherent wisdom in our very design that remained quietly in the background, biding its time until we would begin to reach out and embrace its creative force. That time is upon us. The capacity to manifest happiness, health, abundance, intimacy, and success is clearly present in our design, our genetics, our physiology, and our play on earth: Eden is not lost to us; it was and is our destiny! The mastery of our states of consciousness in holographic space will make Eden real.

I must thank you who read this, for you have been my teachers and my mirrors. I have come to respect the sanctity of your memories and your holographic "Higher Self" or mind. The movements you make to heal your memories open you to the Light. Each memory you heal draws you back into the River. You will draw to yourself on this journey of healing those persons, lessons, and words that will support you on your return home. We write this together to remind ourselves of our unlimited capacity for love: there is nothing new in the universe: all is remembrance! All is play within a river of light!

Our memories of trauma are outdated images of the past. They are static and removed from the flow of white light, and, as such, they are less than true. They impart to us untruths about ourselves on a profound level of awareness. They are all lessons and vehicles for empowerment and reclamation. We now reclaim our membership in the family of light! We did not come to this plane of existence to finally identify ourselves as powerless beings. Admitting our moments and experiences of powerlessness assists us in identifying and healing our traumas and addictions. Paradoxically, this admission provides the "observer stance" required to heal our states of consciousness and stop the shame-induction process. By stepping back from our traumatic experiences and observing, we start to reverse the over-identification with the feelings of powerlessness and worthlessness. We begin to individuate from our trauma histories and, from there, see that we have always kept one foot in the river of power that offers healing and wholeness. We step back from the pain body and begin to remember our connection to the unlimited resources offered us on all levels of being. The truth of the matter is: you are a mystic and child of the light! You have been extended an invitation to embrace your quantum power and participate in the creation of Eden: not the one materially or morally bound by the old mythology, but one that reaches beyond anything we have been told.

In the seminary, I recall one of my favorite scripture passages: the prophecy of a new covenant in Jeremiah 31: 31-34, where the prophet Jeremiah, exasperated at the failure of the "moral responsibility model" invokes a prediction. Though obviously cloaked in the moral failure model and language of Jeremiah's day, the prophet foresaw the breakdown of the old moral exhortation approach. Gently reading the text from our greater understanding of trauma and its impact on our spiritual evolution, notice how the prediction transcends its own context and touches upon fulfillment in our day.

The days are coming, says the Lord, when I will make a new covenant with the house of Israel and the house of Judah. It will not be like the covenant I made with their fathers the day I took them by the hand to lead them forth from the land of Egypt; for they broke my covenant, and I had to show myself their master, says the Lord. But this is the covenant which I will make with the house of Israel after those days, says the Lord. I will place my law within them, and write it upon their hearts; I will be their God, and they shall be my people. No longer will they have need to teach their friends and kinsmen how to know the Lord. All, from least to greatest, shall know me, says the Lord, for I will forgive their evildoing and remember their sin no more.

Jeremiah 31: 31-34

In obvious frustration with the inability of his people to respond appropriately to continuous moral exhortation and to adhere to the commandments, the prophet appeals to a higher vision. Rather than some cognitive learning process, Jeremiah anticipates the solution: the Divine will or law, the "Torah" itself will be imprinted upon the human heart – transferring an inherent knowledge of the Divine will to the human heart which was known to be the "seat of all decision-making." This new covenant would firmly enthrone the Divine will at the source of all choices and decision-making, eliminating the possibility of any great divergence from God's will as evidenced in Israel's past. This oneness with the Divine Mind would spontaneously render up right behaviors as a consequence; once one is united with the Divine Mind, right moral action would follow naturally and easily. Here the path to spiritual union would exist spontaneously and naturally within the movements of the human heart. This immediate knowing would preempt the need for rational, moral education, for the map to wholeness would reside in the heart of the individual. The Divine wisdom would be fully accessible from within.

The reality is: such a map exists within the human heart! The latent potential to return each of our darkest moments to the light was set in place by the very DNA that defines us. The capacity to do more than forgive transgressions – the actual power to heal the disparate states of consciousness behind our illnesses and moral struggles was present in us from our earliest evolution. Our "fight, flight, freeze response" reflects the physiological aspect of this wisdom. The capacity to pause space and time perception until we are prepared to heal our moments of trauma is clearly inherent in our earliest "design." Written in the genetic structure of the human heart and in every cell of our body is the same message, repeated billions of times within our systems. We carry the energetic and physiological capacity to pause consciousness itself until we are prepared to address such overwhelming moments. The physics of consciousness has brought us beyond the limited understanding of the moral responsibility model to face a force that is far greater and more expansive than our moral evolution. In fact, it significantly predates morality, as we currently know it. Trauma preceded "civilization," literature, and probably even verbal communication; it preceded the religious systems that are fairly recent in contrast to humanity's presence on this planet. We were protected before we were even cognizant of our need for protection. There is unimaginable wisdom and potential in our cellular memory.

When we move beyond spiritual teachings that merely focus on the need for moral redemption from some Original Sin and begin to view the greater scope of the Divine plan, we begin to see the healing and reintegration that is present. Jesus as Rabbi (teacher), for instance, went out of his way to touch and heal those who were outcasts, marginal, and those who were simply ill. Apart from the account of the passion itself, almost half of the earlier text in the Gospel of Mark is dedicated to accounts of healing. If we view the account of the death and resurrection of Jesus as intended for more than merely our moral transformation, we begin to understand the relevance of Jeremiah's prophecy of an entirely new relational basis for man's relationship to God. Jesus departs so that we might "know" the will written upon the human heart: that we might experience the Divine Spirit – *ruah* in Hebrew, meaning "breath, wind, spirit," from *within*. As we greet this flow of breath or white light within us, we "know" God in the profound, experiential manner communicated so well by the Hebrew language. Physical healing follows simply and naturally as a by-product of our spiritual enlightenment. In this new healing paradigm, we recognize the fingerprint of the Divine plan in every human being. This spiritual exigency has both an individual and a collective momentum. Like many of our Jewish communities, we come to believe that we are called as a people to manifest the messianic presence on earth. The Christian community speaks of the "Mystical Body of Christ" now manifest in his Spirit dwelling within us. But if this is so, why has the Christian community not served as more of a witness to the healing, nonjudgmental attitude of Jesus instead of the conservatism and moral strictures that resemble the morally rigid sects of Jesus' own day?

When we move beyond the moral failure model and see the life of Jesus within the larger scope, we see in the Divine plan the healing of both our conscious and our subconscious intentionality – not merely that of the conscious, moral mind. In the healing of this intentionality, Eden is made possible. Our capacity to manifest love and truth from a place of clear and singular intentionality emerges. In this purification and healing, we discover our capacity to truly "walk with God" in our everyday lives – and to do so consciously. This is borne of our growing capacity to remain in the eternal present. And this ability increases with the resolution of our trances and the emergence of singular intentionality.

Eckhart Tolle speaks so powerfully in his book, *The Power of Now*, of the importance of remaining in the present. In one portion of his work, entitled: "Nothing Exists Outside the Now," he states the following:

> *Nothing ever happened in the past; it happened in the Now. Nothing will ever happen in the future; it will happen in the Now. What you think of as the past is a memory trace – and you do so now. The future is an imagined Now, a projection of the mind. When the future comes, it comes as the Now. When you think of the future, you do it now. Past and future obviously have no reality of their own.*[42]

We are increasingly one with the Eternal Present of the Divine Mind as we clear our traumas. As we do so, we become singular in our minds and our intentions. Without the voices of trauma to draw us out of the power of the now, we manifest that which we need as we need it. I have seen this abundance, intimacy, and success increase in my life as I commit to my own healing. Though I enjoyed much of my ministry as a priest, I can honestly say that I have never been so spiritually moved as I was the first time that I felt the pain of trauma leave my client and pass through my hands as it did so. It did so in the now! There are no temporal limits to our healing if the present is the only true source and locus of our pain. I physically felt the bodymind healing itself of trauma and releasing the tension that was trapped in my client's body from the perceived moment of abuse.

Like most of us, I was raised and trained in the "moral responsibility" model. My intuitive spiritual experiences in my family, particularly those of my mother, hinted at more, however. Originally I thought that healing and spirituality were the proprietary rights of the religious systems that so generously offered guidance on these paths. Eventually I came to discover that my most spiritual experience was not in some defined ritual or external experience, but in the intimate encounter with the healing power imprinted in the human heart. If you ask people what their most spiritual experiences are, they inevitably respond with the same four top answers: birth of a child, death of someone, an intimate relationship with another person, and a profound experience in nature. The top four answers do not even mention the religious systems; they are all profound movements of the heart. There is truly an innate wisdom and sanctity contained within the human heart. Within our being we know exactly how many traumas we have had and all of the emotions that should have been present at such moments. We hold the ability to draw from this flow of white light and to complete our histories – to finish the parenting that our first spiritual teachers, mom and dad, could not. With these keys, we possess the capacity to unlock the wisdom of the human heart and to heal the blockages to authentic intimacy and manifestation. In our bodies we carry the ability to feel the pain of another and to facilitate the healing of others. As we release the dense and heavy energies of imprinted trauma, we move from a static place of solidity to one of fluidity and light – we gain the capacity to merge with another. In this heightened capacity for intimacy we know the other in ways that transcend speech.

CHAPTER 24

∾⃝

"THE FACE OF EDEN"

Until philosophers are kings, or the kings and princes of this world have the spirit and power of philosophers, and political greatness and wisdom meet in one, and those commoner natures who pursue either to the exclusion of the other one are compelled to stand aside, cities will never rest from their evils.

Plato

One of the reasons that I was so intrigued by the Chalcolithic period of the Middle East was that it was the astoundingly creative period that preceded "urbanism" or "civilization" as we currently know it. The Chalcolithic period in the Middle East occurred earlier than in many other parts of the world. In a land long since overwhelmed by strife, artistic genius once abounded! This period, in particular, was marked by revolutionary advances in metallurgy, beginning with the ability to smelt copper ore and progressing to the discovery of the "lost wax" method of casting metallic objects. This was evidenced, for example, in the finds of the "Cave of the Treasure" that contained hundreds of individually cast elaborate copper objects ranging from ornate scepters and crowns in the form of animals and symbols to carved hippopotamus tusks. At Teleilat Ghassul, Chalcolithic painted frescoes of a spiritual nature were found that preceded other cultures by a thousand years. This period laid the foundation for the "Early Bronze" ages and the formation of cities – the beginnings of "urbanism" – marked by our subsequent preoccupation with "walls" and defensive structures.[43] The walls of the Chalcolithic period were mere perimeter designations and held little defensive value. Once humankind's creative energies were redirected to defense and gathering together for protection from invasion, there were fewer resources and opportunities for higher aesthetic and spiritual expression. Something creative was lost within the struggles for power, survival, and control. Historically, it does not appear that our first effort at gathering together in cities was a defensive one, but one intended to share resources for mutual enhancement and enlightenment. When these resources, however, were redirected to defend ourselves in response to fear and threat, we experienced spiritual trauma and the repression of our "creator within." With the advent of this latest version of "civilization," it would appear that something creative, spontaneous, innocent and artistic was lost. The trauma and dissociation we have encoded over the last 5000 years, in particular, have impacted us profoundly.

In a day and time when the greatest cities of our age remain targets of terrorism and are visited by tsunami, earthquake and hurricane, we dare to speak of a new vision. When we are, as a species, capable of enacting such devastation on an urban populace or fail to respond in a timely manner as people perish, we have become dissociative indeed. In light of these events, we are invited to reflect upon our use of our quantum potential and to consider both our individual and collective contribution to this experience of "city" that we have manifested and maintained.

Cities are ever the mirrors of our collective mind: conscious and subconscious. They manifest our highest achievements and our unresolved shadows. In my training with the Jesuits, I lived for a time in Jerusalem. I loved the smells and sounds that assailed me as I passed through the Old City. I loved the gatherings on Ben Yehuda Street after Shabbat (the Sabbath) ended. My great grandfather was Jewish, and though my friend Wyatt Web stated in his book title that, "It's not about the horse – it's about overcoming fear and self-doubt,"[44] I used to taunt some of my clients and inform them: "It really is sometimes about the horse or certainly does look that way!" You see, my great grandfather was Jewish and was kicked in the head by a horse and died from the concussion. My great grandmother, an Isaac, remarried Catholic, having few Jewish men left available in the little town in Louisiana where they settled. When I left formal ministry, Barry Weinstein, the local rabbi and a friend of mine commented: "I know exactly where your great grandfather's grave is located, and you know, Brent, if it wasn't for that horse, you probably would've been a rabbi instead of a priest!'" I laughed, but realized that he might've been right as well. Traumas shape our lives in unanticipated and unimaginable ways. I have always loved and appreciated my Jewish heritage. My niece and godchild married a charming Jewish podiatrist a few years ago at the Touro Synagogue in New Orleans; it was a beautiful ceremony. They also named their first child "Eve"! Our greatest hope for the future is in the children.

Jerusalem itself, with its overlapping cultures, systems, and sects, is located on the small land bridge we now call Israel, which connects three major continents: a perfect street corner to make a statement or impact history. The Romans, the Greeks, the Assyrians, the Babylonians, the Hittites, and the Egyptians all made their way across this land bridge at one time or another. The site that I excavated in Israel was along one of the most prominent trade routes and showed evidence of Egyptian influence already at 3000 BC, at the time of the first dynasty of Egypt. The land we know as Israel was at the heart of the intercultural communications network of its day. Jerusalem eventually became the spiritual center for Judaism and Christianity, and is one of the major spiritual centers of Islam.

Spiritually, present-day Jerusalem is the perfect metaphor for our collective state of evolution. As I write this, discussion continues as to whether the city should be additionally "split" into more than its various "quarters" to enable the various factions to live in peace. What does this say about our ability to coexist peacefully with one another? The parameters of the city are not the issue or the solution. Here again is an attempt at a material or mechanical solution that serves the concrete thinking of the "child mind." I spent almost two years of my life living in this remarkable city. It remains a city of beauty, mystery, paradox, and contrast.

I recall my visit to the Church of the Holy Sepulcher, one of the most revered sites in Christendom, purportedly built over the sacred site of the crucifixion and possibly the tomb of Jesus. In reviewing the historical details of the site, a story about a ladder surfaced: a ladder put in place for cleaning and repairs as I recall. The various Christian sects represented in the church got into a huge argument about the disposition of the ladder and its use. As a result, it remained for years frozen in its position (and probably still remains) against the outside of the building, an eyesore and attestation of the inability of these groups to communicate effectively with each other and achieve resolution. Apparently, the spiritual significance of the site did not move its occupants enough to insure harmonious communication. Once egos and political maneuvering begin, time and opportunities for healing are lost, as well as effective resolution of an issue or crisis. Inside the church I recall the partitions of the various sects all claiming a piece of this sacred ground. It seemed to me that the church perfectly mirrored the dissociative state of our various religious systems (and political systems) whose spiritual tools have frequently proven ineffective in mending their own breaches. The moral failure model cannot resolve the traumas that so profoundly impact our emotional and spiritual progress. We subsequently find ourselves "stuck" in situations akin to the ladder story! We see tremendous dissociation and discord among the various internal factions of Judaism, Christianity, and Islam. We see the same paralysis appear in the management of crises such as the Hurricane Katrina disaster when the political system evidences its own dissociation and miscommunication. Anger and blame frequently accompany the subsequent confrontations that occur and are good indicators of the degree of trauma still unresolved in the psyche. Trauma influences the decision-making process. We witnessed this situation in New Orleans where a large number of deprived and previously traumatized individuals used their anger to take advantage of the chaos and lawlessness. Time after time we have witnessed that a great percentage of trauma is induced, not by the catastrophic event itself, *but how it is handled by the caregivers – whether it is handled in a compassionate and timely manner!*

But how are we to effectively address larger global or societal issues when we have not addressed the dissociation that so readily compromises our personal decision-making process? The sheer quantity of trauma that many of us hold impacts our listening ability and readily compromises negotiation. Trauma creates unhealthy attachments; it frequently undermines our most rational attempts at reconciliation. We alluded to this in our discussion of "forgiveness and healing." In other words, we may consciously preach peace but act at the same time from a place of such trauma and distrust that we subconsciously sabotage any efforts at compromise or mediation.

Recently I had the privilege to meet with Dr. Ashok Gangadean, Cofounder of the Global Dialogue Institute (www.global-dialogue. com).[45] For many years, his efforts have focused on bringing both individuals and groups to a place of "Deep-Dialogue" where we move from trauma-based, ego-centered thinking into that space where we open to the fundamental meaning of life and all its dimensions.[46] As we grow in our capacity to resolve the traumatic imprinting that has fostered separation on both personal and collective levels, we move, as the Global Dialogue Institute states: "Out of the 'Age of Monologue' into the dawning 'Age of Dialogue,' wherein people are beginning to truly encounter the other in dialogue."[47] As we resolve our traumas and the distortions that they foster in our belief systems, we come to understand more fully how these strong intrapsychic imprints can either inspire and unite us or divide and destroy us. As we still the voices that kept us trapped in the past and unable to fully attend to the present, we become capable of true dialogue with the other.

The traditional moral responsibility model presumed the complete availability of our "free will" to initiate change. Our current understanding of the profound impact that trauma has played in our evolution suggests otherwise. We have witnessed a huge resurgence toward religious and political conservatism and the protection of "moral values" over these past few years. The "moral responsibility" model has never been so hard pressed to produce an answer to our current crises and to address our traumas. Tremendous pressure was created in the spiritual psyche of the populace when the events of September 11, 2001, transpired. Efforts to apply the moral responsibility model came to frustration without a perpetrator firmly in our grasp. It would appear that much of the collective unconscious is still angry and will direct its fury at persons or systems that neglect or reperpetrate; such anger resurfaced in full force after Hurricane Katrina.

One of the principal lessons of trauma resolution gleaned from the events surrounding Sept. 11, 2001, involved the repeated efforts to identify and capture the perpetrators. Our determination to hold accountable the perpetrators, however, failed to take into account the true nature of trauma and the personal encoding that occurs at such moments of overwhelm. Many who believed in the moral responsibility model were greatly surprised that confronting the perpetrators in present time did not necessarily resolve the charge of the original trauma scene. Justice in the present does not necessarily resolve a trauma encoded in the past – at least not as far as the subconscious mind (still trapped in the imagery) is concerned! Capital punishment does not heal a trauma memory! The capture and prosecution of a perpetrator may appear to contain and prevent further traumatization, but it does little to touch the original moment of encoding. We learned long ago that even the execution of a perpetrator does not resolve the actual moment at which the memory was encoded. In the case of capital punishment, the proponents of the moral responsibility model became more confused and frustrated when their feelings of anger and fear returned, having no remaining object for the expression of their unresolved anger now that the offender was dead and well beyond their reach.

Efforts to find a moral solution to resolve the pain of our traumas become increasingly compulsive and desperate when fueled by growing frustration and fear. We see this visibly in the huge surge in "morality" and religiosity following traumatic global events. The morality of the rational mind, however, cannot address the power of the encoding in the subconscious mind. Even the most well-intentioned religious interventions tend to become compulsive and excessive when propelled into motion by the undiminished fear and anger of trauma. Traumatizing solutions, however, merely insure additional trauma in the future. The role of trauma, shame, and unconscious intentionality were not part of our self-understanding in ancient times, though the ancient texts like Genesis reveal our earliest spiritual trauma to somehow involve shame, and not merely moral failure.

Dissociation and trauma not only impact us personally, but also continue to manifest powerfully in the systems around us. The spiritual damage that occurs from exposure to this ongoing dissociation is that we risk becoming compulsive and addicted to our own beliefs in our increasingly desperate search for security; such beliefs, however, are shaped by the distorted thinking of trauma and are separated from close contact with our spiritual core. This risks delusion when based on out-dated trances that leave us in distorted fear, shame, or anger-driven emotional states. When collectively shared with others, this dissociation can generate a "cult-like" mentality or an addictive system such as we have witnessed with those religious sects whose beliefs extended into self-sacrifice and "martyrdom" in the form of suicide bombings or mass suicide. Such distortion happens when our self-definition comes under the profound influence of unresolved shame and trauma – when our core beliefs are shaped by our traumas and our subconscious intentionality. When we do not remain in alignment with our spiritual core and act, instead, from an estranged place of trauma, we make decisions that echo from our deficiency, rather than our fullness. We act primarily from the void. Such decision-making is myopic and off-balance: a decision that bears a compulsive or addictive quality because it originates from the void created by trauma rather than the abundance of serenity and completion. The bridging that is required to end this institutionalized dissociation is found in a new concept of intimacy. Such a reality was suggested two thousand years ago in the vision of the Book of Revelation:

> Then I saw new heavens and a new earth. The former heaven and the former earth had passed away, and the sea was no longer. I also saw a new Jerusalem, the holy city, coming down out of heaven from God, beautiful as a bride prepared to meet her husband. I heard a loud voice from the throne cry out: "This is God's dwelling among men. He shall dwell with them and they shall be his people and he shall be their God who is always with them. He shall wipe every tear from their eyes, and there shall be no more death or mourning, crying out or pain, for the former world has passed away."
> Revelation 21: 1-4

Dissociation is resolved through a new relationship between heaven and earth; the distance between the two dissolves and God makes (his) "dwelling among men." Here, heaven and earth are wed in a new metaphor: a new city -- the New Jerusalem! Perhaps even to find some expression in a reawakened New York or a reborn New Orleans?! Like the "new covenant" prophesied in the Book of Jeremiah, our separation from the Divine Presence dissolves into an *immediate* knowledge and indwelling. There shall be "no more death or mourning, crying out or pain" – there is no dissociation or loss of divine intimacy here! The tenor is that of the height of relational intimacy: "beautiful as a bride prepared to meet her husband." Even heaven and earth are no longer so separated. Our vision of a "new heavens" and a "new earth" seem to correlate with the capacity to abide continuously in the Divine Presence – united with the flow of white light. Here our will is naturally aligned with that of the Divine Mind: **we spontaneously know and manifest our highest good.**

I have no doubt that the social implications of the resolution of our dissociative states would be enhanced communication on the 'horizontal' plane. Not long ago, I cofounded a charity with my friend Yvonne Hedeker, who experienced a life-changing transformation through the resolution of her own trauma memories. As a result, we founded "Michael's Gift," a non-profit charity (www.michaelsgift.org) whose vision includes the following statement:

Michael's Gift is dedicated to the healing of the emotional, psychological, physical and spiritual effects of trauma. We believe that all persons possess an innate ability to heal, given the proper tools and resources. We hold that personal transformation creates the foundation for global change. We are committed to reducing the impact and recurrence of trauma in our world.

Michael's Gift© 2002

We hold both a personal and a collective invitation to transition into this New Jerusalem that awaits us. Our forms of social interaction will change as we remove the obstacles to clear communication and become capable of listening from an authentic place. We cannot love the other consistently when we are constantly interrupted by the voices of violence and shame that remain unresolved within our own psyches. At moments of crisis, we, as a species, will respond from the ethic that mirrors our degree of trauma resolution. We witnessed this in the responses of the populace in the aftermath of Hurricane Katrina. If we do not take seriously the healing of our profound intergenerational trauma patterns, we will not know peace. If we do not reframe our personal trauma histories, we will continue to respond from our personal wounds that bias our ability to listen or negotiate peace. We will be prone to respond from anger or fear. We cannot communicate with those other loving beings when we are not present – when we are trancing and perceiving our reality under the significant distortions induced from another place and time. These places of defense and protection that are held within the mind keep us captive and prevent us from living fully in the present. They also bear the brunt of our unresolved anger and pain and infect our transactions in present time. From such trances we cannot fully see or hear the other. We understand now that the capacity to stay in the "eternal present," the only place of authentic communication, is directly proportionate to our degree of skill in mastering our trance states. These powerful states, if left unresolved, have the ability to easily draw us out of present time in a millisecond. The resolution of these states releases our unhealthy "attachments" to the triggers inserted by past events and opens us up to our full creative potential. Were we to resolve all of our stress and trauma-induced trance states, would we even recognize ourselves? What would the face of this new Eden be?

• **Self-image:** Freed from the distortions of the ego, we find ourselves embracing emotions as opportunities to strengthen our connection to the Source. The notion of defending some static concept of self gives rise to the free, creative expression of an eternal spiritual being spontaneously aligned with his/her highest good. Uniqueness and individuality are cherished as enrichment rather than feared as a cause for rejection. Sadness, fear, and anger are seen as opportunities for healing and invitations to greater intimacy. Crisis and disaster become opportunities for us to shine! We know ourselves as unique refractions of the white light that sustains us at each moment. We recognize ourselves as the mystics we are and were intended to be.

• **Interpersonal Relationships:** Our attractions, communication, and social contact flow from a place of authenticity and are not distorted by the restrictive and often sabotaging intentionality of trauma. True friendships, partnerships, and "soul mates" easily and spontaneously arise when our vision originates from a place of white light. We come to the end of the dynasty of codependency; we will no longer form relationships based on attraction from the void left by trauma and unmet childhood needs. Such attraction has the compulsive and addictive quality that is borne from a vacuum, not the free, unencumbered intimacy that flows from individuals who are already residing at home within themselves. I have long known that at least ninety-five percent of couples' conflicts originate from the unresolved trauma of the past – and most of this was induced prior to the relationship. Relationships are always mirrors of our current state of integration or disintegration. When we are secure within ourselves and abide in present-time awareness, we are able to be patient with others during their own healing process, but we also possess the strength to make the necessary changes should our paths diverge. The healing of oneself and ones trauma history is a "no-lose" situation. Negotiation and compromise manifest easily from such a place.

• **Abundance:** When our intentionality is no longer distorted by the inhibiting voices of trauma, we manifest our highest good. This is immediate and spontaneous. Fear is the projection into the future based on traumatic memory of the past. With the clearing of the emotional body, our creative energy is no longer diverted to contain our traumatic memories, but is now available for conscious manifestation. Eden is the state of abundance where what we need is created as we need it. This is the natural power of our quantum perception when it is freed from the protective constraints of subconscious intentionality. Such manifestation may be financial, occupational, material, or relational in nature. The power to manifest such richness abides within us by our very design.

• **Optimal Health:** Integrative medicine teaches us that many illnesses cannot exist or harm us when our systems are fully balanced. This new medicine treats causes not merely symptoms. Trauma creates an energetic and physiological imbalance that can be resolved. As we learn to love ourselves and master our states of consciousness, we discover our ability to return each of our ego states to optimal health: white light. In such a simple mastery of our trance states, we explore our capacity to manifest the bodymind in its highest form. Within this natural and integrative perspective, health occurs as a natural by-product of spiritual enlightenment.

• **A Physics of Consciousness:** With heightened respect for the power of our trances to impact our psychology, neurology, and physiology, we develop the capacity to see the immediate impact of our altered states. As we learn to map this process within the physiology of the bodymind, a new era of science and medicine emerges. As I write this, we are completing a computer software program that enables us to map and document the self-healing process of the bodymind as it occurs through the resolution of memory. Such a process, already applied effectively with over twelve thousand trauma survivors, will allow us to view our memories, their sequencing, locations, and impact on our physiology – giving us the power to see the relationship between our experiences and our illnesses. The patterns of the soul or higher self emerge as we view these "life-maps" of trauma that so readily reveal our purpose and lessons in this lifetime. This magnificent wisdom is inherent to the bodymind and promptly reveals itself when we honor its language. The body has long been speaking to us about our path to healing and wholeness. We possess the capacity to map the memory history of a pathology or illness, thereby enabling us to "unwind" or sequentially resolve the distortions in consciousness that underlie this healing crisis. The wisdom of the bodymind knows the origins of our pain and is most eloquent and efficient when given its voice. In humility we learn to defer to the wisdom of our design rather than merely impose diagnoses and treat the symptoms of illness. We learn to respect the efficacy and power of consciousness and its impact on the cells and fields of our bodies. We step back and allow the bodymind to disclose the etiology of its healing crisis and its illness. A physics of consciousness emerges.

• **Beyond Justice:** As we move beyond our own fears and traumas, we recognize the power and responsibility of authentic presence. In our interconnectedness we are all parts of one mind and flow of consciousness. Just as we cannot afford to ignore or repress our own states of consciousness without serious impact to the bodymind, we cannot dissociate those elements of our society that mirror the depths of our unresolved traumas. In many cases, we have simply resorted to an "out of sight – out of mind" approach to treating the more dysfunctional "elements" of our society. Aggressive approaches may be used to gain initial management of the terrorism that has spiraled out of control, but the final resolution will not come from war or strategies that induce more anger, fear, and violence. Our leaders have gravely underestimated the traumatic impact of war as a strategy for change. The traumatic imprints and messages of war can live on indefinitely in our memories, in our bodies. In the healing of our traumatic memories, violence is finally disempowered. Each moment of violence that we resolve at its point of origin in consciousness enhances the whole of society. This is readily discernible when we recognize our interconnectedness. As we resolve our trauma-generated fears, we come to know an inner safety that offers a new approach to the treatment of offenders. We act less from fear and a desire to contain the violence and become more focused on healing the source of such breaches in spirit. By actually resolving the violence in our personal histories, we move back into the flow of consciousness, acting less from a static and fear-based place and more from a position of spiritual advantage. Safety will never be ours without the alignment of our intuition and the resolution of the voices within.

• **Mother Earth:** In this last decade we have witnessed catastrophic tsunamis, hurricanes, and earthquakes. Globally, we see nations ravaged by the effects of these natural disasters and recognize the need to transcend our self-protective boundaries and pool our resources to expedite healing and a more timely response to these cyclical traumas of nature. While dissociation can protect us from the overwhelming experiences of our lives, it also restricts our awareness of the intimate connection we maintain with All That Is. There is a danger and a risk in staying overlong behind the trauma-imposed walls we use to survive our pain.

One of the consequences of dissociation is that we can become so focused on personal survival in our own small, private worlds that we fail to see the impact of our choices on the systems and populations around us. For example, there is little doubt that our industrial efforts to improve our quality of life have taken a toll on our environment and resulted in consequences that we are only now beginning to fully comprehend. The consequences of dissociation with respect to our environment will become materially evident in time. Environmental trauma is not new to me. I grew up in the Cancer Belt – one of two areas of the country that register highest in the occurrence of cancer: one in Louisiana, and the other in New Jersey. Both areas were directly adjacent to petrochemical companies: Allied Chemical, Ethyl Corporation, Dow Chemical, etc., who exercised few environmental controls in their early years. I grew up less than two miles away from our nation's leading petrochemical companies. They were on the East bank of the Mississippi River, and we were two blocks from the West bank of the river. The wind frequently blew in our direction. When I attempted to obtain an individual health insurance policy in the late 1980's, I discovered my position within the Cancer Belt and the fact that the cost of health and cancer insurance was higher in these areas. Both of my parents died of cancer, and my father had actually worked in his later years at one of these plants. He was exposed to an agent that was known to cause colon cancer, and though he had been routinely tested mere months before his occurrence of colon cancer, ended up living with a colostomy for over twenty-five years. He ended up dying of lung cancer. Many of the families that lived around us had similar experiences.

It is impossible to speak of trauma without speaking of environmental trauma. While this discussion deserves a book of its own, we must, with the recognition of our oneness with All That Is, recognize the precious role of our Mother, Earth. Years ago it became evident with the melting of the Polar Ice Caps and the environmental evidence that was being amassed, that we would face consequences for these environmental shifts. "Global warming" would surely exact a price on us in time. Our contribution to global warming constitutes "trauma" to the environment. Trauma on such a scale holds the potential for dramatic changes in weather, climate and, as a result, a shift in our definition of what is "habitable" and what is not. As I stated, I come from Louisiana. As a result of "Katrina" and "Rita" or, as some of my relatives referred to it, the "Katrita" Disaster, some of my own relatives' homes and businesses were destroyed. Millions were displaced. Several years ago I was alerted by a friend and Senior Red Cross official that a report had been issued that indicated that "nothing below the third floor of buildings in downtown New Orleans would be dry if the city was hit directly by a category three hurricane." It would prove disastrous. Fortunately, Katrina was not a direct hit. If, however, we combine the factors of global warming and the (supposedly natural) cyclical potential for stronger hurricanes with the erosion of the wetlands, we hold a ticket to disaster. Just as the human body holds a system of checks and balances to alert us to abuses and distortion, so also does our planet. With the environmental trauma involving the erosion of the "wetlands" off the coast of Louisiana, it was clear that the natural barrier to "storm surge" was removed. The coastal cities were laid open for storm exposure/devastation. With the additional failure of maintaining the levees and "cutbacks" in government funding, a direct assault by a hurricane would render much of the city uninhabitable. This information, apparently, was known to our leaders years ago. The dissociation that routinely accompanies bureaucracies rests behind many of the failures that occurred with Katrina. Trauma, you may recall, is not merely the event itself, but is frequently induced by the untimely or inappropriate reaction of the responsible "caregivers" to the crisis itself. Adrenaline and our natural reactions to stress routinely assist us in dealing with immediate physical threat and danger, but the failure to receive timely assistance at the moment of occurrence induces a trauma state that remains embedded in the psyche. Katrina was both a fiasco and a disaster: both bureaucratically and environmentally. It was trauma on a level that the mind has difficulty comprehending.

With the constant bombardment and overstimulation of our senses, it is not surprising that environmental and security warnings were dismissed with events like 9-11 and Katrina. You and I know that, with sensory overwhelm, we fall back upon our tendency to withdraw and dissociate into our own worlds to survive the pain. As a species, we have survived with the help of this mechanism, but it does not resolve the traumas to the environment that we are now witnessing. Trauma to these populations occurred as a direct result of dissociating ourselves from our environment and the voices that gave us warning. The individual and collective states of dissociation we currently hold will not render effective solutions to these growing crises in our environment and society. The matrix thinking that is required to see the interrelationships of these systems and the environment can only come as a result of moving into an awareness of the interdependency that we hold with each other and the environment that we have exploited. Sometimes this exploitation was deliberate as a "sacrifice to higher goals" or an oversight due to the "myopic" vision of an imbalanced intentionality (trauma-driven). Our excessive attachments to money, power, and achievement are the result of trauma encoding in the psyche. We are here to learn to walk the earth without attachments. The attachments that create greed and abuse are the by-product of distorted intentionality. The lesson is simple: ignore these imprints in the psyche, and we may well find ourselves walking home down streets covered in water. This is our mother's own system of checks and balances! We will not be rescued by God from an abuse that we ourselves are creating – at least, not rescued in the manner our egos expect. As we move into a consciousness that fully honors our interdependency with the world that sustains us, we make different choices and make the necessary shifts in our priorities. We cannot dissociate ourselves from the truth of our radical dependency on the earth if we are to protect ourselves and our children's future. We will certainly need to make some different choices if we are to manifest the Eden that we are so capable of generating.

• **Authentic Spirituality:** The lessons of trauma have taught us that any system, when removed from healthy emotional experience, fosters addiction and dysfunction. While trauma can inspire us and form the foundation for our direction in life, if left unresolved overlong, it can bias this process and lead to rigidity and compulsion. This we discovered with the advent of "Family Systems Theory" in the 1960's. For myself, I discovered Systems Theory and the inherent spirituality of the 12 Step programs in the 1980's when my oldest sister intervened on her own system. She invited me to participate in the recovery process. My greatest shock came when I realized that, from an emotional standpoint, the recovering alcoholics that I met were significantly more emotionally available than the priests responsible for my "spiritual formation." This factor eventually shaped my decision to become an addictions counselor.

Looking back, I can see that there were positive spiritual influences in my religious upbringing. I had the opportunity to meet Pope John Paul II five times during my training in Rome. My principal mentor in college and in my theological studies was Polish and was a colleague of his in Warsaw. Pope John Paul II possessed a formidable presence – one that radically altered the politics of Poland and the influence of communism throughout the world. I was beneath the balcony of St. Peter's Basilica the night he was elected, and I remember this as one of the most powerful moments of my life. Here was a man whose passion was shaped by his trauma in Poland, and whose heart was directed in sincere service toward others. He demonstrated that we possess the capability to convert our traumatic experiences into a life work that can inspire others. His life reflected the passion that comes from a profound struggle with political and religious oppression. His defense of his beliefs shaped his spiritual development and fostered an ardent attachment to his religious belief system – one which some held to be overly protective or conservative as a logical response to his history. From a place of compassion, one can understand the polarities that influenced his decision-making. Trauma has the potential to polarize our decision-making process and to foster rigidity. Our decisions will always flow from the degree of spiritual evolution that we have achieved within our own intentionality. These are excellent cases to remind us of the importance of our personal healing and the impact that our biased or unbiased intentionality may have on our entire world.

Another interesting case in the study of trauma has arisen with the election of Pope Benedict XVI in 2005. While conscripted into the Hitler Youth Groups and the German Army during his early development, his attraction to ministry as a priest can be seen as a profound reaction to the immensity of the global trauma that he so personally witnessed. Here resides a passion that could be used for great service or in a polarized counter-reaction to accusations and horrors that indelibly imprint in the holocaust survivor's and the holocaust perpetrator's intentionality. As a Cardinal, his work with the Holy Office was suggestive of doctrinal rigidity and conservatism that is consonant with a zeal born of trauma and as a witness to crimes against humanity. Within the human psyche, however, the counter-reaction to unresolved trauma can launch us onto a path that is fueled by the immensity of the power and untamed anger that is repressed at moments of encoding. This distorted "passion" can cause a parent or leader to become overprotective to the point of disempowerment, or to become overly "zealous" to the extent that thinking becomes "myopic." In recovery from trauma, such as that imposed by an addiction, we have witnessed thousands of cases where religious rigidity is used as a substitute for the "drug of choice" and as a desperate attempt to gain moral control over the compulsive behavior or pattern. Having been given the impression that the only path to healing was that of the "moral model" and the reclamation of our willpower from the vestiges of sin, it is understandable that moral exhortation and the reclamation of our "sinful" exercise of will was perceived to be the path to salvation. This path proved restrictive and even "enabling" when we discovered Systems Theory and the power of addictions in the 1950's and 1960's. It is now considered unethical to utilize "moralizing" and inherently shaming strategies to treat individuals who are driven by the intentionality borne of trauma and addiction.

In response to trauma, the Catholic Church, like many religious systems, has revealed in its writings and doctrinal teachings a traditional tendency toward intellectual disassociation when confused by the onslaught of emotions and the inner voices borne of traumatic experiences. This tendency is an understandable response from the strictures and limited options that were imposed by the old "moral responsibility" model (as discussed earlier in this work). Trauma-based decision making bears a fingerprint, however, and routinely reveals its estrangement from authentic spiritual intimacy. Decisions based on trauma frequently serve to reinforce patterns of shame and alienation. Such decisions can simply be measured by the "fruit" they produce: (Luke 6:44-45) "Each tree is known by its yield ... Each man speaks from his heart's abundance" (or lack thereof). The decisions and directions chosen by Pope Benedict XVI will reveal his own clarity or the residual bias of trauma, and as such, will move us, one way or another, toward an answer to this question both personally and collectively: Do we continue on the path of disassociation, or do we focus on resolving our traumas and move into a place of clear intentionality and authentic spiritual intimacy? Authentic, balanced spiritual leadership would be most helpful at this time in our evolution.

In light of the profundity of our personal and collective trauma experiences, the invitation is obvious: We are at a turning point in our spiritual evolution, where language and strategies that induce shame and dissociation are readily identified as spiritual abuse. The greatest proof of this history of dissociation is found in reading the writings of the "mystics" and witnessing their efforts to know authentic spiritual experience while constrained by the thought processes of the "moral failure" model. As the old moral responsibility model gives way to the more comprehensive trauma resolution or "Integrated Consciousness Model," we come to focus more on mastery of our states of consciousness and less on the adherence to moral precepts that are always conditioned by the health of our intentionality (conscious and unconscious). As we bring into harmony both our conscious and subconscious intentionality, "Quantum Spirituality" emerges that is far more "orthodox" and consonant with the truths of our natures and our power as cocreators of our reality. The truth of this is revealed in the power it offers us to love unconditionally and to shape every aspect of our reality.

• **The Body Politic:** Long has it been understood that truth and history both proceed as a dialectic process: thesis, antithesis, synthesis. Such is the path of evolution and growth. When we challenge the status quo, it shifts in response to the challenge, and from the dialogue that ensues, a new state of consciousness emerges. This is the lesson of "Systems Theory." With a "bipartisan" system, however, the duality that is created and sustained by trauma can be fostered, so that, rather than moving upward when facing a challenge, larger and larger gaps are created. Instead of seeing the challenge of insights that each party offers, thereby leading to enlightenment and growth, the parties additionally polarize into their respective positions and virtually immobilize the system altogether. If these parties remain polarized and move farther into defense, they subvert the original goal of synthesis that comes from shared wisdom and compromise. In other words, a system itself built on duality runs the risk of perpetuating the divisions created by trauma and solidifying the resistance and homeostasis so common to dysfunctional systems. Politics has not been historically founded on an inherently integrative model, but on one that tends to support dissociation. The starting point for the resolution of *interpersonal violence* and conflict is the resolution of *intrapersonal violence* and conflict. The starting point for the resolution of all duality is the individual psyche where all such splitting originates and is predisposed from our extensive pre-history of trauma.

There is no question that our personal trauma histories impact our decision-making ability. The political arena is one of the premier locations for demonstrating this concept. In positions of responsibility, our leaders are entrusted with immense power to act in the best interests of our society and culture. But how much trauma or "Post Traumatic Stress" do our leaders hold? Personal trauma inserts a potential for biased or myopic decision-making that can result in the excessive use of force or in paralysis when action is needed. This has been the case from humankind's earliest evolution. I have noticed that those in positions of great power in the public eye frequently convince themselves that they hold equal power in their internal arena. Trauma results in the dissociation of power into fear and anger. It may also take the form of shame, powerlessness, or sadness, but it is merely a different face of the same splitting of energy that occurs at such overwhelming moments. If we allow our personal traumas and the distorted emotions that accompany them to become significant in the decision-making process, we permit the delusional aspect of our outdated memories to influence our current choices. Such choices, when wielding the immense power that leadership holds in America, can be catastrophic or abusive. Trauma encodes in such a profound way that any situation resembling our original pain will trigger a similar surge of emotion: it is this surge, originating from another place and time that can bias our choices on a subtle level. Such distortion holds the capacity to twist our interpretation of the raw data or "intelligence" that we do receive, irrespective of its objective accuracy. We may then find ourselves using military intervention prematurely or excessively in reaction to our emotional response to the supposed threat. In our alliances with big business and corporate America, we may find ourselves just distant enough from the plight of the common man to miss the cues and warnings that could circumvent a disastrous delay in response to crisis. You and I have all reacted excessively or been immobilized from a place of trauma within our lives at one time or another, and we may well have traumatized others in the process. How often do we take out our frustrations on those around us when they are not the actual source of our discontent?

Perhaps we will never know if some of our country's decisions were truly excessive or not, but our best opportunity for balanced decision-making is to remain clear and centered within ourselves so as not to act from a distorted intentionality. We have a need for such balanced leadership in our government as well. I must admit that when I heard President George W. Bush state: "That man tried to kill my Daddy!" I felt some trepidation that his personal trauma was influencing the decision-making process and causing us to act prematurely or excessively. The other emotional stance that occurs as a result of trauma is visible when, instead of acting from excessive anger, we become too fearful, detached, and paralyzed and are unable to make a decision or act in a timely manner. Trauma can leave us immobilized in fear and codependently outward looking for a source of direction for our decisions. Trauma distorts the decision-making process, and we all carry some degree of trauma. I believe, however, that we all seek to act from the best of our intentionality and wisdom at most times. But the hidden power of trauma-induced subconscious, repressed intention is powerful and readily warps our decision-making process before we are even aware that we are under its influence. Frequently, our "attachments" to issues, causes, etc. can be directly tracked to our personal experiences. I have seen this most commonly in our choices of careers.

It is my hope that, with greater understanding of the power of the human mind to store memory and pain, we choose leadership that is multidimensional in its thinking and open to its own humanity and healing. To be perfectly human is to make mistakes and learn from them! We make fewer of them, I find, when we are in touch with our own traumas and emotions, and make an effort to resolve the excessive emotional charges that bias our intentionality. These are powerful lessons we have all had reason to contemplate in recent times. Looking back at the political condition of America and the huge polarities that have emerged in recent times, we have sufficient cause to consider the influence of trauma and the directions our emotions have pushed us in making certain choices. How much of the body politic is influenced by trauma-driven motivation? We do not want to elect from the excessive bias induced from trauma-based fear, anger, or shame, though these "triggers" are now readily utilized as campaign strategies. I suspect that the manipulation of the collective unconscious through the deliberate media stimulation of these trauma triggers is now becoming evident to all. One can almost anticipate the announcement of "intelligence data" suggesting the possibility of a new nuclear threat from terrorists prior to an election. Fear is a powerful motivator for those still holding the triggers of past traumas. Such excessive fear manipulates and triggers the reaction of the subconscious mind, biasing our choices without our even realizing it. The voice of excessive fear and threat is that of subconscious intentionality and will only serve to amplify the distortion in the future and return to us in consequence. Fear tactics manipulate us by triggering the body of fear that we already hold resolved in the subconscious; the same is true of anger. We must make our decisions from a conscious place of balance that weighs all voices with equal import. In order to listen from a balanced place, we must resolve our own trauma histories. This is an important key to peace. This is the challenge that we face in the body politic and the selection of our leadership.

• **Authentic Intimacy:** With the resolution of our body-shame and the "lightening" of the fields of consciousness, true intimacy becomes possible. Sex is no longer a substitute for frustrated communication on other levels, but becomes more integrated into the larger definition of self. Trauma inserts a weight, heaviness, and density that impact all levels of communication. As we reclaim our "breath" held from the moments of paused trauma, we merge with our friends and partners in ways that honor our nature as "spirit" or *ruah* in Hebrew (meaning "breath," "wind," or "spirit"). True encompassing "tantra" becomes possible. In the reclamation of ourselves, we become available to truly listen and attend to both the divinity and the remarkable humanity that manifests before us. After working with so many trauma survivors, it is easier to recognize the healer and mystic that resides within each of us. Such intimacy awaits us as we release the dense burden of trauma that inhibits our capacity for merger. We are redefining intimacy as we clear the vast body of trauma that has so profoundly affected human relationality.

• **Mystical Union:** The greatest impact of trauma on the human psyche is spiritual. The moments of overwhelm in our lives insert contradictory voices that hold primacy until they are addressed. They profoundly affect our spiritual intimacy and our deepest level of communication. The current impact of trauma on our spirituality is beautifully summarized for us in a passage written by the artist Bill Worrell. I came across the passage in an art gallery in Tubac, Arizona. The passage recognizes the spiritual immaturity created by trauma – the spiritual codependency that emerges as the natural side effect of so many pauses in our flow of consciousness. We see the spiritual effects of our entrapment in the child-mind:

We are such children.
How great is our need for guidance.

How can we possibly hear Great Spirit
When we are always talking,
Always giving Great Spirit instructions,
Always telling Great Spirit what to do for us?

How can we receive the gifts Great Spirit offers
When we are always busy seeking other things.

Great Spirit sings songs of peace.
We cannot hear them because we are busy
Telling Great Spirit to give us peace.

Great Spirit lays before us great treasures.
We cannot see them because we are busy
Telling Great Spirit to show us prosperity.

Great Spirit sings to us of great love.
We do not hear the melody
Because we are busy
Telling Great Spirit to show us love.

We are such children.
We babble so –
And think we are praying.[48]

Bill Worrell
April 27, 2000,
at 9:52 a.m.

Authentic spiritual intimacy and prayer come when we are able to remain still and recognize the voice that is continuous and unabating in its assurances of love. The capacity to "walk with God," to be continuously aware of our connection to Source has never been closer in our evolution. Our dependency on external guidance diminishes as we learn to recognize the wisdom that we hold within. The voice within grows stronger as we resolve the false messages imposed by trauma. Our natural intuition and alignment to our highest good flows spontaneously without the interruption of the static states of mind that so desperately hold onto pain and fear to protect us. As we clear the emotional and energetic blockages to intimacy, we move back into the main flow of the river – the Divine Mind in all its power, purity, and wisdom. The experiential knowledge of All That Is comes easily and spontaneously when we remove the obstacles to our innate creative flow. We are quantum creators by nature. The act of perception is creative. When our perception of reality is freed from the biases and unhealthy attachments caused by trauma, we act directly from our contact with the Source without the distortions held in the fields of the subconscious mind. Duality of mind and inner conflict resolve as our intentionality is healed. We become simpler in our perception, needs, and manifestation. We become singular in our intentionality. Thought, emotion, and action all work smoothly together without the polarities of dissociation and trauma. We attract that which we need as we need it. We abide in the present where all intimacy occurs. We reach a still point where time and space cease to be and we are simply one with All That Is. In such a state, there is no "need," for all is present and complete; all is whole.

Beyond the restrictions of space and time, we are never alone, for we are in union with the one flow of consciousness. The ego is pacified and dissolves in the realization that we do not lose ourselves in such mystical intimacy, but attain our fullest potential when we are at home in the fullness of light. Death loses its power in the offering of such unimaginable union. In the radiance of the light, we do not dissolve into some amorphous mass of consciousness, but are highlighted more precisely in our uniqueness and individuality, all the while knowing deeper peace and union than we ever thought possible. Any remaining shadows become invitations to greater intimacy and beckon us to states of consciousness that surpass anything that we were ever promised by the systems. The unresolved traumas of the systems warped their vision of our spiritual potential. With the dissolution of the intra-psychic partitions created by trauma, we move into multi-dimensional or matrix thinking. We can see the whole and the parts at the same time when we become fully aware of all aspects of self – without fear! We also come to recognize our fellow humans as our "other-selves." As we move out of the age-old trances that limited our access to personal, interpersonal, social, global, and spiritual intimacy, a new perspective of life is born. No longer do we lose such immense energy and power warring within our own minds and hosting opposing voices and intentions. Freely and spontaneously we act from an uncomplicated center – freed of the baggage of the past and wholly focused on the only reality that is: the unlimited love and intimacy proffered us by the present moment. Ever has such intimacy awaited us in the eternal now! Infinitely patient and hospitable is the Divine Mind in its summons home. All of the currents of our lives, including the lessons of trauma, exist only through their dependency on the primordial flow of the One Light. As such, all is lesson; all is safe; all is invitation to know love in its fullness.

Of the many lessons of the last years, there is one that stands out above all others: We have never fully left or lost touch with the Divine Mind – with the river of white light that sustains all creation. In working with so many trauma survivors, I have never found one that did not have essential contact with the inherent flow of goodness, light, and purity that can heal all. I have never found one that did not know, somewhere within his or her being, exactly what gesture, word, or expression of love should have been present at each moment of his/her existence. We are spiritual beings whose home is the light. Scaled down in vibration to take on this body of matter, we are given an opportunity for conscious ascendance and enlightenment. Our conscious minds may have fallen under the illusion of the five senses for a time and even become so entranced as to believe the lessons of trauma to be fatal, but the truth is, looking down from the observer stance of the higher self, these are only lessons offered to enrich our appreciation of who and what we are as Children of the Light.

As we move out of our spiritual infancy, we move into a higher ethic based on the mastery of our states of consciousness. We accept our stewardship of the light of consciousness and wield this divinity from full awareness that we are quantum creators. We hold a gift, a creative power that has never left our hands for a moment in our evolution. When wielded, however, from an unconscious place, this power can readily manifest as fear, anger, sadness, and shame. By participating in the conscious reclamation of this creative power, we feel the actual transformation from darkness to light. We grow in gratitude and appreciation of our spiritual nature. Moreover, we actually contribute to the river of white light with the healing of each moment of our pain and trauma. In this immersion and illumination, we come to know the Divine Mind in its uniqueness and individuality. Far from being threatened in our own identity, we become incapable of trauma and overwhelm, for we live as one with the Source of all consciousness. In such proximity to the Source, we no longer need to reframe any static states of consciousness, for the dynamic outpouring of love preempts their occurrence. As we are reminded in the Book of Revelation 21: 3b-4:

He shall dwell with them and they shall be his people and he shall be their God who is always with them. He shall wipe every tear from their eyes, and there shall be no more death or mourning, crying out or pain, for the former world has passed away.

And again in the Book of the prophet Jeremiah: (Jeremiah 31: 31-34)

I will place my law within them, and write it upon their hearts; I will be their God, and they shall be my people. No longer will they have need to teach their friends and kinsmen how to know the Lord. All, from least to greatest, shall know me, says the Lord…

In our capacity to bridge the gaps created within our own psyche through trauma, we are invited to participate in our healing. The quantum capacity for creation has been passed to us. We are stewards of that body of light that generates our universe. How and where we focus our attention, therefore, is creative and transformative. Eden is not a mythological abstraction, but an expression of the original invitation to embrace our divinity. Eden is not a shame-based projection from the past detailing the defectiveness of our nature. It is the standing invitation to embrace our true nature as cocreators and stewards of the flow of consciousness. The obstacle to an Edenic existence clearly comes, not from some primordial moral failure, but from our alienation from the One Mind and the shame that reinforces such illusions of separation. As we master our states of consciousness, using that inherent wisdom written on the human heart, the past and the future dissolve, giving rise to the mystical knowledge that we have always been securely held within the womb of white light that sustains all. The master plan for our healing and the path to enlightenment are clearly contained within us. This wisdom beckons us to focus our quantum creativity on the manifestation of Eden by abiding in the Light.

There is a path or gateway to joy and abundance that resides in the human heart: in the very cells and fields of the bodymind. It is our spiritual nature and birthright to enter Eden at our own pace and in a manner that honors our invitation to create – and to learn to create from a "conscious" place. Jesus was heralded in early Christian literature as the "New Adam." The essence of his message was that the kingdom of spiritual intimacy with God is within us. His physical departure totally hinged on this point: we must come to the recognition of Spirit within. In our dissociative history, we got caught up in the "where" of God/Divinity/spirituality and missed the main point.

Do you recall the stages of self-esteem induction (or shame induction if it takes the form of negative encoding) that I spoke of earlier? On the earth plane, all imprinting of worth originates initially from the outside. Eventually it becomes internalized. If this process continues, it achieves autonomy. With further reinforcement, the message becomes identified with self, and, finally, moves into a continuous higher (holographic) cycle that is continuously accessible. As we internalize the messages of unconditional love, we begin to trust them to be true. This goodness and light begins to achieve autonomy and require less conscious recall to be felt and known. A fundamental sense of spiritual worth begins to "abide" in us – requiring less conscious maintenance on our own part. By remaining more consistently in the pure flow of consciousness, we come to identify with the white light. In this identification, we move beyond the old restrictions of our subconscious intentionality and start to act spontaneously and powerfully from a higher state of awareness. We begin to know ourselves as light and to act as "light from light." This affords us access to the power and resources of the "Superconscious" Mind, which transcend the traditional parameters of consciousness, as we have known it. As we move into the Higher Self or "Holographic Mind," we begin to recognize this fundamental property as native to our Mind. Hologram theory understands the universe to be the projection from some ultimate light source. All of matter and created reality is the interplay of light and energy from some ultimate source, according to the physicists. In learning to master our states of consciousness – those traumatic images that have daunted us in our evolution, we finally come to see the depth of our invitation: to share in the intimacy of the Divine Mind. We have been gifted with the capacity to bring light to bear and heal any state of consciousness. As we know from physics, every fragment of a hologram contains the whole. Hence, as holographic beings in a holographic universe, we appear to contain, in some mysterious way, as aspects of the Divine Mind, the whole! If sufficient light is poured into a holographic fragment, the whole is manifested. Such is our potential. The consequence of this realization may take some time for us to digest.

We have been maturing spiritually throughout our evolution on earth, but are we prepared to realize the depths to which the Divine Mind has committed itself to bring us home? We are now learning that this quantum, creative power is so inherent to us as to be inseparable from our management of consciousness itself. To be alive, whether conscious or unconscious, is to be creating at every moment. Our path of evolution up to this point has been largely influenced by the subconscious imprinting of trauma. We hold within the cells and fields of our bodymind an invitation to quantum mastery. Mysticism, therefore, is not some extraordinary experience outside of our ordinary perception; it is the fabric that underlies our very existence. We are at play in a holographic universe that possesses consciousness. There is only one Mind, in truth. As we learn to master the universe that is most immediately ours in this bodymind, we will see the healing spread outward to the whole. This is our blessing as holographic beings in a holographic universe: every part immediately and profoundly affects the whole. "We are one with All That Is; we are one with the Divine Mind!"[49]

Notes

1. The film, *What the #$*! Do We Know!?* was produced, directed, and written by William Arntz in 2004. It is a film that explains much about quantum mechanics and its impact on the human psyche.
2. Thomas S. Kuhn, "The Structure of Scientific Revolutions," *International Encyclopedia of Unified Science,* II, 2 (1962).
3. Rabbi Yonassan Gershom, *Beyond the Ashes: Cases of Reincarnation from the Holocaust* (Virginia Beach, VA: ARE Press,1992).
4. Brian Weiss, *Many Lives, Many Masters* (New York: Simon & Schuster, 1988).
5. Michael Talbot, *The Holographic Universe* (New York: Harper Collins Publishers, 1991).
6. Robert North, S.J., *Ghassul* 1960: Excavation Report (Rome: Pontifical Biblical Institute, 1961).
7. Pessah Bar-Adon, *The Cave of the Treasure* (Jerusalem: The Israel Exploration Society, 1980).
8. Gary Zukav, *The Seat of the Soul* (New York: Simon and Schuster, Inc. 1989), p. 137.
9. The city of Lachish is cited in the following: Joshua 10:3, 5, 23, 31-35, 12:11, 15:39; II Kings 14:19, 18:14,17, 19:8; II Chronicles 11:9, 25:27, 32:9; Nehemiah 11:30; Isaiah 36:2, 37:8; Jeremiah 34:7; Micah 1:13.
10. Don Miguel Ruiz, *The Four Agreements* (San Rafael, CA: Amber-Allen Publishing Company, 1997), p. 29.
11. Talbot, pp. 11ff.
12. In the liturgy of the Catholic Church, the Nicene Creed declares Jesus as "light from light, true God from true God."
13. Eckhart Tolle, *The Power of Now* (Novato, CA: New World Library, 1999), pp. 29-33.
14. Wyatt Webb, *It's Not About the Horse – It's About Overcoming Fear and Self-Doubt* (Carlsbad, CA: Hay House, Inc., 2002).
15. Karl Pribram, the neurophysiologist, coined the term, "holonomic," indicating that memory encoded in the physical body follows the laws (nomos, means "law" in Greek) of a hologram, but is not equally present in every part of the body/system as would be the case for a truly "holographic" system. In the latter, every part of the hologram contains the whole equally. Memory in the physical body would be overwhelming if it were encoded equally in every part of the system.
16. Harville Hendrix's book: *Getting the Love You Want* (New York: Harper Perennial, 1988). In the first half of his book, he talks about the "unconscious marriage," while in the second half, he speaks of creating the "conscious marriage."

17. "Hermeneutic" is an inclusive term that incorporates speech, translation, and commentary as part of the understanding of a text. "Hermeneutics" is the science of meaning, particularly as applied to biblical texts. See Raymond Brown, The Jerome Biblical Commentary (Englewood Cliffs, NJ: Prentice-Hall, Inc., 1969). The article entitled: "Hermeneutics," pp. 605-623.

18. John Bradshaw, *Healing the Shame that Binds You* (Deerfield Beach, Florida: Health Communications, Inc., 1988).

19. "Ontology" is a philosophical term referring to the systematic study of "being." The position taken by the early fathers of the church was that something "primordial" happened on the level of "being" when the "Original Sin" occurred. This was a laudable attempt to explain how something profound and enduring had happened in our history that the simple "moral failure" model could not fully explain. The psychology of dissociation provides insights that may assist us in clarifying the original theological efforts to explain the "split" that occurred in the order of "being."

20. The Catholic Church went out of its way to tell Martin Luther that human nature was most certainly not "negative" or "sinful" in its natural orientation, as Lutheranism tended to posit.

21. Brent Baum, *The Healing Dimensions* (Tucson, AZ: Healing Dimensions, A.C.C. in collaboration with West Press, 1997). See www.healingdimensions.com for availability of this text or also www.amazon.com.

22. John and Linda Friel, *Adult Children: The Secrets of Dysfunctional Families* (New York: Health Communications, Inc., 1990).

23. Friel, pp. 56-57.

24. It has been the same with the medical profession – addressing symptoms and behaviors, but not the cause.

25. "Recidivism" is a term that refers to a tendency to relapse into a previous condition or mode of behavior.

26. Michael Talbot, *The Holographic Universe* (New York: Harper Collins Publishers, 1991).

27. Brent Baum, *The Healing Dimensions* (Tucson: Healing Dimensions A.C.C. & West Press, 1997).

28. The elaborated version of Hans Selye's General Adaptation Syndrome is found in Ernest Rossi and David Cheek, *Mind Body Therapy* (New York: W.W. Horton & Co., 1988), p 166.

29. Cheek & Rossi, p. 166.

30. "Homeostasis" is defined by the American Heritage Dictionary (Boston: Houghton Mifflin Company, 1983), p. 332, as "a state of physiological equilibrium produced by a balance of functions and of chemical composition within an organism." As applied here, it refers to the tendency of either a healthy or unhealthy system to maintain the current state of subsistence – the "status quo."

31. Louise Hay, *Heal Your Body* (Carson, CA: Hay House, Inc., 1982).

32. Doc Childre & Deborah Rozman, *Transforming Anger* (Oakland, CA: New Harbinger Publications, Inc., 2003), p. 5.

33. Barbara Brennan, *Hands of Light* (New York: Bantam Books, 1988), p. 182.

34. Gary Zukav, *The Dancing Wu Li Masters* (New York: William Morrow & Co., Inc, 1979).

35. Gary Zukav, *The Seat of the Soul* (New York: Simon and Schuster, Inc., 1989) p. 137.

36. James Redfield, *The Celestine Prophecy* (New York: Warner Books, Inc., 1993).

37. See Neale Donald Walsch, *Conversations with God, Book I* (Charlottesville, VA: Hampton Roads Publishing Company, Inc., 1995), pp. 33-34.

38. Deepak Chopra, *Quantum Healing* (New York: Bantam Books, 1989), pp. 122-124.

39. Bernie Siegel, *Love, Medicine and Miracles* (New York: Harper and Row, 1986).

40. John Bradshaw, *Healing the Shame that Binds You* (Deefield Beach, Florida: Health Communications, 1988).

41. These terms were utilized and demonstrated effectively by Terry Kellogg in his educational videotape series entitled: "Return to Intimacy," produced by Paradox Productions in 1989.

42. Tolle, p. 41.

43. Pessah Bar-Adon, *The Cave of the Treasure* (Jerusalem: The Israel Exploration Society, 1980).

44. Wyatt Webb, *It's Not About the Horse – It's About Overcoming Fear and Self-Doubt* (Carlsbad, CA: Hay House, Inc., 2002.)

45. See www.global-dialogue.com and the Global Dialogue Institute for a description of the Institute's goals and Dr. Ashok Gangadean's pioneering work in "Deep-Dialogue."

46. Global Dialogue Institute: "The Power and Promise of Deep-Dialogue," p. 1. As found on the web site: www.global-dialogue.com.

47. Global Dialogue Institute, p. 1.

48. Poem by Bill Worrell entitled: *We Are Such Children*. Presented at his Gallery in Tubac, Arizona. Written on April 27, 2000, at 9:52 a.m.

49. Cited from a prayer invocation of Yogiraj Vethathiri Maharishi.

Bibliography

Bar-Adon, Pessah. *The Cave of the Treasure.* Jerusalem: The Israel Exploration Society, 1980.

Baum, Brent. *The Healing Dimensions.* Tucson, AZ: Healing Dimensions, A.C.C. and West Press, 1997.

Bradshaw, John. *Healing the Shame that Binds You.* Deerfield Beach, Florida: Health Communications, Inc., 1988.

Brennan, Barbara. *Hands of Light.* New York: Bantam Books, 1988.

Brown, Raymond. "Hermeneutics." *The Jerome Biblical Commentary.* Englewood Cliffs, NJ: Prentice-Hall, Inc., 1969, pp. 605-623.

Catholic Biblical Association of America. *The New American Bible.* Huntington, Indiana: Catholic Publishers, Inc., 1976.

Cheek, David and Ernest Rossi. *Mind Body Therapy.* New York: W.W. Horton & Co., 1988.

Childre, Doc and Deborah Rozman. *Transforming Anger.* Oakland, CA: New Harbinger Publications, Inc., 2003.

Chopra, Deepak. *Quantum Healing.* New York: Bantam Books, 1989.

Friel, John and Linda. *Adult Children: The Secrets of Dysfunctional Families.* New York: Health Communications, Inc., 1990.

Gangadean, Ashok. *Meditative Reason: Toward Universal Grammar.* Peter Lang: Revisioning Philosophy Series, 1993. Cofounder of the Global Dialogue Institute.

Gershom, Rabbi Yonassan. *Beyond the Ashes: Cases of Reincarnation from the Holocaust.* Virginia Beach, VA: A.R.E. Press, 1992.

Hay, Louise. *Heal Your Body.* Carson, CA: Hay House, Inc., 1982.

Hendrix, Harville. *Getting the Love You Want.* New York: Harper Perennial, 1988.

"Homeostasis." *The American Heritage Dictionary.* Boston: Houghton Mifflin Company, 1983, p. 332.

Kellogg, Terry. "Return to Intimacy." A videotape series produced by Paradox Productions, 1989.

Kuhn, Thomas S. "The Structure of Scientific Revolutions." *International Encyclopedia of Unified Science,* 1962, II, No.2.

North, Robert. Ghassul 1960: Excavation Report. Rome: Pontifical Biblical Institute, 1961.

Redfield, James. *The Celestine Prophecy.* New York: Warner Books, Inc., 1993.

Ruiz, Don Miguel. *The Four Agreements.* San Rafael, CA: Amber-Allen Publishing Company, 1997.

Siegel, Bernie. *Love, Medicine and Miracles.* New York: Harper and Row, 1986.

Talbot, Michael. *The Holographic Universe.* New York: Harper Collins Publishers, 1991.

Tolle, Eckhart. *The Power of Now.* Novato, CA: New World Library, 1999.

Walsch, Neale Donald. *Conversations with God. Book I.* Charlottesville, VA: Hampton Roads Publishing Company, Inc., 1995.

Webb, Wyatt. *Five Steps for Overcoming Fear and Self-Doubt.* Carlsbad, CA: Hay House, Inc., 2004.

Webb, Wyatt. *It's Not About the Horse – It's About Overcoming Fear and Self-Doubt.* Carlsbad, CA: Hay House, Inc., 2002.

Weiss, Brian. *Many Lives, Many Masters.* New York, NY: Simon & Schuster, Inc. 1988.

Zukav, Gary. *The Dancing Wu Li Masters.* New York: William Morrow & Co., Inc, 1979.

Zukav, Gary. *The Seat of the Soul.* New York: Simon and Schuster, Inc., 1989.